DISASTERS AT SEA

DISASTERS AT SEA

Every ocean-going passenger ship catastrophe since 1900

Milton H. Watson

Foreword by Frank O. Braynard

Second edition updated and expanded by William H. Miller

Patrick Stephens Limited

First published in 1987
Second edition March 1995

British Library Cataloguing in Publication Data
A catalogue record for this book is available
from the British Library

ISBN 1 85260 505 7

Library of Congress
catalog card no. 94 79681

*Patrick Stephens Limited is an imprint of Haynes
Publishing, Sparkford, Nr Yeovil, Somerset
BA22 7JJ.*

Printed and bound in Great Britain by
BPC Hazell Books Ltd
A member of
The British Printing Company Ltd

Contents

Dedication

To my mother,
Avis Watson,
who brought me into this world and did
everything in her power to make sure I was
healthy, comfortable and contented.

Acknowledgements

Many wonderful people assisted me in writing this volume but I would like to express my particularly sincere and warm thanks to three special people. Firstly, my thanks to Frank O. Braynard, maritime historian extraordinaire and collector of maritime artifacts, for writing the foreword, for his encouraging words, and for providing many fine photographs. Secondly, my thanks to Theodore Scull, author, lecturer and world traveller, who provided research materials, pictures, constructive criticism and helpful suggestions. The third on the list is William H. Miller, maritime author and lecturer, who through his enthusiasm provided me with encouragement, many useful contacts and photographs.

Other individuals who provided photographs and information regarding certain ships were: Mr C. Spanton Ashdown of Alcoa Steamship Company; Ms Laura Brown of the Steamship Historical Society of America /University of Baltimore Library; Mr Luis Miguel Correia; Mr Alex Duncan; Mr P.M. Heaton for information on the ships of Lamport & Holt; Mr Arnold Kludas; Miss K. Langrish of Lloyd's Register of Shipping, London; Mr Richard Morse; Mr Tom Rayner; Mr Antonio Scrimali; Mr Scott Seifert and Mr James Shaw.

Companies, libraries and museums that provided information and photographs were: Airfoto (Malaysia); Alexander Turnbull Library, Wellington, New Zealand; Associazone Marinara Aldebaran of Trieste; The British & Commonwealth Shipping Company representing Union-Castle Line; Canadian Pacific; Chantier de l'Atlantique, Saint Nazaire; Compagnie Générale Maritime for French Line and Messageries Maritime; Compagnie Maritime Belge; Den Kongelige Gronlandske Handel, Denmark; B.V. Kon. Mij. 'De Schelde', Vlissingen, Nederland; Furness Withy Group representing Royal Mail Lines; Fremantle Port Authority; Hamburg-South America Line; *Illustrated London News* Picture Library; Mariners' Museum; Maritiem Museum 'Prins Hendrik', Rotterdam; Ministry of Transport New Zealand; Mitchell Library, State Library of NSW, Sydney; National Archives, Washington DC; P&O Lines; Puget Sound Maritime Historical Society; *South China Morning Post,* Hong Kong; Mr Norman J. Brouwer of South Street Museum and Library; United States Coast Guard; Woods Hole Oceanographic Institution and Mr Cliff Parsons of World Ship Society Photo Library.

Finally, I would like to extend a special thank to a dear and dedicated colleague, Ms Terry Fenster, who took time from her busy schedule to proof-read my manuscript. And to all those who provided interesting items of information and who are not personally mentioned, I extend to you my thanks.

Foreword to the second edition
by Frank O. Braynard FRS

When I was asked to contribute the Foreword to the first edition of this book, I wrote that Milton Watson was the future, and that with young historians and ship lovers like him around, there was hope for the future, at least in so far as maritime historic works are concerned.

I liked the way he went about this book. His background was two decades of genuine love of great ocean liners, a variety of different and most interesting travel experiences and a self-taught skill in both research and writing. Salt in a remarkable bit of persistence and you had all the elements needed in a good maritime scholar. Then add to this the facility that a computer can offer (for he had his own computer and knew how to use it) and you had a real contender.

I read several of Milton Watson's travel diaries, written for distribution to his friends, and knew that he could write. I watched him delve into the widest variety of sources, many not easy even to locate, let alone use. I saw this work start from scratch, and I admired what I saw. It offered a needed compendium of information in a concise and most worthwhile way. At the time I predicted that it might become a standard reference work, perhaps with a number of reprints.

It was a pleasant experience to provide some photos for this new work. But the real satisfaction was seeing Milton Watson growing and learning and creating. His sad passing a while back has left a large hole in the area of maritime history. However, when it came to bringing his *Disasters at Sea* up to date, the publishers were fortunate in being able to persuade Bill Miller to undertake the assignment. He has done an outstanding job, and I know that the new Watson-Miller book will be as popular as its first edition.

Introduction

One of the neglected aspects of passenger ships is their demise. Most liners plied the oceans and seas safely and when retirement arrived the company quietly disposed of them. Unfortunately, some liners cheated their owners and the scrapyards and instead, went on to make headlines by meeting a fateful end. Since 1900, I have discovered that some 200 passenger ships either burned, foundered, exploded, collided, were torpedoed, hit a mine or broke down with disastrous consequences.

When contemplating the ships to be included in this work, I decided that certain criteria had to be met. The first criterion was that each ship had to be in commission or undergoing refitting to re-enter passenger service at the time of the accident. The second criterion was that the liner had to be either scuttled, abandoned, scrapped or sunk as a result of the incident. The third was necessary in order to keep the book within manageable proportions — I decided to exclude minor vessels such as overnight inter-island and inter-coastal ships, with the exception of two whose disasters proved significant in maritime history. Finally, I excluded all wartime sinkings except for five cases which involved non-requisitioned ships engaged on their regular commercial routes.

In writing this volume information was gathered from many sources. Particularly useful were the newspaper accounts from *The New York Times* and *The Times* of London. In addition, *Dictionary of Disasters at Sea During the Age of Steam 1824–1962* and court documents, available from the National Archives, provided supplementary material. Statistics were obtained from the *Lloyds Registry of Shipping, Marine News* and the works of Noel Bonsor and Arnold Kludas. I was also allowed to pry into the extensive private libraries of Theodore Scull and Frank O. Braynard, both of whom were gracious enough to give me constructive criticism. All data was cross-checked with two or more sources if it was available and where wide discrepancies in statistics and stories existed, I decided to use what I believed to be the most reliable source.

The layout of the book is straightforward. It is divided chronologically into ten chapters with a brief overview of each ten-year period. The ships are then listed according to the date misfortune occurred. Below each ship's name is listed the owner followed by the ship's statistics, career outline and description of the tragedy that befell her. All ship dimensions are rounded up to the nearest foot.

As a ship enthusiast, I enjoyed researching and writing this book. I can only hope that you will get as much pleasure and knowledge from reading it as I did from producing it.

Milton Watson
Bronx, New York, September 1986

Introduction to the 2nd edition

The late Milton Watson was a good friend and a devoted ship enthusiast and historian. But very sadly he passed away in September 1988. Not quite 40, he was far too young. Producing this book had been one of his greatest joys. Along with two other completed works, *US Passenger Ships Since 1945* and *Flagships of the Line*, he had other titles on the drawing-board. Regrettably they will never see the light of day. But I am very sure that Milton would be delighted, ecstatic even, over the great success of the first edition of *Disasters At Sea*. Now we are bringing it up to date.

There have been over 20 passenger ship disasters since Milton concluded with the *Admiral Nakhimov* tragedy in August 1986. The causes are as varied as ever. Fire claimed the greatest number, 11 in all; four were lost, or at least 'declared to be beyond economic repair', by groundings; three others sank. Finally, one capsized, ironically quite close to the very scrapyard where she would have been broken up. In a way it seems to be an unwritten final chapter in the story of P&O's *Uganda*, one of Britain's most popular and beloved liners.

Nationally, Greek ship owners have suffered the greatest recent losses, eight passenger vessels in all; and four of these belonged to the same owner, the Epirotiki Lines. All of these Greek ships had long and varied careers. Otherwise, three ships were once well-known transatlantic liners: the *American Star* was the former *America*, the one-time pride of the entire US merchant fleet; the *Pallas Athena*, which, as the *Flandre*, was France's first brand new Atlantic liner after the Second World War; and the *Lavia*, once Cunard's *Media*, which had been the first new North Atlantic passenger ship to come into service after that war. Another ship, the *Ramada*

al Salaam, was once one of America's finest passenger ships, the *Santa Paula*.

While the Soviets lost two larger liners within months of one another during 1986, two of their smaller pasenger ships were swept by fires later in 1986 and then in 1988. The *Logos* is the smallest passenger ship mentioned in this recent group and is perhaps the most unusual: she served as a missionary book fair. And at least three ships — the *Stardancer/Pegasus*, the *Danae* and the *Ocean Princess* — were declared complete losses, but then were either resurrected or at least saved pending some future decision on repairs.

Generally we were unable to include large ferries because of space limitations, but such large-scale catastrophes as those that befell the ferries *Herald of Free Enterprise* and *Estonia* could not be ignored. In addition, three ex-ferries sailed also as cruise ships, and therefore also warranted inclusion. The loss of the *Scandinavian Star* was especially tragic since her fiery demise was the result of an onboard arsonist. Then double tragedy certainly followed the two ships named *Sally Albatross*: the first burned and was mostly scrapped, but some of her remains did, in fact, find their way into a brand new successor of the same name. Then, quite coincidentally, she met with tragedy as well.

Sadly, tragic endings for passenger ships, both great and small, will continue. In due course, I expect, *Disasters At Sea* will need another update.

Bill Miller
Secaucus, New Jersey, USA, winter 1994–95

Chapter 1

The only way to cross

In the first decades of the century ship travel was the only way to cross large expanses of ocean. There were no jets to zip people across the Atlantic Ocean in as little as four hours or to fly passengers from Europe across the vast expanses of Asia to Australia in twenty hours. No, it was six days' journey across the Atlantic if a person boarded an express liner or perhaps as much as 35 days' travel to Australia. Comforts — private facilities, air conditioning, gourmet meals and live entertainment — were rare and on some routes non-existent. Captains navigated their ships through stormy oceans and seas without modern navigational aids, and pilots guided the liners in and out of fog-enclosed harbours by instinct.

It is therefore truly amazing that with the hundreds of passenger ships plying the oceans and seas only 46 met disaster in the first ten years of the century: 34 were by groundings, seven collided, two burned, two disappeared and one was overwhelmed by a cyclone. Fog contributed to most of these groundings, with either the pilot or captain misjudging the harbour's landmarks.

Many of the ships lost in the first decade of this century were built in the 1880s and early 1890s, and by the turn of the century were degraded to the carriage of Third Class or Steerage only. For that reason many companies did not list the passenger complement of their respective vessels. Many of the ships that met

untimely ends in the first decade had unusual characteristics. The *Dakota* was the largest American-built ship at the time; and the *Neustria* unhappily became the first ship in the 20th century to simply disappear. The *Republic* was the fastest ship on the Boston run, while the *Slavonia* was the only Cunard liner to be lost at sea during peace time: and the *Lucania*, at one time, was the largest and fastest ship in the world.

Cuvier
Lamport & Holt, Liverpool

Builders: A. Leslie & Co, Hebburn-on-Tyne, 1883.
Particulars: 2,229 gross tons, 302ft × 37ft.
Machinery: Compound engines, single screw, speed 10 knots.
Passengers: 80 First Class.

Date of disaster: 9 March 1900.

Lamport & Holt was founded in 1845. Its fleet sailed to North and South America, South Africa and India. The *Cuvier* was one of two sister-ships built for Lamport's South American service, a route that the company opened in 1863. She left Liverpool on her maiden voyage on 11 November 1883.

Under the command of Captain William

The Union Line Mexican, *in a picture dating back to her pre-1883 three-mast period* (Union Castle Line).

Spratly, the *Cuvier* was sunk in a collision with the SS *Dovre* off East Goodwin lightship on 9 March 1900, with the loss of 26 lives. This was the first of seven Lamport & Holt disasters, and gained for the *Cuvier* the dubious distinction of being the first passenger ship to be lost in the 20th century.

Mexican
Union Steamship Co Ltd, Southampton

Builders: Sir James Laing, Sunderland, 1883.
Particulars: 4,661 gross tons, 378ft × 47ft.
Machinery: Triple-expansion engines, single screw, speed 14 knots.
Passengers: 350 in three classes.

Date of disaster: 5 April 1900

Union Line decided to answer the Castle Line challenge of two sparkling liners by building three sister-ships of their own. In a two-year period Union Line introduced the *Athenian, Moor, Mexican* and *Tartar*. All four were generally similar, reverting back to the three-mast pre-1860 style. They were all employed in the company's England-South Africa service.

Under the command of Captain Copp, the *Mexican* left Cape Town for Southampton on 4 April 1900 with 104 passengers and mails. In the early hours of 5 April, the *Mexican* encountered dense fog. Proceeding dead slow, she collided with the British SS *Winkfield* some

eighty miles from Cape Town. The *Mexican* began to sink slowly and the *Winkfield*, which was only slightly damaged, managed to rescue all of the *Mexican's* passengers and mails. Twelve hours after the collision, the *Mexican* disappeared beneath the waves.

Devenum
Linha de Navegação de J.H. Andresen, Oporto

Previous name: *Rosecliffe* (1888-90).

Builders: Craig, Taylor & Co, Stockton, 1888.
Particulars: 2,298 gross tons, 273ft × 40ft.
Machinery: Triple-expansion engine, single screw, speed 10 knots.
Passengers: 13 First Class, 250 Third Class.

Date of disaster: 3 June 1900.

The Andresen Line was founded by Jan Hinrick Andresen, a Danish-born entrepreneur who settled in and became a citizen of Portugal. The company started operation in 1887, and the *Devenum* was the company's third ship, named after Andresen's birthplace. She joined the other units of the line and sailed between Oporto, Bilbao and New York.

Ten years after her purchase on 3 June 1900, the *Devenum* was wrecked ten miles north of Oporto.

Saale
North German Lloyd, Bremen

Builders: Fairfield Shipbuilding & Engineering Co, Glasgow, 1886.
Particulars: 4,967 gross tons, 440ft × 48ft.
Machinery: Triple-expansion engines, single screw, speed 17 knots.
Passengers: 150 First Class, 90 Second Class, 1,000 Third Class.

Date of disaster: 30 June 1900.

The two-funnel, four-mast *Saale* was one of three sister-ships built for the express service between Bremen, Southampton and New York. During the winter of 1896 and 1897 the *Saale* was refitted and her masts were reduced to two.

North German Lloyd ships docked in Hoboken, New Jersey and occupied Piers One, Two and Three. On the afternoon of 30 June 1900, a fire started among the cotton stored on Pier Three. Beside the cotton, barrels of turpentine and oil were also stored on the pier: soon they were ablaze. Docked that day were the North German Lloyd liners *Kaiser Wilhelm Der Grosse, Saale, Main* and *Bremen.* The strong wind fanned the flames the length of the pier and over to the tied-up ships. The *Kaiser* got up steam and pulled away with minor damage but the other ships were pulled out ablaze. People on the deck of the *Saale* jumped into the Hudson River: others trapped inside screamed for help through the open portholes,

Saale *departing New York* (Frank O. Braynard collection).

too small for them to get through. The *Saale* finally sunk on the Jersey flats. Between her decks were the charred and twisted bodies of 99 victims.

The *Saale* was never returned to passenger service. She was sold in 1900 and renamed *J.L. Luckenbach,* a US cargo steamer with one funnel. In 1921 she was renamed *Princess,* and finally, in 1923, *Madison,* all under US ownership. Her end came in 1924 at the scrapyards in Italy.

As a result of the Hoboken disaster, portholes on ships were made bigger so that a person could escape through them in an emergency.

The Saale *burning in Upper New York Bay* (Hoboken Public Library/Theodore W. Scull collection).

City of Rio de Janeiro
Pacific Mail Steamship Co, New York

Builders: J. Roach & Son, Chester, 1878.
Particulars: 3,548 gross tons, 345ft × 39ft.
Machinery: Triple-expansion engines, single screw, speed 14 knots.
Passengers: 100 First Class, 500 Steerage.

Date of disaster: 22 February 1901.

The *City of Rio de Janeiro* was built for United States and Brazil Mail Steamship Co in 1878. Purchased by Pacific Mail in 1881, the *City of Rio de Janeiro* was employed on the California-Far East service.

The *City of Rio de Janeiro* left Yokohama on 2 February 1901 with 201 persons aboard under the command of Captain Ward. The liner reached San Francisco during the early morning of 22 February under dense fog. The *City of Rio de Janeiro* picked up her pilot, Fredrick Jordan, who warned of possible danger if Captain Ward persisted in attempting the passage through the Golden Gate. The Captain insisted and proceeded. The *City of Rio de Janeiro* struck rocks and sustained extensive damage below the waterline. Within an hour, the ship pitched forward and went down taking 72 passengers and 32 crew members, including her Captain, with her.

Left City of Rio de Janeiro — *note the sails on the forward mast* (Courtesy of the Steamship Historical Society collection/University of Baltimore Library).

Below Union Castle's *Tantallon Castle at anchor* (Union Castle Line).

Tantallon Castle
Union-Castle Line, London

Builders: Fairfield Shipbuilding Co, Glasgow 1894.
Particulars: 5,636 gross tons, 440ft × 51ft.
Machinery: Quadruple-expansion engines, single screw, speed 16 knots.
Passengers: 200 First Class, 170 Second Class.

Date of disaster: 7 May 1901.

The *Tantallon Castle* was a three-masted liner originally built for Castle Line's mail service between England and South Africa. In May 1895, she carried 384 passengers to England, at that time a record for the South African service. In February 1900, Union Line and Castle Line amalgamated to form Union-Castle Line.

At the end of her long voyage from England, the *Tantallon Castle* encountered fog some forty miles outside Cape Town, and as a result ran on to a shoal a few hundred yards to the north-west of Robben Island, at 3:20 pm on 7 May 1901. Captain de la Cour Travers sounded the ship's siren and fired distress guns and rockets. Calm was maintained on board until the local steamer *Magnet* arrived on the scene at five o'clock and took on all the *Tantallon Castle's* 120 passengers and some of her crew. The remaining crew, with the assistance of harbour tugs, tried to free the ship. However, all attempts were in vain, for within a few days the sea rose and the great Atlantic battered the vessel into a mass of junk strewn about the beaches.

Lusitania
Elder Dempster, Liverpool

Builders: Laird Bros, Birkenhead, 1877.
Particulars: 3,912 gross tons, 380ft × 41ft.
Machinery: Triple-expansion engines, single screw, speed 12 knots.
Passengers: 70 First Class, 85 Second Class, 700 Steerage.

Date of disaster: 26 June 1901.

Elder Dempster was founded in 1852 under the banner of African Steam Ship Company, whose activities were confined to West Africa. On 3 November 1891, the company entered the North Atlantic trade with the *Alexander Elder*. In 1900 the company purchased the *Lusitania* and placed her on the Liverpool-Canada run, which she started on 31 March 1900. Back in 1877 this vessel had inaugurated Orient Line's service to Australia, making the passage from London to Melbourne in forty days and six hours with a compound engine: the *Lusitania* was re-engined in 1886.

Nearing the end of a voyage, the *Lusitania* mistook her course in a dense fog and ran over a reef and hung against a cliff near Renews, Canada, twenty miles north of Cape Race, before daybreak. Panic-stricken passengers stampeded to the boats, but the officers and crew managed to bring order to the evacuation. Later, furious rainstorms and a heavy sea finished off the liner.

Lusitania *in Orient Line's colours. She was sold in 1900 to Elder Dempster* (P & O Group).

Armenia
Anchor Line, Glasgow

Builders: D. & W. Henderson Ltd, Glasgow, 1881.
Particulars: 3,396 gross tons, 364ft × 38ft.
Machinery: Compound engines, single screw, speed 11 knots.
Passengers: 40 First Class.

Date of disaster: 29 June 1901.

Anchor Line built the *Armenia* for their Indian service, their main source of revenue. She plied that route from 1881 to 1890. In April 1890 and thereafter, she made some voyages to New York.

On 29 June 1901 the *Armenia* was wrecked near St John, New Brunswick. There was no loss of life.

Mexico
Compañiá Transatlántica Española, SA, Barcelona
Previous name: *Trentham Hall* (1875–85).

Builders: London & Glasgow Co, Glasgow, 1875.
Particulars: 2,101 gross tons, 332ft × 34ft.
Machinery: Compound engines, single screw, speed 10 knots.
Passengers: Data not available.
Date of disaster: 7 July 1901.

The four-masted Armenia *of Anchor Line* (Courtesy of the Steamship Historical Society collection/ University of Baltimore Library).

After trading for several years as the *Trentham Hall,* the vessel was bought by the Spanish and renamed *Mexico.* Her first voyage under her new owners commenced on 23 March 1900, from Liverpool to Montevideo and Valparaiso. Two more round voyages followed in July and December 1900.

Misfortune struck *Mexico* on her homeward passage on 7 July 1901, when she struck rocks and wrecked herself six miles south of Vianno do Castello, Portugal. All 580 persons aboard were saved.

Grecian
Allan Line, Glasgow

Builders: Wm Doxford & Sons, Sunderland, 1880.
Particulars: 3,613 gross tons, 361ft × 40ft.
Machinery: Compound engines, single screw, speed 11 knots.
Passengers: 50 First Class, 270 Second Class, 500 Steerage.

Date of disaster: 9 February 1902.

Allan Line started in the transatlantic business in 1854 when the *Canadian* sailed on her

Allan Line's Grecian *(The Mariners' Museum).*

maiden voyage. The *Grecian* was launched on 16 October 1879, and within a year, by 21 April 1880, she was ready and despatched on her maiden voyage from Glasgow to Quebec and Montreal. In December 1880 she undertook a few trips between Glasgow and South America, and was chartered as a troopship for the Egyptian Expedition between 1882 and 1886. The *Grecian* was returned to her owners and commenced her first sailing on 16 September 1886, between London and Canada.

On 9 February 1902, nearing the end of a voyage from Liverpool, the *Grecian* was wrecked at Sandwich Point, seven miles southeast of Halifax, Nova Scotia.

Waesland
American Line, New York
Previous name: *Russia* (1867–80).

Builders: J. & G. Thomson, Glasgow, 1867.
Particulars: 4,752 gross tons, 435ft × 42ft.
Machinery: Triple-expansion engines, single screw, speed 14 knots.

The Waesland *sailed for two owners before she was sold to American Line (Courtesy of the Steamship Historical Society collection/University of Baltimore Library).*

Passengers: 120 First Class, 1,500 Steerage.

Date of disaster: 5 March 1902.

When the *Russia* was built, she was 358 ft long, carried 235 First Class passengers and had inverted engines. Together with the *Scotia* and *Persia* of Cunard Line, she carried out a fortnightly service between Liverpool and New York. In 1880 the *Russia* was sold to Red Star Line. She was lengthened to 435 ft, given another mast (now four), fitted with compound engines, and altered to carry 1,600 passengers. Tonnage was increased from 2,960 to 4,752. Renamed *Waesland,* she commenced her first voyage in 1880. On 11 February 1895 she was purchased by the American Line and started sailing under that company's flag on 11 September 1895.

The *Waesland* was sunk in a collision with the SS *Harmonides* off Anglesey on 5 March 1902. Two people lost their lives..

The Lake Superior's *fore mast was fitted to accommodate sails* (Courtesy of the Steamship Historical Society collection/University of Baltimore Library).

Lake Superior
Elder Dempster, Liverpool
Previous name: *Evans* (1884–99).

Builders: J. & G. Thomson, Glasgow, 1884.
Particulars: 4,562 gross tons, 400ft × 44ft.
Machinery: Triple-expansion engines, single screw, speed 11 knots.
Passengers: 190 First Class, 80 Second Class, Third Class unknown.

Date of disaster: 31 March 1902.

The *Evans* sailed for fifteen years for the Beaver Line before being purchased in 1899 by Elder Dempster, who renamed her *Lake Superior* and despatched her on the Liverpool-Canada run.

On 31 March 1902 she was wrecked near St John, New Brunswick with no loss of life. The *Lake Superior* was salvaged and scrapped where she lay.

Camorta
British India Steam Navigation Co, London

Builders: A. & J. Inglis, Glasgow, 1880.
Particulars: 2,119 gross tons, 285ft × 35ft.
Machinery: Compound inverted engines, single screw, speed 11 knots.
Passengers: Data not available.
Date of disaster: April 1902.

British India was formed in 1862 to provide a passenger and mail service between England and India. Service was later extended to Australia, East Africa and the Persian Gulf. The iron-hulled *Camorta* joined the fleet in 1880 for the London-India service. She made one trip out to Australia in 1883, and was transferred in 1886 to Netherlands India Steam Navigation Co. She was transferred back to British India in 1886.

The *Camorta* left Madras in April 1902 with 650 passengers and a crew of 89 for Rangoon, Burma. A cyclone blew up in the Gulf of Martaban and the *Camorta* was overwhelmed, taking with her the entire ship's complement.

Bretagne
Société Générale des Transports Maritimes (SGTM), Marseille

Builders: Forges et Chantiers de la Méditerranée, La Seyne, 1877.
Particulars: 2,209 gross tons, 289ft × 39ft.
Machinery: Compound engine, single screw, speed 11 knots.
Passengers: Data not available.

Date of disaster: 12 September 1903.

The *Bretagne* was SGTM's sixth ship, and she was almost exclusively employed on the Marseille–South America service. However, when demand required additional tonnage on SGTM Mediterranean service, the *Bretagne* was switched accordingly.

The *Bretagne* wrecked herself at Bahia on 12 September 1903. Fortunately no lives were lost.

Kurfurst
Deutsche Ost Afrika Linie, Hamburg

Builders: Reicherstieg Werft, Hamburg, 1901.
Particulars: 5,655 gross tons, 411ft × 48ft.
Machinery: Triple-expansion engines, twin screw, speed 13 knots.
Passengers: 100 First Class, plus Second and Third (numbers unknown).

Date of disaster: 6 May 1904.

The *Kurfurst* was a two-masted, one-funnel liner built exclusively for the Hamburg–East Africa colonial trade.

During foggy conditions the *Kurfurst* was wrecked near Sagres on the coast of Portugal on 6 May 1904, with no loss of life.

Norge
Scandinavian American Line, Copenhagen
Previous name: *Pieter de Coninck* (1881–89).

Builders: A. Stephen & Sons, Glasgow, 1881.
Particulars: 3,310 gross tons, 340ft × 41ft.
Machinery: Compound engines, single screw, speed 11 knots.

Top *One of the first ships with engines aft was SGTM's* Bretagne (Courtesy of the Steamship Historical Society collection/University of Baltimore Library). **Above Right** *German colonial steamer* Kurfurst (Courtesy of the Steamship Historical Society collection/University of Baltimore Library). **Right** *The* Norge *underway for Scandinavian American Line.* (Courtesy of the Steamship Historical Society collection/University of Baltimore Library).

76 -- BRETAGNE

Passengers: 50 First Class, 150 Second Class, 900 Steerage.

Date of disaster: 28 June 1904.

The *Norge* joined the Scandinavian American fleet as their third ship in 1898, after serving nine years with Thingvalla, another Danish company engaged in North Atlantic shipping. The *Norge* sailed from Stettin, Copenhagen and Christiania, Christiansand to New York. She commenced her maiden voyage on that route on 29 November 1898.

The *Norge* left Copenhagen on 22 June 1904 for New York with 700 emigrants and a crew of eighty. Six days later, she ran on to the rocks at Rockall. In an attempt to refloat her, the Captain ordered reverse engines, but in the process of refloating the vessel was severely holed. As a result, the *Norge* began to sink quickly. Approximately 550 persons perished.

Australia
Peninsular and Oriental Steam Navigation Co, London

Builders: Caird & Co, Greenock, 1892.
Particulars: 6,901 gross tons, 466ft × 52ft.

Machinery: Triple-expansion engine, single screw, speed 17 knots.
Passengers: 265 First Class, 140 Second Class.

Date of disaster: 29 June 1904.

The *Australia* was the biggest ship yet built at Greenock, and was one of two sister-ships designed for the Australia service. She commenced her maiden voyage on 25 November 1892 from London to Sydney. In April 1893 she created a new record for the Australian run by steaming from London to Adelaide in 26 days, 16 hours.

The *Australia* left London on 13 May 1904 for another routine voyage to Australia. Nearing the end of that trip, on the approach to Port Phillip, near Melbourne, the pilot made an error in judgment connected with the navigation lights. As a result, the *Australia* went aground on the Corsair Rock off Point Nepan at about 2:00 am on 20 June. All on board — 294 people — were safely taken off, and her cargo and fittings were brought ashore and sold for £30,000. The *Australia* was then declared a total loss, and a few days later she was gutted by fire.

The four-masted Australia *built for P & O's Australian service* (P & O Group).

Damara
Furness, Withy & Co, London

Builders: A. Stephen & Sons, Glasgow, 1885.
Particulars: 1,779 gross tons, 275ft × 35ft.
Machinery: Compound engines, single screw, speed 10 knots.
Passengers: 40 First Class, 20 Second Class.

Date of disaster: 7 February 1905.

The *Damara* started her twenty-year career sailing for Halifax Steam Navigating Co in 1885. Handed over to Furness in 1886, the *Damara* began her first voyage between London – Halifax and St John, New Brunswick on 6 May 1886.

The *Damara* foundered off Musquodoboit on 7 February 1905 while on a voyage from Liverpool to Halifax.

Orizaba
Orient Line, London

Builders: Barrow Shipbuilding Co, Barrow, 1886.
Particulars: 6,077 gross tons, 460ft × 49ft.
Machinery: Triple-expansion engines, single screw, speed 15 knots.
Passengers: 126 First Class, 154 Second Class, 400 Third Class.

Date of disaster: 16 February 1905.

The *Orizaba* became the 22nd vessel to enter service on the Australia route for Orient Line. She commenced her maiden voyage on 30 September 1886, and, like most ships of her day, the *Orizaba's* first mast was fitted with square yards to accommodate auxiliary sails.

On 16 February 1905, the *Orizaba* was approaching Fremantle when, due to poor visibility attributed to forest fires, she sailed to the west of Rottnest Island instead of the east. As a result, she ran aground and holed herself under her engineroom — becoming a total loss. She was the second (the wrecking of the *John Elder* in January 1892 was the first) and last peacetime misfortune to visit the popular Orient Line.

Orizaba *sailing through the Suez Canal* (P & O Group).

Chodoc
Compagnie des Chargeurs Réunis, Marseille

Builders: Forges et Chantiers de la Méditerranée, La Seyne, 1898.
Particulars: 4,686 gross tons, 413ft × 42ft.
Machinery: Triple-expansion engines, single screw.
Passengers: Data not available.

Date of disaster: 23 June 1905.

Chargeurs Réunis was created in 1872 to maintain a service between France and South America. Later the company branched out to other areas. The *Chodoc* was acquired from Cie

Rohilla Maru *pictured here as P & O's* Rohilla (P & O Group).

Nationale de Navigation in October 1904, and placed on Chargeurs' Far East service.

The *Chodoc* ran aground near Gardafui on 23 June 1905, and was declared a total constructive loss.

Rohilla Maru
Toyo Kisen Kabushiki Kaisha, Tokyo
Previous name: *Rohilla* (1880–1900).

Builders: Caird & Company, Greenock, 1880.
Particulars: 3,869 gross tons, 387ft × 39ft.
Machinery: Compound engines, single screw, speed 14 knots.
Passengers: Data not available.

Date of disaster: July 1905.

The *Rohilla* was an iron-hulled liner employed on the England-Bombay and England-Australia routes for P&O Line from 1880 to 1900. She was purchased by the Japanese in 1900, renamed *Rohilla Maru* and placed on various routes.

In July 1905, she was wrecked at Ujina in the China Inland Sea.

Cyril
Booth Line, Liverpool
Previous name: *Hawarden Castle* (1883–1904).

Builders: John Elder & Co, Glasgow, 1883.
Particulars: 4,380 gross tons, 381ft × 48ft.
Machinery: Triple-expansion engines, single screw, speed 14 knots.
Passengers: 160 First Class, 90 Second Class Third Class.

Date of disaster: 5 September 1905.

Booth Line started out as an import company founded in 1860 by Alfred Booth and an American named Walden. The company decided to go into the South American shipping business and in 1865 ordered their first ship, which started England-Brazilian service in February 1866. The company prospered and in 1904 purchased the *Hawarden Castle,* a ship christened by Mrs Gladstone, wife of the Prime Minister of that name. Renamed *Cyril,* the ship plied the Liverpool-Amazon River route, extending into Manus.

Booth Line's 39-year safety record was shattered when on 5 September 1905, one of their own ships, the *Anselm,* collided with and sank the *Cyril* in the Amazon River.

The Cyril *which shattered Booth Line's 39-year safety record* (Courtesy of the Steamship Historical Society collection/University of Baltimore Library).

Bavarian
Allan Line, Glasgow

Builders: William Denny & Bros, Dumbarton, 1899.
Particulars: 10,376 gross tons, 520ft × 59ft.
Machinery: Triple-expansion engines by Denny, twin screw, speed 16 knots.
Passengers: 240 First Class, 220 Second Class, 1,000 Steerage.

The Allan Line steamship Bavarian *at Indian Cove, after breaking in two* (Arnold Kludas collection).

Date of disaster: 3 November 1905.

The *Bavarian* was launched on 11 May, delivered 18 August, and commenced her maiden voyage from Liverpool to Montreal on 24 August 1899. When commissioned, the *Bavarian* was the first ship in the Canadian Trade to exceed 10,000 tons. After two voyages, the *Bavarian* was taken over by the British government for use as a troop transport in the Boer War. The *Bavarian* resumed her regular schedule on 9 October 1902.

On 3 November 1905, the *Bavarian* was stranded on Wye Rock off Montreal, later breaking in two. In November 1906 the hulk of the *Bavarian* was towed to Quebec where it was scrapped the following year.

Caobang
Messageries Maritimes, Marseille

Builders: Forges et Chantiers de la
Méditerranée, La Seyne, 1902.
Particulars: 6,762 gross tons, 446ft × 47ft.
Machinery: Triple-expansion engines, twin
screw, speed 14.5 knots.
Passengers: Data not available.

Date of disaster: 4 January 1906.

Like the *Chodoc*, the *Caobang* was purchased
from Cie Nationale de Navigation in August
1904, and placed on Messageries Maritimes Far
East service.

The *Caobang* was lost due to fog on
4 January 1906, when she went aground at
Poulo Condor, becoming the first of eight
Messageries Maritimes tragedies.

Etolia
Elder Dempster, Liverpool

Builders: Harland & Wolff, Belfast, 1887.
Particulars: 3,270 gross tons, 346ft × 41ft.
Machinery: Triple-expansion engines, single
screw.
Passengers: Data not available.

Date of disaster: 10 June 1906.

The steel and iron hull of the *Etolia* supported
two masts and one funnel and served in the
England-West Africa service, though occasional
transatlantic voyages were also made.

On 10 June 1906, while on a voyage from St
John, New Brunswick to Barrow, the *Etolia*
was wrecked near Cap Sable with no loss of
life.

Sirio
Società Italiana di Trasporti Maritimi Raggio & Co, Genoa

Builders: Robert Napier & Sons, Glasgow,
1883.
Particulars: 4,141 gross tons, 380ft × 42ft.

Machinery: Three-cylinder compound
engines, single screw, speed 13 knots.

Passengers: 80 First Class, 40 Second Class,
1,200 Third Class.

Date of disaster: 4 August 1906.

When the *Sirio* commenced her maiden
voyage from Genoa to South America on 15
July 1883, she was one of the finest liners on
that route, but after Raggio commissioned two
more vessels to complement the *Sirio*, the
company went into liquidation. Their ships,
including the *Sirio*, were sold to the
Navigazione General Italiana (NGI) in 1885.
The *Sirio* continued on the Genoa-
Montevideo-Buenos Aires route. Considered
too slow in comparison with her new fleet
mates, the *Sirio* was given triple-expansion
engines in 1891, increasing her speed to 15
knots.

The *Sirio* sailed from Genoa for Montevideo
and Buenos Aires via Cadiz in August 1906,
with 645 passengers and a crew of 127. En
route to Cadiz, Captain Paradi decided to
shorten the run by taking his ship as close as
possible along the dangerous rocky ledges
surrounding the Hormigas Island. The result
was that the *Sirio* struck Hormigas Island at full
speed. Within minutes the stern started to sink
and the passengers, mainly immigrants,
stampeded forward in their panic, fighting each
other with knives for the boats and life buoys.
Fishing boats in the area raced to the scene and
rescued whom they could. When it was over, it
was found that some 442 people had died.

In an investigation that followed, it was
stated that 'the *Sirio* was engaged in the
clandestine embarkation of Spanish immigrants
along the coast... which explains why the
vessel followed a course never taken by ships
of equal draught'.

Facing Page Top Caobang *built in 1902* (Courtesy
of the Steamship Historical Society collec-
tion/University of Baltimore Library). **Middle** *Elder
Dempster's* Etolia *built in 1887* (Courtesy of the
Steamship Historical Society collection/University
of Baltimore Library). **Bottom** Sirio *was one of the
finest Italian ships operating to South America*
(Courtesy of the Steamship Historical Society collec-
tion/University of Baltimore Library).

Prinzessin Victoria Luise
Hamburg American Line, Hamburg

Builders: Blohm & Voss, Hamburg, 1900.
Particulars: 4,409 gross tons, 408ft × 47ft.
Machinery: Quadruple-expansion engines, twin screw, speed 15 knots.
Passengers: 200 First Class.

Date of disaster: 16 December 1906.

Hamburg-American was one of the first European companies to engage in cruises. This idea arose when the company sought better ways to utilize their express steamers during the lean winter months. At the instigation of Albert Ballin (director of the line) the experiment was tried, and in January 1891, the *Augusta Victoria* was sent on a pleasure cruise from Hamburg to the Mediterranean. The cruise was a great success and in subsequent years cruises were run to a variety of destinations. To accommodate affluent cruise passengers in luxurious style, the company introduced the yacht-like *Prinzessin Victoria Luise* in 1900, complete with a clipper bow. When transatlantic traffic necessitated the need for additional tonnage, the *Prinzessin Victoria Luise* was pressed into that service. Her first sailing from Hamburg to New York was undertaken on 5 January 1901. Until her ultimely demise in 1906, she made only six round transatlantic voyages, with the rest of her time spent cruising the world.

Prinzesin Victoria Luise *displaying her beautiful lines* (Courtesy of the Steamship Historical Society collection University of Baltimore Library).

On 12 December 1906 the *Prinzessin Victoria Luise* departed New York on a cruise to Port Antonio and Kingston, both in Jamaica, with 74 passengers, of whom three were accompanied by their maids. On the homeward passage along the coast of Jamaica, the ship was sailing without a pilot. The *Prinzessin Victoria Luise* was following a course set by her Captain, H. Brunswig. During the night of 6 December the *Prinzessin Victoria Luise* ran on the rocks under the lighthouse off Port Royal. Panic among the passengers followed the impact and for a time confusion prevailed. The officers had to reassure them that there was no immediate danger, and once this became evident to the frightened passengers the tumult subsided. The next morning the passengers were landed without mishap and transferred to various hotels. Later that afternoon a storm came up, and the *Prinzessin Victoria Luise,* lying on a ledge of rocks, began to take a heavy pounding from the tempestuous seas.

Sensing that he had plotted the incorrect course, sometime during the night of 16 December Captain Brunswig locked himself in his cabin and committed suicide by blowing his brains out.

After nineteen years of service the Imperatrix *was wrecked* (Courtesy of the Steamship Historical Society collection/University of Baltimore Library).

Imperatrix
Lloyd Austriaco, Trieste

Builders: Lloyd Austro-Ungarico, Trieste, 1888.
Particulars: 4,213 gross tons, 390ft × 45ft.
Machinery: Triple-expansion engines, single screw, speed 14 knots.
Passengers: Data not available.

Date of disaster: 24 February 1907.

The *Imperatrix* was built with a steel hull and had three masts and one funnel. Her trading career was spent between Europe and Asia.

On 24 February 1907 the *Imperatrix* ran on the rocks near Cape Elaphomnisi, Crete. Foreign warships rescued most people aboard but forty members of the crew lost their lives. Once abandoned, the *Imperatrix* sank stern first.

Dakota
Great Northern Steam Ship Co, New London

Builders: Eastern Shipbuilding Co, New London,1905.
Particulars: 20,714 gross tons, 630ft × 74ft.
Machinery: Triple-expansion engines, twin screw, speed 14 knots.
Passengers: 300 First Class, 2,400 Steerage.

Date of disaster: 7 March 1907.

Dakota *was the largest American-built ship until surpassed in 1928* (Puget Sound Maritime Historical Society).

Dakota *going down on 7 March 1907* (Arnold Kludas collection).

The *Dakota* was the largest American-built passenger ship at the time of her commission, and held that distinction until surpassed in 1928 by the *Virgina*. Together with the *Minnesota*, the two giants were a source of pride to the citizens of Seattle and the Pacific Northwest. James Hill, proprietor of the Great Northern Railway, designed the two ships to ferry the passengers and freight from his trains across the Pacific to the Orient. A unique feature on each ship was an opium den located on the far stern on Main Deck for the use of Chinese passengers.

On 7 March, 1907 the *Dokota* ran aground forty nautical miles from Yokohama on a submerged reef, forcing passengers and crew to abandon ship. Sixteen days later on 23 March, the *Dakota* broke up during a storm and was shortly thereafter scrapped on the spot. The Captain spent the remainder of his life as a night watchman in a San Francisco shipyard.

Poitou
Société Générale des Transports Maritimes

(SGTM), Marseille
Previous names: *Batavia* (1883–93); *Soembing* (1893–1903).

Builders: Koninklijke Maatschapij de Schelde, Flushing, 1883.
Particulars: 2,679 gross tons, 320ft × 37ft.
Machinery: Two-cylinder double-expansion engines, single screw, speed 12 knots.
Passengers: Data not available.

Date of disaster: 7 May 1907.

The *Poitou* was a secondhand vessel purchased by SGTM for their South American service. The *Poitou* started sailing under her new flag on 30 December 1903.

During a voyage to Montevideo, the *Poitou* was wrecked off San Jose Ignacio, on the Uruguaian coast on 7 May 1907. In the collision and subsequent evacuation, twenty persons lost their lives.

Tartar
Canadian Pacific, London

Builders: Aitken & Mansel, Glasgow, 1883.
Particulars: 4,339 gross tons, 377ft × 47ft.
Machinery: Triple-expansion engines, single screw, speed 14 knots.
Passengers: 160 First Class, 160 Second Class, 100 Third Class.

Date of disaster: 17 October 1907.

Built originally for Union Line's mail and passenger run to South Africa, the *Tartar* was acquired by Canadian Pacific to participate in the Klondyke Gold Rush of 1897. With few changes, and the same name, Canadian Pacific sent her out in March 1898. Between July 1899 and April 1900, the *Tartar* was chartered to the United States government.

On 17 October 1907, the *Tartar* was in a collision with the coastal steamer *Charmer* resulting in the *Tartar* being beached at English Bay, British Columbia. In 1908 she was sold to Japanese shipbreakers and broken up in Osaka.

Borussia
Hamburg American Line, Hamburg

Builders: Germaniawerft (Fried Krupp AG), Kiel, 1906.
Particulars: 6,951 gross tons, 421ft × 54ft.
Machinery: Quadruple-expansion engines, twin screw, speed 13 knots.
Passengers: 62 First Class, 40 Second Class, 1,776 Third Class.

Date of disaster: 22 October 1907.

Catering basically to an emigrant clientele, the *Borussia* was launched on 24 March 1905. Completed, the *Borussia* was despatched on her first voyage from Hamburg to Rio de Janeiro on 25 September 1906.

While coaling in Lisbon on 22 October 1907, the *Borussia* foundered. Three crewmen died.

Newark Castle
Union-Castle Line, London

Builders: Barclay, Curle & Co, Glasgow, 1901.
Particulars: 6,224 gross tons, 414ft × 51ft.
Machinery: Triple-expansion engines, twin screw, speed 12 knots.
Passengers: Data not available.

Date of disaster: 12 March 1908.

The *Newark Castle* was one of four steel-hulled sister-ships built for the West African and Mauritius service.

She left Durban for Mauritius on 12 March 1908 with 115 persons, of whom 46 passengers and 69 crew. Six hours later, around 6:00 pm, after leaving port, the *Newark Castle* ran

Top *Acquired by Canadian Pacific in 1897, the* Tartar *sailed until 1907 (Canadian Pacific).* **Above Right** Borussia *was an emigrant carrier in the South American trade (Courtesy of the Steamship Historical Society collection/University of Baltimore Library).* **Right** Newark Castle *was built for Union-Castle's African service (The Mariners' Museum).*

NGL's Hohenzollern (The Mariners' Museum).

ashore in Richard's Bay near the Umhlatuzi River. The sea was calm and the passengers were sent off in the ship's boats. Unfortunately, one capsized in an attempt to reach shore and drowned three persons. The Captain and most of the crew remained on board and with the assistance of a tug freed the liner. The *Newark Castle* then drifted away and grounded again on a sandbank some seven miles distant, eventually becoming a total wreck.

Hohenzollern
North German Lloyd, Bremen
Previous name: *Kaiser Wilhelm II*
(1889–1901).

Builders: A.G. Vulcan, Stettin, 1889.
Particulars: 6,661 gross tons, 450ft × 51ft.
Machinery: Triple-expansion engines, single screw, speed 16 knots.
Passengers: 120 First Class, 80 Second Class, 1,000 Third Class.

Date of disaster: 10 May 1908.

When the *Kaiser Wilhelm II* was commissioned in 1889, she was the longest vessel in the North German Lloyd fleet. The *Kaiser Wilhelm II* first saw service on the North Atlantic between Bremen and New York.

Later in October 1889, she started a series of voyages to Australia via the Suez Canal. In November 1892, the *Kaiser Wilhelm II* was switched to the Genoa-New York route. Seven months later, on 5 June she sank at her berth in Genoa. Refloated, she resumed service in July that year. In 1900 the *Kaiser Wilhelm II* was renamed *Hohenzollern* with no change in service.

On 10 May 1908, while on a trip in the Mediterranean, the *Hohenzollern* was stranded at Alghero, Sardinia. She was refloated and sold for scrap in Italy.

Cap Frio
Hamburg-South America Line, Hamburg

Builders: Reicherstieg Werft, Hamburg, 1900.
Particulars: 5,732 gross tons, 411ft × 48ft.
Machinery: Quadruple-expansion engines, single screw, speed 12 knots.
Passengers: 80 First Class, 500 Third Class.

Date of disaster: 30 August 1908.

Due to an increase in emigrant traffic from Europe to South America and a demand for

Hamburg-South America Line's Cap Frio (Hamburg South America Line).

First Class accommodation in both directions, Hamburg-South America Line decided to build five *'Cap'* class liners of which *Cap Frio* was the first. *Cap Frio* started her maiden voyage from Hamburg on 2 March 1900, and headed for Rio, Montevideo and Buenos Aires.

During a tropical storm off Brazil on 30 August 1908, the *Cap Frio* was blown aground. In the process she holed herself and sank near the city of Bahia.

Velasquez
Lamport & Holt, Liverpool

Builders: Sir Raylton Dixon & Co, Middlesbrough, 1906.
Particulars: 7,542 gross tons, 466ft × 59ft.
Machinery: Triple-expansion engines, single screw, speed 12 knots.
Passengers: Data not available.

Date of disaster: 16 October 1908.

The first three voyages of the *Velasquez* were between Liverpool and Buenos Aires. In 1907 she was switched to Lamport's highly successful New York-Buenos Aires run.

On 16 October 1908, during dense fog, the *Velasquez* stranded near Santos, Brazil. There were no casualties, but she became a total loss.

Neustria
Fabre Line, Marseille

Builders: Claparede & Cie, Rouen, 1883.
Particulars: 2,926 gross tons, 328ft × 40ft.
Machinery: Compound engines, single screw, speed 12 knots.
Passengers: 18 First Class, 1,100 Steerage.

Date of disaster: October/November 1908.

Fabre was founded in 1865 with services confined to the Mediterranean. Transatlantic sailings were inaugurated in 1882. The *Neustria,* their fifth ship on the route, was also their first French-built ship and their largest vessel at the time of her commissioning. She was employed on the Marseille-New York run with a stop in Spain. During the Spanish America War, the *Neustria* was chartered by Spain to repatriate Spanish troops from Cuba.

On 27 October 1908, the *Neustria* sailed from New York to Marseille and was never heard from or seen again. Her name was deleted from the 1909–10 edition of *Lloyd's Register of Shipping.*

Republic
White Star Line, Liverpool
Previous name: *Columbus* (1903).

Builders: Harland & Wolff, Belfast, 1903.
Particulars: 15,378 gross tons, 585ft ×
58ft.
Machinery: Quadruple-expansion engines,
twin screw, speed 16 knots.
Passengers: 200 First Class, 2,000 Steerage.

Date of disaster: 23 January 1909.

The *Columbus* sailed on her maiden voyage
between Liverpool and Boston on 1 October
1903, under the banner of Dominion Line. In
December 1903, she was sold to White Star
Line and renamed *Republic*. The *Republic*
became White Star's flagship on the Boston-
Liverpool run, and she also held the record for
the fastest passages between Boston and
Queenstown. During the winter months, the
Republic was engaged in the emigrant traffic
between Boston/New York and Naples/Genoa.

Above *A striking view of the* Republic *taken before
1912* (Harland & Wolff).

Below *The hapless* Republic *is abandoned in mid-
Atlantic. To the left is the* New York *and right
background, the* Lucania *(Frank O. Braynard
collection).*

Outward bound from New York to the
Mediterranean with 442 passengers and
supplies for the US battleship fleet, the
Republic collided with the Italian emigrant
steamer, *Florida*, 175 miles east of Ambrose
Lightship at 5:30 am on 23 January 1909. The
Republic sent out the first SOS distress call in
sea history, on the new infant wireless system.
The liners *Baltic, Furnessia,* and *La Lorraine*
answered the call for assistance. Once she was
evacuated the US revenue tug *Gresham* took
the *Republic* in tow. However, next morning
she sank. The fact that only four people were
killed can be attributed to the ability of the new
wireless system to send out a distress call and
attract the attention of potential rescue vessels.

Slavonia
Cunard Line, Liverpool
Previous name: *Yamuna* (1902–1904).

Builders: Sir James Laing, Sunderland, 1902.
Particulars: 10,606 gross tons, 526ft × 60ft.
Machinery: Triple-expansion engines, twin screw, speed 13 knots.
Passengers: 71 First Class, 74 Second Class, 1,954 Third Class.

Date of disaster: 10 June 1909.

The *Yamuna* sailed for British India until purchased in 1904 by Cunard Line. Renamed *Slavonia*, Cunard placed her on their secondary Trieste-New York route.

On a voyage from New York to Trieste with 410 passengers, the *Slavonia* went aground two miles south-west of Flores Island on 10 June 1909. Captain A.G. Dunning sent out a wireless call for help and the German steamers *Princess Irene* and *Batavia* responded. All the passengers were taken to the German ships. As the vessel began to fill with water and bang against the edges of the coral reef, the crew started to abandon her. The *Slavonia* was written off as a total loss and was the only Cunard ship to be lost at sea in peacetime.

Cunard's Slavonia *was engaged in the New York-Mediterranean service* (Courtesy of the Steamship Historical Society collection/University of Baltimore Library).

The Slavonia *going under stern first by the rocks* (Richard Morse collection/The Mariners' Museum).

Waratah
Blue Anchor Line, London

Builders: Barclay, Curle & Co, Glasgow, 1908.
Particulars: 9,339 gross tons, 465ft × 59ft.
Machinery: Quadruple-expansion engines, twin screw, speed 14 knots.
Passengers: 128 First Class, 160 Third Class.

Date of disaster: July 1909.

Blue Anchor's answer to the *Pericles* of the Aberdeen Line was the *Waratah*, the largest and finest ship ever built for them. The *Waratah*, named after an Australian wild flower, left London on her maiden voyage to Australia via Cape of Good Hope on 6 November 1908. In addition to passenger cabins, provision was made in the *Waratah* for the carriage of several hundred emigrants in temporary quarters.

On her second homeward voyage, the *Waratah* left Durban on 26 July 1909 with 92 passengers bound for Cape Town. The next day at sea, she passed Clan Line's *Clan Macintyre*. The two ships exchanged flash signals since the *Waratah* was not equipped with wireless. That was the last encounter the *Waratah* had with another ship. She was never heard from or sighted again. Mystery surrounded her disappearance. Foul weather was reported in her vicinity. Could she have foundered or capsized due to rough weather? Was there an explosion and flash fire? No one knows. An extensive search made by the British government and other interested parties revealed nothing — not a piece of wreckage or a single body. On 16 December 1909 the *Waratah* was posted missing at Lloyds.

Blue Anchor never recovered from the loss of the *Waratah,* and in January 1910, its fleet was purchased by Peninsular & Oriental Steam Navigation Co. Six months later in July 1910, Blue Anchor went into voluntary liquidation and within a year its name and flag disappeared from the shipping world.

Maori
Shaw, Savill & Albion Co Ltd, London

Builders: Swan & Hunter, Wallsend, 1893.
Particulars: 5,200 gross tons, 403ft × 48ft.
Machinery: Triple-expansion engines, single screw, speed 11 knots.
Passengers: Saloon, Third, 200 emigrants.

Date of disaster: 4 August 1909.

The *Maori* was basically a cargo liner that catered for a limited number of passengers on her England-New Zealand run. Emigrant

The Steerage liner Langton Grange (The Mariners' Museum).

quarters were erected in the cargo 'tween decks, while Saloon and Third Class were carried in the superstructure.

The *Maori* left Cape Town on the night of 4 August 1909 at 11:30 pm. On board were 55 crewmen and a cargo consisting of explosives. A north-westerly gale was growing and soon after leaving the shelter of Table Bay, the vessel was driven inshore and crashed upon the rocks near Deseker Point. Because the *Maori* swung around after the collision, the vessel was hidden from the coast road. However, during the afternoon of 5 August, a fisherman discovered the wreck, informed the Cape Town police, and they in turn rushed out. Only 21 crewmen were saved.

Langton Grange
Houlder Bros & Co Ltd, London

Builders: Workman, Clark & Co, Belfast, 1896.
Particulars: 5,851 gross tons, 420ft × 54ft.
Machinery: Triple-expansion engines, single screw, speed 12 knots.
Passengers: 26 First Class, 230 Third Class.

Date of disaster: 5 August 1909.

Houlders Bros' business activities started in December 1849, and were always concentrated in Australia. They entered the shipping business as agents in 1862, sailed their first chartered ship in 1876, and their own ship in 1893. The *Langton Grange* was the fifth ship built for them, and she commenced her maiden voyage from England to Australia in 1896.

While on a voyage in ballast from Clyde to Newport, the *Langton Grange* was wrecked on 5 August 1909, on the North Bishops, Pembrokeshire.

Lucania
Cunard Line, Liverpool

Builders: Fairfield Shipbuilding & Engineering Co, Glasgow, 1893.
Particulars: 12,952 gross tons, 622ft × 65ft.
Machinery: Triple-expansion engines, twin screw, speed 21 knots.
Passengers: 600 First Class, 400 Second Class, 1,000 Steerage.

Date of disaster: 14 August 1909.

The *Lucania* was the first Cunard ship to abandon sail power. Launched and completed in 1893, the *Lucania* commenced her maiden voyage from Liverpool to New York on 2 September 1983, as the largest ship in the world. First Class passengers had nothing but

The Lucania *anchored at Liverpool* (Courtesy of the Steamship Historical Society collection/University of Baltimore Library).

praise for her interiors. Magnificently appointed, the *Lucania* had the first 'single' staterooms, a dining room 100ft long and 64ft wide (situated amidships), a drawing room, a smoking room with a real fireplace and a library — all decorated and furnished in various period styles — Elizabethan, Italian Renaissance, and so on. In October 1893, the *Lucania* captured the coveted 'Blue Riband' by speeding from Queenstown to Sandy Hook at an average speed of 20.75 knots. In May 1894 she sped eastbound at 21.81 knots. Her westbound performance improved in October 1894 with an average speed of 21.95 knots.

On 14 August 1909, while lying at Huskisson Dock in Liverpool, the *Lucania* was consumed by fire and badly damaged. The cost of repairs and her 'modern' competition made the *Lucania* unsuitable for overhaul. Therefore later that year she was sold for scrap in Swansea.

Laurentian
Allan Line, Glasgow
Previous name: *Polynesian* (1872–93).

Builders: R. Steele & Co, Greenock, 1872.

Particulars: 3,983 gross tons, 400ft × 43ft.

Machinery: Triple-expansion engines, single screw, speed 13 knots.

Passengers: 36 First Class, 1,000 Steerage.

Date of disaster: 6 September 1909.

The *Laurentian* was always employed on the North Atlantic, even as the *Polynesian*. When first built she had compound engines and carried 120 passengers in First Class with 850 more in Third. A refit was given to her in 1893 by Workman & Clark & Co, Belfast. Renamed *Laurentian,* her route varied between Glasgow and America, putting into either Boston, New York or Philadelphia.

Under the command of Captain Henry Imne, the *Laurentian,* left Boston with forty passengers and a general cargo. On 6 September 1909, the *Laurentian* steaming under dense fog, ran aground at Mistaken Point, Tripassey Bay. All on board were safely taken off, before the ship was abandoned as a total loss.

The Laurentian *was built in 1872* (The Mariners' Museum).

Umhlali
Bullard, King & Co (Natal Line), London

Builders: Sir James Laing & Son Ltd,
Sunderland, 1905.
Particulars: 3,388 gross tons, 348ft × 43ft.
Machinery: Triple-expansion engines, single
screw, speed 13 knots.
Passengers: 75–100.

Date of disaster: 15 September 1909.

The *Umhlali* was the sixth vessel owned by
Natal Line, a company founded in the late
1880s to trade between England and South
Africa. The *Umhlali* had two masts and one
funnel, and her spaces catered to large amounts
of cargo.

Bound from England to Durban, the *Umhlali*
encountered fog near the end of her long
southward journey and ran aground near Cape
Point on 15 September 1909. She was declared
a total loss and abandoned.

La Seyne
Messageries Maritimes, Marseille
Previous name: *Etoile du Chile* (1873–88).

Builders: Forges et Chantiers de la
Méditerranée, La Seyne, 1873.
Particulars: 2,379 gross tons, 312ft × 38ft.
Machinery: Compound engines, single screw,
speed 10 knots.
Passengers: Data not available.

Date of disaster: 14 November 1909.

The *La Seyne* was an iron-hulled vessel
renamed and refitted in 1888. She was a mail
steamship that plied the France-Indochina
trade.

On her way to Singapore at 4:00 pm on 14
November, 1909, the *La Seyne* collided in the
Rheo Straits with the British India liner *Onda*.
The *La Seyne* sunk in two minutes, a record,
with the loss of 101 persons out of her
complement of 162. The survivors (those not
drowned or attacked and eaten by sharks),
were picked up by the *Onda*.

Chapter 2

The teens

This decade opened with the *General Chanzy* destroyed by weather, the abandonment of the *Korea,* followed by the foundering of the *Pericles,* the pride of Aberdeen Line, the grounding of the *Lisboa,* flagship of Empresa Nacional. Despite the fact that 38 ships met disaster during this decade, the maritime event that dominated this period was the sinking of the *Titanic.* The *Titanic* was the British answer to the German greyhounds and White Star's answer to the Cunard speed queens. On board for the maiden crossing of the *Titanic* were the aristocracy, rich and famous of both America and England, who sat, slept and dined in palatial splendour. However, misfortune struck and the liner went down with a heavy loss of life.

The headlines were soon again ablaze with marine news when the popular Cunard liner *Lusitania* was torpedoed. The Germans posted warnings against British merchant shipping, yet Cunard continued sailings with their most valuable liner. Questions are still raised today as to why she sank so quickly when only one torpedo was fired. Her cargo manifest for that voyage provides some clues. Other wartime casualties included the *Vandyck* and *Ancona,* both on commercial voyages at the time of their demise.

Equally catastrophic, but often neglected, was the collision involving the *Empress of Ireland.* When she went down 840 passengers died, one of the highest death tolls in peacetime. The loss of life in maritime disasters was the highest during this decade — 5,165 — of which 1,392 were war related.

General Chanzy
Compagnie Générale Transatlantique, Le Havre

Builders: Compagnie Générale Transatlantique, St Nazaire, 1891.
Particulars: 2,257 gross tons, 346ft × 36ft.
Machinery: Triple-expansion engines, single screw, speed 10 knots.
Passengers: Data not available.

Date of disaster: 10 February 1910.

The *General Chanzy* was engaged in French Line's West Indies service transporting civil servants, mails and general cargoes. The vessel was also utilized in other services.

The *General Chanzy* left Marseille on 9 February 1910 bound for Algiers with 87 passengers and a crew of seventy under the veteran Captain Cayol, a Chevalier of the Legion of Honour. To avoid a raging storm in the Mediterranean, Captain Cayol sailed his ship along the coast as far as Barcelona before heading south. The vessel took shelter under the Islands of Minorca and Majorca. During the night of 10 February, the engines of the

General Chanzy failed and the liner was at the mercy of the sea. The powerless vessel was hurled against the rocks on the coast of the island of Minorca, near the town of Ciudadela. On striking the rocks, the vessel broke up and went down almost immediately. All souls were lost expect one, Marcel Rodel, an Algerian customs official who clung to a piece of wreckage and was later picked up by a fisherman at daylight.

News of the tragedy caused consternation and grief in Marseille, where many of the people were from. Rescue vessels despatched from France, Spain and the Balearic Islands reported, upon reaching the scene, a raging storm and a large number of bodies floating in the sea near the wreck.

Korea
Russian American Line, Copenhagen

Builders: Flensburger Schiffbau, Flensburg, 1899.
Particulars: 6,123 gross tons, 409ft × 50ft.
Machinery: Triple-expansion engines, single screw, speed 14 knots.
Passengers: 50 First Class, 1,350 Steerage.

Date of disaster: 1 March 1910.

The *Korea* was launched for the East Asiatic Co, a Danish concern. In 1906 she was purchased by the Russian American Line, a company formed at the instigation of Albert Ballin, general manager of Hamburg-America Line. The *Korea* commenced her first voyage from Libau to New York on 14 September 1906.

On 15 February 1910, she sailed from Narvik to New York with a cargo of ore. During the voyage the *Korea* was abandoned. No explanation was given and she was not listed in *Lloyd's Register of Shipping* after the 1909–10 edition.

Pericles
Aberdeen Line, Aberdeen

Builders: Harland & Wolff, Belfast, 1908.
Particulars: 10,925 gross tons, 518ft × 62ft.
Machinery: Quadruple-expansion engines, twin screw, speed 14 knots.
Passengers: 100 First Class, 400 Third Class.

Date of disaster: 31 March 1910.

The *Pericles* made her maiden voyage between London and Sydney in July 1908. She quickly proved quite popular on this route because of her lavish First Class appointments and her comfortable Third Class accommodation, the latter being well in excess of the standards of the day.

The *Pericles* left Brisbane for London with 300 passengers under the command of Captain A. Simpson. On 31 March 1910 the *Pericles* struck an uncharted underwater reef six miles off Cape Leewin, West Australia. The calm sea and clear sky enabled all the passengers an crew to take to the lifeboats and land safely on the island. Two and a half hours after striking the reef the *Pericles* went down.

For three years the Pericles *was the flagship of Aberdeen Line* (Courtesy of the Steamship Historical Society collection/University of Baltimore Library).

Lisboa
Empresa Nacional de Navegação, Lisbon

Empresa Nacional flagship Lisboa (Luis Miguel Correia collection).

Builders: D. & W. Henderson & Company Ltd, Glasgow 1910.
Particulars: 7,412 gross tons, 432ft × 54ft.
Machinery: Triple-expansion engines, twin screw, speed 16 knots.
Passengers: 120 First Class, 64 Second Class, 144 Third Class, 1,000 Fourth Class.

Date of disaster: 23 October 1910.

When the *Lisboa* was introduced into service, she became the flagship of Empresa Nacional.

The *Lisboa's* duty was to maintain a maritime link between Portugal and her African colonies in southern Africa. In carrying out her assignment, the *Lisboa* departed Lisbon on her maiden voyage to Angola, South Africa and Mozambique on 18 June 1910, arriving back in Lisbon on 11 September. Her second voyage commenced on 1 October. Fifteen days later she arrived and departed Luanda, Angola.

With 250 passengers aboard, Captain Menezes guided his ship southward toward Cape Town, the *Lisboa's* next stop. At 10:50 pm on 23 October 1910, the *Lisboa* ran aground on Soldier's Reef near Paternoster Point, sixty miles north of Cape Town. A distress call was sent out and a Norwegian fishing vessel rushed to the scene. All except seven people were rescued. The Norwegian vessel then took possession of the *Lisboa* and hoisted the Norwegian flag. The ship's own flag was later raised, but it did not matter. The *Lisboa* was a total loss.

Messageries Maritimes' Colombo *at dockside* (Courtesy of the Steamship Historical Society collection/University of Baltimore Library).

Colombo
Messageries Maritimes, Marseille

Builders: Forges et Chantiers de la Méditerranée, La Seyne, 1882.
Particulars: 3,731 gross tons, 380ft × 40ft.
Machinery: Compound engines, single screw, speed 13.5 knots.
Passengers: Data not available.

Date of disaster: November 1910.

Purchased from Cie Nationale de Navigation in 1904, the *Colombo* was given an overhaul then placed in the France-Indochina service.

During a typhoon in November 1910, the *Colombo* became disabled and was towed to Tourane. Damaged beyond repair, she was subsequently broken up for scrap in Saigon.

Delhi
Peninsular & Oriental Steam Navigation Co, London

Builders: J. Caird & Co, Greenock, 1905.
Particulars: 8,090 gross tons, 470ft × 56ft.
Machinery: Quadruple-expansion engines, twin screw, speed 16 knots.
Passengers: 163 First Class, 180 Second Class.

Date of disaster: 13 December 1910.

The *Delhi* was an intermediate mail steamer that served on the London-Bombay route.

The *Delhi* sailed from London bound for Bombay with 85 First Class passengers, among whom were the Duke and Duchess of Fife (The Princess Royal) and their two daughters, Princess Alexandra and Princess Maud. Also on board in the cargo holds were gold and silver bullion worth £295,925. At about 2 o'clock in the morning of 11 December 1911, the *Delhi* ran aground in very rough weather some two miles from Cape Spartel. An SOS call was immediately sent out and the French cruiser *Friant*, the British cruiser HMS *Duke of Edinburgh* and the British battleship HMS *London* sped to the scene.

Despite the rough seas, and the swamping of two lifeboats, all persons were brought to land. Sadly, the Moorish authoritities were not cooperative, therefore the crews from the navy ships had to procure conveyances to carry the exhausted and sodden passengers to Tangiers, ten miles away. The gold and silver bulliion was ultimately salved.

New Guinea
McIlwraith, McEacharn & Co, London

Builders: W. Doxford & Sons, Sunderland, 1885.
Particulars: 2,674 gross tons, 300ft × 40ft.

Above *The P & O colonial steamer* Delhi *(Tom Rayner collection).* **Below** *The stricken* Delhi *listing to starboard (Tom Rayer collection).*

Machinery: Compound engines, single screw, speed 11 knots.
Passengers: Data not available.

Date of disaster: 13 February 1911.

McIlwraith and Co was a firm closely associated with British India. The *New Guinea* in fact was chartered to British India for her entire career trading between England and Australia.

The *New Guinea* was wrecked west of Green Cape Lighthouse on 13 February 1911, while on a voyage from Melbourne to Sydney. The bay was located in New South Wales and carried the unhappily prophetic name 'Disaster Bay'.

Lusitania
Empresa Nacional de Navegação, Lisbon

Builders: Sir Raylton Dixon & Co, Middlesbrough, 1906.
Particulars: 5,557 gross tons, 421ft × 51ft.
Machinery: Triple-expansion engines, twin screw, speed 15 knots.
Passengers: Data not available.

Date of disaster: 18 April 1911.

When the *Lusitania* was commissioned she was one of the largest and finest ships in the Portuguese mercantile marine. The *Lusitania* was engaged in the company's southern Africa

Lusitania *docking in Lourenco Marques (Maputo), Mozambique* (Luis Miguel Correia collection).

The Asia *of Pacific Mail Steamships* (Courtesy of the Steamship Historical Society collection/University of Baltimore Library).

run, connecting Portugal to her Africa colonies of Angola and Mozambique.

The *Lusitania* departed Mozambique for Lisbon on 8 April 1911 with 200 Europeans, 450 indentured natives bound for Sao Thome, and a crew of 150. During the evening of 18 April, when round the Cape of Good Hope in poor visibility, the *Lusitania* attempted to enter Table Bay harbour. Instead, she struck on the Bellows Rocks.

The waters were calm and the weather cooperative to enable lifeboats to be launched. HMS *Forte* and the tug *Scotsman* also aided in the evacuation. Unfortunately, one of the lifeboats capsized, drowning an officer and three passengers. The *Lusitania* remained fast for four days until she was washed off by swells, sinking in deep water.

Asia
Pacific Mail Steamship Co, New York
Previous name: *Doric* (1883–1906).

Builders: Harland & Wolff, Belfast, 1883.
Particulars: 4,744 gross tons, 440ft × 44ft.
Machinery: Triple-expansion engines, single screw, speed 15 knots.

(Merida *departing New York for Havana* (Courtesy of the Steamship Historical Society collection/University of Baltimore Library).

Passengers: Approximately 80 First, plus Steerage.

Date of disaster: 22 April 1911.

The *Asia* had a long career with three different companies. As the *Doric* she was owned by White Star Line and chartered to Shaw Savill for use on the England-New Zealand service. In 1895 she was re-engined and transferred to trans-Pacific service for the Occidental & Oriental Steamship Co, then in 1906 the *Doric* was sold to Pacific Mail Steam Ship Line and renamed *Asia*. They placed her on the transpacific run between San Francisco and the Orient.

On 22 April 1911 the *Asia* struck the Finger Rock at Taichow Island off the China coast and sank.

Merida
New York & Cuba Mail Steamship Co, New York

Builders: William Cramp & Sons Co, Philadelphia, 1906.
Particulars: 6,207 gross tons, 416ft × 50ft.
Machinery: Triple-expansion engines, twin screw, speed 17 knots.
Passengers: 189 First Class, 48 Second Class, 24 Steerage.

Date of disaster: 12 May 1911.

When the *Merida* was completed in 1906 she was a first class mail and passenger steamer, and considered the best in the fleet of express liners for Ward Line. She was of steel construction with a wood sheathing and had three decks fore and aft.

The *Merida* left Havana for New York on Tuesday, 9 May 1911 with 188 passengers and a crew of 131 under the command of Captain Robertson. Two days later the *Merida* encountered dense fog. At 12:30 am on 12 May, fifty miles north-east of Cape Charles, the *Merida* was struck by United Fruit's *Admiral*

Not exactly a liner, the Milton *did provide space for Third Class/Steerage passengers* (Tom Rayner collection).

Farragut. The *Admiral Farragut* immediately sent out a wireless call to summon help from the *Hamilton* of Old Dominion Steamship Company. In the interim, the *Admiral* took on the passengers and crew from the sinking *Merida*. Since the *Admiral* was herself badly holed and her forward compartment filled with water, the survivors were transferred to the *Hamilton* when she arrived on the scene. The *Hamilton* delivered the passengers and crew to Norfolk on 12 May at 7:00 pm. Five hours after the impact the *Merida* sank, and the *Admiral Farragut* proceeded to New York.

Milton
Lamport & Holt, Liverpool

Builders: D. & W. Henderson Ltd, Glasgow, 1888.
Particulars: 2,679 gross tons, 310ft × 39ft.
Machinery: Triple-expansion engines, single screw, speed 11 knots.
Passengers: Data not available.

Date of disaster: 15 June 1911.

Lamport & Holt had a policy of naming their ships after scientists, philosphers and poets. In

The sleek Empress of China (Canadian Pacific).

The Papanui *steaming away* (Dickie collection/ Alexander Turnbull Library).

1888 they took delivery of their 64th vessel and named it after the great English poet, *Milton*. The *Milton* departed on her maiden voyage from Liverpool to Rio and Buenos Aires on 2 October 1888. Within a month, the new ship was involved in a collision in the River Plate with the *Archimedes*, another Lamport ship. Damage was slight to both vessels. The *Milton* spent the next 23 years engaged in the South American trade.

On 15 June 1911 while on a voyage from London to Santos, the *Milton* was wrecked near Cabo Espichel, Portugal.

Empress of China
Canadian Pacific, London

Builders: Naval Construction & Armaments Co Ltd, Barrow, 1891.
Particulars: 5,905 gross tons, 456ft × 51ft.
Machinery: Triple-expansion engines, twin screw, speed 16 knots.
Passengers: 50 First Class, 150 Second Class, 400 Third Class.

Date of disaster: 27 July 1911.

Launched by Lady Stafford on 25 March 1891, the sleek *Empress of China* commenced her positioning voyage on 15 July 1891 from Liverpool to Suez, Hong Kong and Vancouver, her home port. From Vancouver, the *Empress of China* voyaged to Japan and Hong Kong until, lying at her pier at Vancouver, the *Empress of China* slowly sank and settled on the mud bottom during the night of 23 October 1907. It could not be positively ascertained, but it was presumed that her seacocks had been opened by accident. She was refloated, repaired and placed back in service.

During fog off Nojima, some 35 miles from Yokohama, on 27 August 1911, the *Empress of China* was wrecked. All the passengers and crew, together with the mails, were safely taken off. She was later refloated, but this time the damage was too extensive to repair, and therefore the *Empress of China* was sold for scrap.

Papanui
Australian Shipping Company, Wellington

Builders: William Denny & Bros, Dumbarton, 1898.
Particulars: 6,582 gross tons, 430ft × 54ft.
Machinery: Triple-expansion engines, single screw, speed 13 knots.
Passengers: 35 First Class, 45 Second Class, Steerage.

Date of disaster: 11 September 1911.

The *Papanui* started trading on the London, Cape Town, Auckland and Wellington route for New Zealand Shipping on 12 January 1899. In 1905 she was relegated to secondary service in the carriage of general cargo and emigrants between London and New Zealand.

After leaving Hobart on 14 December 1909, the *Papanui* ran aground on uncharted rocks. She was refloated and docked at Melbourne for a general survey. The company decided she was not worth repairing and sold her to H.C. Sleight and H.B. Blake, both of New Zealand. They decided to fix her up before sailing her to Japan for a refit. However, the local authorities would not certify the *Pananui* as seaworthy.

Sleight and Blake therefore transferred the *Papanui* to Nicaraguan registry and sailed her without a pilot to Nagasaki for her refit into a passenger vessel. Repaired, she was placed under the banner of Australian Shipping Co, and she departed Melbourne on 10 May 1910, with a full load of passengers to witness the coronation of King George V. On 25 August at London, she embarked 324 passengers for the return trip to New Zealand.

The *Papanui*'s homeward passage was via Las Palmas and the Cape. Shortly after crossing the Equator on 5 September a fire was discovered smouldering in her coal bunker. For five days, the Captain and his crew attempted to extinguish the fire, but to no avail. Faced with no alternative the Captain headed his ship toward St Helena arriving there on 11 September. He put his passengers and crew ashore then beached his ship, which was now fully ablaze, at James Bay. Completely gutted, the wreck lay there for several years until the heavy seas pounded it to pieces.

Calderon
Lamport & Holt, Liverpool

Builders: Workman, Clark & Co Ltd, Belfast, 1900.

Particulars: 4,083 gross tons, 378ft × 47ft.
Machinery: Triple-expansion engines, single screw, speed 11 knots.
Passengers: Data not available.

Date of disaster: 23 January 1912.

The *Calderon* was commissioned for the Liverpool-Rio-Santos trade on 21 July 1900.

Commencing a voyage from Glasgow to Santos, the *Calderon* collided with the *Musketeer* in the Mersey River on 23 January 1912 and broke in two.

Oceana
Peninsular & Oriental Steam Navigation Co, London

Builders: Harland & Wolff, Belfast, 1888.
Particulars: 6,610 gross tons, 468ft × 52ft.
Machinery: Triple-expansion engines, single screw, speed 16.5 knots.
Passengers: 240 First Class, 150 Second Class.

Date of disaster: 16 March 1912.

When the *Oceana* was first introduced into service, she was placed on the London-Colombo-Melbourne-Sydney trade. In 1905 she was replaced by the larger and newer *Mooltan,* and P & O switched the *Oceana* to the London-Bombay route. For this new service the *Oceana* recieved an extensive refit.

Having just departed London for Bombay with forty passengers aboard, the *Oceana* was

The Calderon *loading cargo at Manchester* (Tom Rayner collection).

Oceana *being coaled* (P & O Group).

smashed into by the German sailing barque *Pisagua* off Beachy Head in the English Channel at 4:00 am on 16 March 1912. The *Oceana* sustained a 40ft hole on her side, but managed to stay afloat for six hours. During that time the officers and crew quickly shepherded the passengers into the lifeboats. Nine lives were lost when a lifeboat overturned whilst being launched but the speedy arrival of harbour craft prevented the loss of more lives.

The largest luxury liner at the time was the Titanic (Courtesy of the Steamship Historical Society collection/University of Baltimore Library).

Titanic
White Star Line, Liverpool

Builders: Harland & Wolff, Belfast, 1912.
Particulars: 46,328 gross tons, 883ft × 93ft.
Machinery: Triple-expansion engines, triple screw, speed 21 knots.
Passengers: 1,034 First Class, 510 Second Class, 1,022 Third Class.

Date of disaster: 14 April 1912.

White Star's answer to the German four-stackers and the Cunard speed queens — *Lusitania* and *Mauretania* — was a trio of large luxurious moderate speed liners. The first to be delivered for the Southampton-New York

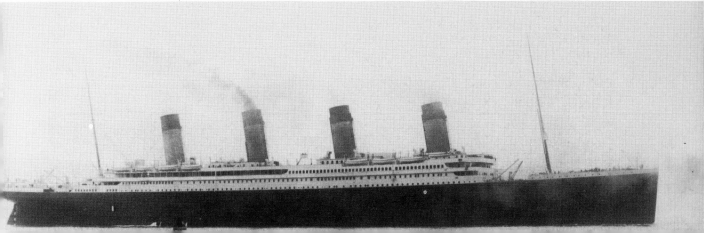

A stern shot of the ill-fated Titanic (Frank O. Braynard collection).

service was the *Olympic* in 1911. Next on line was the *Titanic* in 1912, to be followed in 1914 by the *Britannic* (whose rumoured name before April 1912 was to be *Gigantic*). Nature prevented the *Titanic* from reaching New York, and a world calamity sunk the *Britannic*, cheating her from commercial service.

The *Titanic* was launched unceremoniously on 31 May 1911, and was delivered to White Star Line on 2 April 1912. Under the command of veteran Captain Edward J. Smith, the largest and most luxurious liner of her day set out on her maiden voyage on 10 April 1912, from Southampton to New York. After stops at Cherbourg and Queenstown, the *Titanic* had a passenger complement of 322 First Class, 277 Second Class and 709 Third Class and a crew of 898.

During the initial stages of the *Titanic's* voyage, little attention was paid to her, since it was little more than a repeat of the *Olympic's* maiden journey the year before, then the largest liner. But, once the *Titanic* sank, it made for irresistible copy. The most opulent liner on its maiden voyage, with a passenger list larded with names from America's and Britain's rich and famous collectively worth $250 million, the shortage of lifeboats, a death toll kindest to First Class and heaviest to Third, and the gallantry of a few who remained on board to die with their spouses, all played their part in making the *Titanic* tragedy one of the most famous in the world.

On a calm crystal clear evening on 14 April, the *Titanic* was ploughing along at 22.5 knots. At 11:40 pm lookout Frederick Fleet reported, 'Iceberg right ahead'. In charge of the bridge at that hour was First Officer William Murdoch, who ordered to Quartermaster Hitchens, 'Turn the wheel hard-a-starboard'. Murdoch then yanked the engine-room telegraph to 'Full speed astern.' He then pushed the button closing all watertight doors. Breathless seconds passed. It was too late. Seconds after giving the orders, the *Titanic* collided with the iceberg. Latest findings suggest that the ice caused the massive steel plates of the *Titanic's* starboard side to buckle, immediately flooding the first six (forepeak, No 1 hold, No 2 hold, No 3 hold, No 5 boiler room and No 6 boiler room) watertight compartments.

The Captain and Thomas Andrews, Managing Director of Harland & Wolff, examined the damage but when Mr Andrews explained that while she could perhaps float with her first four compartments waterlogged she could not expect to float with six flooded, Captain Smith ordered Chief Officer Henry T. Wilder to uncover the lifeboats. This was at five minutes past midnight. Ten minutes later, the Captain requested First Radio Operator John George Phillips to send out a call for assistance. Phillips began tapping out the letters 'CQD' — the international call of distress at the time, followed by 'MGY' the call letters of the *Titanic*.

It was during the impending and actual evacuation of the *Titanic* that the appalling shortage of lifeboats was noticed. There were twenty lifeboats on board with a total capacity of 1,178 people. On this voyage there were 2,206 people aboard. Therefore, 1,028 souls were already doomed. Compounding the problem, the first lifeboat (No 7) was lowered at 12:45 am with only nineteen or twenty people.

Right Titanic's *port and starboard cranes taken at a depth of 13,000 ft.* (Woods Hole Oceanographic Institution). **Below Right** *Anchor chains and windlass on* Titanic's *bow* (Woods Hole Oceanographic Institution).

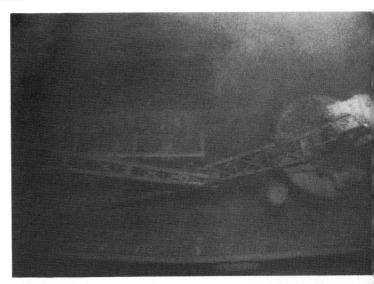

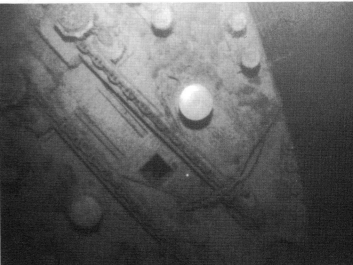

Many passengers particularly in First Class, believed the *Titanic* was 'unsinkable'. That word 'unsinkable' was first used in a souvenir issue of *Shipbuilder* dedicated to the new White Star ships. It was preceded by the word 'practically' which was conveniently dropped from the newspaper columns surrounding the excitement of the new ship. Calm remained on board until near the end, with the band coming out on deck to serenade the passengers. By 2:05 am the last boat and collapsible were away.

At this time the *Titanic* was rapidly going down. In the distance, approximately nineteen miles away, lay the steamer *Californian,* with her wireless shut down for the night and her watchman unresponsive to the new distress calls of the rockets. The lights in the *Titanic* went out as the engines broke loose from their mountings. At 2:20 am the world's largest ship foundered in position 41°46'N, 50°14'W. The Cunard liner *Carpathia* arrived on the scene at 4:10 am, rescued 703 people, and later brought them to New York. For 815 passengers and 688 crew members there were no rescuers.

White Star Line never fully recovered from this tragedy, but because of it, sea travel was made safer. The findings of the British Inquiry were published on 30 July 1912. Among the many recommendations that were implemented, the most important were: that lifeboats and rafts should be carried for all persons on board (of which one or more must be powered with some form of mechanical propulsion); that all ships should have a boat drill, a fire-drill and a watertight door drill as soon as possible after leaving the original port of departure; and finally, that all ships should have a wireless telegraph worked by a sufficient number of trained operators to secure a continuous service by night and day.

A team of American and French researchers, under the sponsorship of the Wood Hole Oceanographic Institution (American) and the Institute for Research and Exploitation of the Sea (French), ended 73 years of speculation on 1 September 1985 when they found the *Titanic* lying at the bottom of the ocean 370 miles off Newfoundland. This discovery was made possible by a high-tech marriage of supersensitive sonar and powerful cameras that were attached to a submersible craft called *Argo,* developed by Dr Robert D. Ballard. As it scanned the ocean bottom, the *Argo* was able

to transmit the images to the pilot ship *Knorr*. Eleven more dives in 1986 in the submersible *Alvin* showed that the liner split in two as it sank 13,000ft to the ocean floor. The 300ft bow section lies embedded in 50ft of mud 1,970ft away from the stern, and they face in opposite directions. Scattered about are huge sections of hull plating, a large piece of decking, cargo cranes, bedsprings, dishes, bottles, basins, window frames, light fixtures, balustrades and hundreds of other items including passengers' personal effects.

With the discovery came word of salvage. British salvage expert John Pierce wanted to raise the liner using inflatable canvas bags; Texas oil millionaire Jack Grimm also wanted a go at the rumoured treasure below; and the Commercial Union Insurance Company of London, a descendant of the insurance firms that insured the ship, said that it would consider salvage offers. However, to date the wreckage remains undisturbed within an area bounded by 41° 55' and 41° 35' N, 50° 20' and 49° 55' W.

Oravia
Pacific Steam Navigation Co, London

Builders: Harland & Wolff, Belfast, 1897.
Particulars: 5,321 gross tons, 421ft x 49 ft.
Machinery: Triple-expansion engines, twin screw, speed 15 knots.
Passengers: Data not available.

Date of disaster: 16 November 1912.

Pacific Steam Navigation was the brainchild of the American, William Wheelwright, who settled in Guayaquil in 1833. He later moved to Chile and there started a steamship business. The *Oravia* was the 31st vessel to sail under the PSN banner. Her maiden voyage started from Liverpool on 1 July 1897 and proceeded to Rio de Janeiro, Montevideo and Valparaiso, a route on which she was to spend her entire trading career.

During a voyage to Callao carrying a general cargo, the *Oravia* was wrecked on Billy Rock at the entrance of Port Stanley, Falkland Islands, on 16 November 1912.

Veronese
Lamport & Holt, Liverpool

Builders: Workman, Clark & Co Ltd, Belfast, 1906.
Particulars: 7,063 gross tons, 465ft x 59 ft.
Machinery: Triple-expansion engines, single screw, speed 12 knots.
Passengers: Data not available.

Date of disaster: 16 January 1913.

The *Veronese* was built specifically for the South American trade sailing from various British ports. Her maiden voyage commenced on 28 January 1906.

The *Veronese* left Liverpool on 12 January 1913, under the command of Captain Charles

The Veronese *resembled a cargo vessel more than a passenger liner* (Courtesy of the Steamship Historical Society collection/University of Baltimore Library).

Turner. Three days later she called at Vigo, after which she is believed to have had a complement of 117 passengers and a crew of 98. During the early morning of 16 January, in hazy weather, the *Veronese* stranded on the Boa Nova rocks off Leixoes, Portugal. Enormous seas made rescue impossible until late morning when the sea abated. Two days later, with the assistance of Portuguese gunboats, 172 persons reached shore alive: 43 lost their lives.

Federal Steam's Devon *aground at Pencarrow Head. Note the people on the forepart waiting to be rescued* (Tom Rayner Collection).

Devon
Federal Steam Navigation Co, London

Builders: R. & W. Hawthorn, Leslie & Co Ltd, Hebburn, 1897.
Particulars: 5,489 gross tons, 420ft × 54ft.
Machinery: Triple-expansion engines, single screw, speed 11 knots.
Passengers: 12 First Class, 156 Third Class.

Date of disaster: 25 August 1913.

Federal Steam was formed in 1895 to trade between England, Australia and New Zealand. The two-masted schooner-rigged *Devon,* the second vessel built for Federal, had a considerable amount of cargo space.
     Federal Steam suffered its first loss on 25 August 1913, when the *Devon,* nearing the completion of her voyage from Montreal to

Wellington, was wrecked on Pencarrow Head, near Wellington, New Zealand.

Volturno
Uranium Steamship Company, London

Builders: Fairfield Shipbuilding & Engineering Co Ltd, Glasgow, 1906.
Particulars: 3,581 gross tons, 340ft × 43ft.
Machinery: Triple-expansion engines, twin screw, speed 14 knots.
Passengers: 24 First Class, 1,000 Third Class.

Date of disaster: 9 October 1913.

Volturno *afire in the Atlantic with the* Grosser Kurfurst *in attendance on the left* (Richard Morse collection/The Mariner's Museum).

The *Volturno* was a typical emigrant steamer that operated up to the outbreak of the First World War. She ran for three different companies between 1906 and 1910, principally on the same route — Europe to America with emigrants. Purchased by Uranium, the *Volturno* sailed on her first voyage between

Cobequid *plied the South American route for RML* (Furness, Withy Group).

Rotterdam and New York in 1910.

The *Volturno* left Rotterdam on 2 October 1913, with 22 First Class passengers, 539 Steerage and a crew of 96 bound for New York. Among her cargo was a quantity of barium oxide and various other chemicals, together with peat moss, rags and straw bottle covers. In mid-Atlantic on 9 October, smoke was seen coming out of the No 1 hatch. The ship's fire fighters reached the scene and shortly thereafter an explosion caused the ship to catch fire. The roaring gale force winds helped fan the flames. An SOS was sent and ships in the vicinity answered.

The first ship to arrive was the Cunard liner *Carmania,* followed by the German liner *Grosser Kurfurst* and the Atlantic Transport Line's *Minneapolis.* By 4:00 pm seven more rescue ships arrived. All saw a blazing vessel being tossed about by an angry sea, which hampered the rescue effort. The terrified passengers who were huddled on deck with their life-jackets boarded the lifeboats, and once lowered were picked up by the waiting ships. During the launching process and in the rough seas, four lifeboats were smashed. The next day, the *Volturno* sank, taking with her 136 lives.

Empress of Ireland *bedecked with flags* (Canadian Pacific).

Cobequid
Royal Mail Lines, London
Previous name: *Goth* (1893–1913).

Builders: Harland & Wolff, Belfast, 1893.
Particulars: 4,791 gross tons, 401ft × 47ft.
Machinery: Triple-expansion engines, single screw, speed 12 knots.
Passengers: 56 First Class, 97 Second Class, 200 Third Class.

Date of disaster: 13 January 1914.

The *Goth* was one of Union Line's three intermediate liners built specifically to sail across the restrictive bars at East London and Durban. In 1913, the *Goth* was purchased by Royal Mail Lines, renamed *Cobequid,* and placed on their South American service.

On a voyage from Demerara to St John with passengers and a cargo of sugar, the *Cobequid* was wrecked on Trinity Ledge, Newfoundland on 13 January 1914, and declared a total loss.

Empress of Ireland
Canadian Pacific, London

Builders: Fairfield Shipbuilding & Engineering Co, Glasgow, 1905.
Particulars: 14,191 gross tons, 570ft × 66ft.
Machinery: Quadruple-expansion engines,

twin screw, speed 18 knots.
Passengers: 310 First Class, 350 Second Class, 800 Third Class.

Date of disaster: 29 May 1914.

The *Empress of Ireland* and her sister-ship *Empress of Britain,* were the fastest ships on the Liverpool-Quebec run when they were commissioned. The *Empress of Ireland* was not an ostentatious luxury liner like the *Amerika* or *Kaiser Wilhelm Der Grosse,* but instead was designed to provide fast, comfortable transportation between two points.

On Thursday, 28 May 1914, at approximately 4:27 pm, the *Empress of Ireland* set sail from Quebec with 87 First Class, 253 Second and 717 Third Class passengers and about 1,100 tons of general cargo for Liverpool. In command was Captain Kendall. Around 1:30 am on 29 May, the *Empress of Ireland* dropped off her pilot at Father Point. As the *Empress* was leaving the pilot station, the Norwegian collier, *Storstad,* loaded with 11,000 tons of Nova Scotia coal, was slowly approaching it from the opposite direction. First Mate Alfred Toftenes of the *Storstad* sighted lights six or eight miles away and he reckoned the ship would pass the *Storstad* green-to-green. Fog rolled in from the shore and engulfed the two ships. Visibility was reduced considerably as each ship tried to sight the other's lights. The *Storstad* watched the approaching lights loom closer and tried to change course. It was too late. Captain Kendall 'first ordered full speed ahead' to avoid collision, then 'Go Astern'. Captain Thomas Andersen of the *Storstad* arrived on the bridge of his ship only a few minutes before impact, after being informed by Toftenes that it was 'hazy'. Captain Andersen ordered three whistle blasts. As the whistles sounded, the *Storstad* slid gently into the *Empress*. Captain Kendall then ordered 'Full Ahead' in an effort to beach his crippled liner but the engines would not respond. A hole 25ft deep and 14ft wide had been made and water poured into the *Empress* at 60,000 gallons a second. As the *Empress* listed, more of the gash slipped below water.

As Captain Kendall sensed an inevitable

sinking, he ordered his crew to prepare the lifeboats. Practically all the passengers were sleeping at the time. Those passengers fortunate enough to be awake found their life-jackets and proceeded to the Boat Deck. Ten minutes after the collision, the *Empress of Ireland* lurched violently and fell on her side. Shortly after, her stern rose toward the night sky, and the *Empress of Ireland* went down 150ft to the river bed.

Canadian Pacific rules stated that in the event of fog or snow in the St Lawrence, hands were to be stationed at the watertight doors, ready to close them. Captain Kendall did not order any men to stand by the doors when he sighted the fog; therefore, they were unclosed during and after the collision and were one of the reasons why the *Empress of Ireland* sank so quickly.

The death toll was monumental. Out of 1,057 passengers, only 217 survived. Gone were 840 — 80 per cent of them — the greatest passenger death toll in maritime history during peace-time. 248 crew members survived out of 420.

The *Empress of Ireland* story is often a neglected one, for three reasons: The *Empress* was not a luxurious ship; she was not on the fashionable New York-Liverpool or Southampton route; and finally, the outbreak of World War I and its senseless slaughter caused even her terrible fate to pale by comparison.

Vandyck
Lamport & Holt, Liverpool

Builders: Workman, Clark & Co, Belfast, 1911.
Particulars: 10,328 gross tons, 511ft × 61ft.
Machinery: Quadruple-expansion engines, twin screw, speed 15 knots.
Passengers: 280 First Class, 130 Second Class, 200 Third Class.

Date of disaster: 26 October 1914.

Completed in August 1911, the *Vandyck* sailed across the Atlantic to New York and then on her maiden voyage from New York to Buenos Aires on 8 September 1911. On this route she was one of the largest and finest vessels in the Lamport & Holt fleet.

On a voyage from Buenos Aires to New York with over 200 passengers, the *Vandyck* was intercepted during the early morning of 26 October 1914, by the German light cruiser *Karlsruhe* in the South Atlantic. The passengers and crew were placed on the steamship *Asuncion,* previously captured, and sent to Pará (Brazil). After the German crew boarded the liner and helped themselves to provisions, the *Karlsruhe* opened fire on the *Vandyck,* finishing her off with explosive charges.

Norfolk
Federal Steam Navigation Co, London

Builders: Sunderland Shipbuilding Co, Sunderland, 1900.
Particulars: 5,310 gross tons, 421ft × 54ft.
Machinery: Triple-expansion engines, single screw, speed 13 knots.
Passengers: 12 First Class, 52 Second Class.

Date of disaster: 8 November 1914.

Cunard's speed queen Lusitania **photographed before 1912 (Courtesy of the Steamship Historical Society collection/University of Baltimore Library).**

Like the *Devon,* the *Norfolk* was built to trade between England and her colonies in the South Pacific. During the South African war between 1899 and 1902 the *Norfolk,* along with all the Federal line's ships, participated in the carriage of New Zealand troops to Cape Town in the course of their regular voyages.

Homeward-bound between Melbourne and Sydney, a fire broke out aboard the *Norfolk* on 7 May 1915. Unable to control the blaze, the Captain decided to beach his ship, which was done on Ninety Mile Beach, Victoria. Lying exposed, she broke in two during heavy weather.

Lusitania
Cunard Line, Liverpool

Builders: John Brown & Co, Clydebank, 1907.
Particulars: 31,550 gross tons, 787ft × 88ft.
Machinery: Steam turbines, quadruple screw, speed 25 knots.
Passengers: 563 First Class, 464 Second Class, 1,138 Third Class.

Date of disaster: 7 May 1915

In 1903 the task fell on Cunard Line to wrestle the 'Blue Riband' from the German greyhounds and to remove the threat of an American stranglehold (the Morgan combine of IMM) on

the Atlantic ferry. Working in close cooperation with the British Admiralty on design and specifications, the blueprints called for two giant liners that could maintain an average speed of 24 knots. In addition, an agreement dated 31 July 1903, between the Admiralty, the Board of Trade, the Postmaster General and the Cunard Steamship Company Ltd, stipulated that fittings should be so arranged as to provide for armament in the event of their being taken over by the Admiralty and used as armed cruisers. In such a case, the Admiralty should give one month's notice.

The first of Cunard's luxury liners was the *Lusitania*. When she commenced her maiden voyage on 7 September 1907 from Liverpool, she was the largest and one of the most elegant ships in the world. On her second westbound voyage, 5 October 1907, the *Lusitania* also proved to be the fastest ship in the world. She steamed from Queenstown to Ambrose Light at an average speed of 23.99 knots. On her return, she broke all existing records by maintaining an average speed of 23.61 knots, thus capturing the 'Blue Riband' for England. In November 1907, the *Lusitania* was eclipsed in size by her sister, the *Mauretania*. The twins battled it out for the 'Blue Riband' with the *Lusitania* achieving an average speed of 25.85 knots during a crossing in 1909, but the *Mauretania* proved to be the faster of the two, and from 1909 she flew the 'Blue Riband' for the next 22 years.

In anticipation of hostilities in Europe, the *Lusitania* was given a secret refit in May 1913. The No 1 boiler was converted to a magazine, a second magazine was converted from part of the mail room and the shelter deck was adapted to take four six-inch guns on either side. When war was declared in August 1914, the *Lusitania* was immediately sent to drydock. On 17 September 1914, the *Lusitania* entered the Admiralty fleet as an armed auxiliary cruiser, and was entered as such on Cunard's ledger. The liner continued the Liverpool-Queens-town-New York run on a monthly basis.

Despite an announcement by the Germans that all the seas around the British Isles would

be considered a war zone and that any vessel wearing the British flag was liable to be sunk, the *Lusitania* prepared for another 'slow' (21 knots) crossing. During the last few days in April 1915, the *Lusitania* loaded the following items: 1,248 cases of three-inch shrapnel shells (filled), 4,927 boxes of cartridges, 1,639 ingot bars of copper, 74 barrels of fuel oil, several hundred packages of sundries, 329 cases of lard, 184 cases of accoutrements (for Booth and Company — haversacks, pouches, etc), 323 bales of raw furs, 3,863 boxes of cheese, 600 cases of canned goods, 696 tubes of butter and 500 cases of candy. Practically all of the 'lethal' cargo was loaded directly adjacent to the bulkhead leading into No 1 boiler room. On 1 May 1915, the *Lusitania* was given clearance to sail based on a one page manifest. A little after noon on 1 May, with veteran Cunard Captain William Thomas Turner in command, the *Lusitania* commenced the second leg of her 101st voyage to Liverpool. On board were 290 First Class, 600 Second, 367 Third Class passengers and a crew of 702; along with 1,400 tones of 'general cargo'.

The voyage was uneventful until the *Lusitania* approached the Irish coast. Starting on 6 May, the Admiralty sent out a series of wireless messages to the *Lusitania* about German submarine activity off the Irish coast, which Captain Turner acknowledged. As a precautionary measure, he followed the guidelines for navigating an 'unarmed' liner through hostile waters. Captain Turner ordered all the lifeboats hanging on davits to be swung out and lowered to promenade deck, double lookouts were posted at the bridge, bow and stern, all passenger portholes were blacked out, and he ordered closed all watertight doors and bulkheads not essential to the working of the ship.

The Admiralty assigned the cruiser *Juno* to escort the *Lusitania* to Liverpool once she got to Ireland. However, the Admiralty considered the *Juno* unsuitable for exposure to submarine attack without escort, and again with the known knowledge of German U-boats' activity in the area, ordered the *Juno* to return to Queenstown. The seas around Ireland were now unguarded, making one wonder about Winston Churchill's comment in 1914 that, 'She *(Lusitania)* is just another 45,000 tons of live bait'.

Kapitän-Leutnant Walter Schwieger of *U-20* had been ordered to locate and sink either the *Mauretania* or *Lusitania*. On Friday 7 May at 1:20 pm Kapitän Schwieger sighted his prey. The *Lusitania* by now had reduced speed to 18 knots and was not zigzagging, but sailing in a 'perfectly straight line'. At 2:10 pm, Kapitän Schwieger fired one torpedo. It struck the *Lusitania's* starboard side right below the bridge near the bulkhead leading to No 1 boiler room. The immediate result was the flooding of the starboard coal bunkers and a 15-degree list. Within seconds a second explosion followed. This was the 'cargo', not a second torpedo.

Though there was no panic on board, there was a considerable amount of excitement, rush and much confusion as the increasing list rendered the launching of the port side boats ineffective. As a result, the passengers crowded over to the starboard side where the number of boats was not enough to accommodate everyone. After 18 minutes the *Lusitania* went down off Old Head of Kinsale. Survivors were few. Out of 1,159 passengers and 702 crew members, 374 and 289 survived respectively.

Inquiries into the disaster were held on both sides of the Atlantic. Survivors claimed negligence and carelessness on the part of Cunard in connection with the navigation of the *Lusitania* and in respect to the conduct of her officers and crew. In the *Opinion of Court* handed down by Judge Julius M. Mayer in the United States District Court for the Southern District of New York dated 23 August 1918, Cunard Line was exonerated and 'The cause of the *Lusitania* sinking was the illegal act of the Imperial German government, through its instrument, the submarine commander...'

Marowijne
United Fruit Company, New York

Builders: Workman, Clark & Co, Belfast, 1908.

Particulars: 3,191 gross tons, 340ft × 43ft.
Machinery: Triple-expansion engines, single screw.
Passengers: 40 First Class.

Date of disaster: August 1915.

Named after a river in Dutch Guyana, the *Marowijne* was purchased from the Dutch West India Company in 1908 after a plant disease wiped out the firm's banana plantation in Guyana. The *Marowijne* was placed under American registry and assigned to sail from New Orleans to Central America, carrying 40,000 bunches of bananas in her refrigerated cargo space.

On Friday, 13 August 1915 at 11:00 am the *Marowijne* sailed from Belize, British Honduras. Except for a single life preserver picked up later by another ship, the *Marowijne* was never heard from or seen again. It is suspected that she was overwhelmed by a hurricane that was roaring in the Gulf of Mexico, the same one that devastated Galveston, Texas on 17 August.

The *Marowijne* was the only peacetime disaster to befall the company, and she was the third passenger ship of this century to simply disappear at sea.

Marowijne *was one of four ships United Fruit purchased from the Dutch* (Courtesy of the Steamship Historical Society collection/University of Baltimore Library).

Athinai
National Steam Navigation Co Ltd of Greece, Piraeus

Builders: Sir Raylton Dixon & Co Ltd, Middlesbrough, 1908.
Particulars: 6,742 gross tons, 420ft × 52ft.
Machinery: Triple-expansion engines, twin screw, speed 14 knots.
Passengers: 300 First Class and Second Class, 2,000 Steerage.

Date of disaster: 19 September 1915.

National Greek Line, as it was commonly known, was one of the pioneers in establishing a sea link between Greece and America. Operations were inaugurated in 1909 with the steamer *Patris*. The *Athinai* was their fifth ship, acquired from the defunct Hellenic Transatlantic Steam Nav Co in 1914. National continued operating the *Athinai* between Piraeus and New York with intermediate calls in Italy.

On 28 February 1914, the *Athinai* arrived in New York with 480 passengers, of whom three had cerebro-spinal meningitis. All the passengers were removed to Hoffman Island, with the cerebro-spinal ones being sent to Swinlum Island. The Health Officer of the Port of New York later visited the vessel and filed a libel and complaint suit against the *Athinai* and her engines, boilers, tackle, apparel and furniture, all a cause of action for violation of a Public Health law. A lien of $4,551.50 was held against the *Athinai* on 30 July 1914, until it was discharged and cancelled on 23 August 1916.

On 16 September 1915, the *Athinai* sailed from New York to Piraeus with a small passenger list, but a large general cargo and many bags of mails. According to the wireless received by the Anchor liner *Tuscania*, the *Athinai* caught fire in mid-Atlantic on 19 September, and was abandoned by her passengers and crew, who were all rescued by the *Tuscania*.

Highland Warrior
Nelson Line, London

Builders: Cammell, Laird & Co Ltd, Birkenhead, 1911.
Particulars: 7,485 gross tons, 414ft × 56ft.
Machinery: Triple-expansion engines, single screw, speed 13 knots.
Passengers: 80 First Class, 40 Second Class, 400 Third Class.

Date of disaster: 3 October 1915.

Hugh Nelson, who established a meat factory at Zarate, near Buenos Aires, wanted an economical way to ship his produce from Argentina to England. The result was the formation of a shipping company in 1889. A fleet designed to carry passengers started operation in 1901. A building programme of

Highland Warrior *was one of ten ships designed by A.R.T. Woods* (Courtesy of the Steamship Historical Society collection/University of Baltimore Library).

ten ships commenced in 1910, all designed by the line's general manager, A.R.T. Woods. The *Highland Warrior* was the final vessel in the series. She started her maiden voyage between Glasgow and River Plate on 28 August 1911.

On 3 October 1915, the *Highland Warrior* was wrecked north of Cape Prior on the north-west coast of Spain.

Ancona
Italia Società di Navigazione a Vapore, Genoa

Builders: Workman, Clark & Co, Belfast, 1908.
Particulars: 8,885 gross tons, 482ft × 58ft.
Machinery: Triple-expansion engines, twin screw, speed 14 knots.
Passengers: 60 First Class, 120 Second Class, 2,500 Third Class.

Date of disaster: 8 November 1915.

The *Ancona* was detailed on Italia's new service between Genoa, Naples, Palermo, New York and Philadelphia on 26 March 1908. In 1909 First Class was increased from sixty to

120, but in 1910 was reduced back to sixty with space provided for 120 Second Class passengers.

The *Ancona* left Naples on 6 November 1915 on a routine transatlantic voyage to New York. On Monday, 8 November, the *Ancona* was sighted by a submarine flying the Austrian flag. The submarine gave chase and fired at the liner. At about 1:00 pm, the *Ancona* was torpedoed. The death toll was heavy as the liner began to sink fast. Of the 446 persons on board, 194, of whom eleven were Americans, lost their lives. The survivors were picked up by the French cruiser *Pluton*. The American government demanded satisfaction from the Austrian government. It was then revealed that the submarine was the German *U-38* flying the Austrian flag. This was indeed sad since Italy was not at war with either Germany or Austria.

The Ancona *was torpedoed despite the fact that Italy was not at war* (The Mariners' Museum).

Thessaloniki
National Steam Navigation Co Ltd of Greece, Piraeus
Previous name: *City of Vienna* (1889–1914).

Builders: Workman, Clark & Co Ltd, Belfast, 1889.
Particulars: 4,682 gross tons, 421ft × 47ft.
Machinery: Triple-expansion engines, single screw, speed 12 knots.
Passengers: 50 First Class, 50 Second Class, 1,900 Third Class.

Date of disaster: 5 January 1916.

The *Thessaloniki* joined National Greek Line in 1914 after 25 years of service for City Line (Ellerman) and Allan Line. The petite *Thessaloniki* commenced service on 16 February 1914, from Piraeus, Patras and Palermo to New York.

On 25 November 1915 the *Thessaloniki* departed Piraeus. En route to New York with 49 Cabin and 128 Steerage passengers the *Thessaloniki* encountered heavy weather in mid-Atlantic. During the course of the voyage her engines and boiler room became flooded due to the storm and she started to drift helplessly. At 2:30 pm on Wednesday, 22 December 1915, Captain Goulandis sent out a wireless call for assistance. The call was received by the Italian liner *Stampalla* which relayed the message to their agents in New York and then proceeded to the scene. The *Stampalla* arrived alongside the *Thessaloniki* at 11:15 pm and remained at their disposal until released the next morning at 8:30

Alone again, Captain Goulandis did all he could to keep his ship afloat. Finally, on 29 December, when everything Captain Goulandis did failed, he assembled his frightened passengers, who were beginning to question his wisdom and leadership, in the main lounge and announced that he was going to send out a SOS call for help.

On 31 December the streamer *Florizel* arrived on the scene, followed by the National liner *Patris*. Starting at 9:30 on 1 January, the storm-wearied passengers were ferried over to the *Patris*, which returned immediately to New York. Most of the crew went over to the

Florizel. Then the *Florizel* made an attempt to tow the *Thessaloniki* to port, but this proved fruitless. Therefore, on 5 January Captain Goulandis, who had remained on board, ordered the seacocks opened before he too departed the dying ship. The *Thessaloniki* sank 350 miles east of Sandy Hook.

Principe de Austurias
Pinillos, Izquierdo y Compañiá, Cadiz

Builders: Russell & Co, Port Glasgow, 1914.
Particulars: 8,371 gross tons, 460ft × 58ft.
Machinery: Quadruple-expansion engines, twin screw, speed 15 knots.
Passengers: 144 First Class, 150 Second Class, 1,750 Third Class.

Date of disaster: 3 March 1916.

The *Principe de Asturias* was one of the finest ships in the Spanish mercantile marine, built exclusively to serve the former Spanish empire in South America. She commenced her sailings between Barcelona and Buenos Aires in August 1914, in conjunction with her sister-ship *Infanta Isabel*.

Nearing the end of a normal Atlantic passage, her sixth voyage, the *Principe de Asturias* encountered thick fog off the coast of Brazil. At 4:15 am on 3 March 1916, she struck rocks off Sebastiao Point. The impact was so violent that she ripped her bottom open causing several boilers to explode resulting in fire. The *Principe de Asturias* broke in two, capsized and sank within ten minutes. Out of the 395 passengers and 193 crew members, only 173 were rescued. One of the reasons advanced for the grounding and sinking of the *Principe de Asturias* was that many of her passengers were German and for that reason the Captain was trying to avoid interception by British cruisers stationed near the Brazilian coast.

Chiyo Maru
Toyo Kisen KK, Yokohama

Builders: Mitsubishi, Nagasaki, 1908.
Particulars: 13,426 gross tons, 575ft × 61ft.

速　機　排　總　深　幅　長
力　關　水　噸　　　サ
　　　量　數
貳　ス　一　一　三　六　五
十　チ　三　三　十　十　百
一　|　四　四　九　三　四
節　ム　二　二　呎　呎　十
　　タ　五　六　餘　餘　七
　　|　〇　噸　　　　　呎
　　ビ　噸　　　　　　餘
　　ン
　　パ
　　|
　　ソ
　　ン
　　ス
　　三
　　軸

S.S. "CHIYO MARU"
東洋汽船株式會社造船地洋丸

Above *Toya Kisen's* Chiyo Maru (Courtesy of the Steamship Historical Society collection/University of Baltimore Library).

Right Chiyo Maru *breaking up on Tam Kan* (Courtesy of the Steamship Historical Society collection/University of Baltimore Library).

Machinery: Turbines (Parsons), triple screw, speed 18 knots.
Passengers: 275 First Class, 75 Second Class, 800 Third Class.

Date of disaster: 31 March 1916.

The *Chiyo Maru* was one of three sister-ships built for the Hong Kong-San Francisco service which went via Yokohama.

On 31 March, 1916, the *Chiyo Maru* ran aground twenty miles south of Hong Kong on the island of Tam Kan. The ship broke in two and was declared a total loss.

Tongariro
New Zealand Shipping, London

Builders: R. W. Hawthorn, Leslie & Co Ltd, Hebburn, 1901.
Particulars: 7,661 gross tons, 457ft × 58ft.
Machinery: Triple-expansion engines, twin screw, speed 14 knots.
Passengers: 40 First Class, 50 Second Class, 80 Third Class.

Date of disaster: 30 August 1916.

The *Tongariro* was one of the final units in the building programme initiated by New Zealand Shipping in 1898. She commenced her maiden voyage from England to New Zealand via South Africa on 12 September 1901. With new tonnage on line, the *Tongariro* was relegated to secondary service in 1911 with accommodation for Third Class and emigrants only. Although the Shipping Controller governed the accommodation space on the *Tongariro* during the war, she did maintain her routine voyage runs to New Zealand.

With only a general cargo, the *Tongariro* sailed from London for another routine voyage to Wellington. Nearing the end of that voyage in poor visibility, the *Tongariro* ran aground on Bull Rocks, off Portland Island, New Zealand. After attempts to refloat her failed, her 93-member crew was taken off and rescued by the coastal steamer *Koutunui* and the *Westralia*. The *Tongariro* later broke in two and was abandoned as a total loss.

Maitai
Union Steam Ship Co of New Zealand Ltd, Wellington

Previous name: *Miowera* (1892–1908).

The Tongariro *at Nelson, New Zealand* (Jones collection/Alexander Turnbull Library).

The tiny Maitai *was engaged in a regular transpacific service* (Dickie collection/Alexander Turnbull Library).

Builders: Swan & Hunter, Newcastle, 1892.
Particulars: 3,393 gross tons, 345ft × 42ft.
Machinery: Triple-expansion engines, single screw, speed 14 knots.
Passengers: 233 First Class, 127 Second Class.

Date of disaster: 25 December 1916.

The *Maitai* started her career as the *Miowera* of the New Zealand Australasian Steamship Company. Under that company's banner, the *Miowera* made her positioning voyage to Australia in October 1892, then commenced her maiden voyage on 17 December between Australia and New Zealand. In 1893 the *Miowera* was transferred to the newly formed Canadian-Australian Mail Line and placed on their transpacific route. She departed Sydney for Brisbane, Honolulu and Vancouver on 18 May 1893. During her third northbound voyage to Vancouver the *Miowera* was stranded on 2 October 1893, at the entrance to Pearl Harbor. The passengers and mails were taken off; then the vessel was refloated.

Temporary repairs were made at Esquimalt, before the trip to the Tyne in England, where *Miowera* was given a complete overhaul and refit. Before returning to the Antipodes the *Miowera* undertook three cruises to Norway. She then departed London on 1 September 1894 for Sydney where she resumed her regular itinerary. In August 1897 Wellington, New Zealand was added to the schedule. The *Miowera* was chartered in 1901 to Union SS Co and remained on the Vancouver route. Seven years later Union purchased the vessel, renamed her *Maitai* and finally altered her itinerary in 1911 to Wellington, Raratonga, Tahiti and San Francisco. In addition to the *Maitai*'s Pacific voyages, she was used as a relief ship on the trans-Tasman trade.

While at anchor in the roadstead at Avarua, Rarotonga, on 25 December 1916, the chain cable parted and the *Maitai*'s bow, owing to the current and ocean swell, sung rapidly to starboard bringing her parallel with the reef. Captain Charles McLean took all the necessary measures to keep his vessel off the reef, but owing to the poor ocean conditions, was unable to get her out to sea.

The *Maitai* was driven upon the reef and became a total wreck. A court of inquiry was unable to find out why the chain parted and credited the Master with doing all he could to save his ship.

Kristianiafjord
Norwegian America Line, Christiania

Builders: Cammell, Laird & Co, Birkenhead, 1913.
Particulars: 10,669 gross tons, 530ft × 61ft.
Machinery: Quadruple-expansion engines, twin screw, speed 15 knots.
Passengers: 101 First Class, 216 Second Class, 700 Third Class.

Date of disaster: 15 July 1917.

The *Kristianiafjord* was the first ship built for Norwegian America Line. She inaugurated their North America service when she sailed from Christiania on 4 June 1913. On board for the occasion was the King of Norway and many prominent members of his government, who accompanied the liner on her coastal run to Bergen. There, the royal party disembarked and the *Kristianiafjord* continued to New York.

On a voyage from New York to Norway with

The Kristianafjord *pioneered Norwegian America Line service* (Courtesy of the Steamship Historical Society collection/University of Baltimore Library).

906 passengers aboard, the *Kristianiafjord* ran aground near Mistaken Point, seven miles from Cape Race. The passengers were safely taken off; then the liner was abandoned by her crew as a total constructive loss.

Toscana
Italia Società di Navigazione a Vapore, Genoa

Builders: N. Odero & Co, Genoa, 1900.
Particulars: 4,113 gross tons, 363ft × 43ft.
Machinery: Triple-expansion engines, single screw, speed 12 knots.
Passengers: 42 First Class, 1,320 Third Class.

Date of disaster: 5 February 1918.

Italia was a company founded in May 1899, and under the control of Hamburg America Line. Their first ship, *Toscana,* was launched in a fully completed condition on 26 October 1900, and began her maiden voyage from Genoa to South America on 4 November 1900. In August 1917, Italia ceased operation and ownership of the *Toscana* was passed on to the new shipping concern of Transoceanica Societa Italiana di Navigation.

The *Toscana* was sunk in a collision with the French vessel *Molière* on 5 February 1918, near Gibraltar.

Highland Scot
Nelson Line, London

Builders: Russell & Co, Port Glasgow, 1910.
Particulars: 7,604 gross tons, 414ft × 56ft
Machinery: Triple-expansion engines, single screw, speed 13 knots.
Passengers: 80 First Class, 40 Second Class, 400 Third Class.

Date of disaster: 6 May 1918.

The *Highland Scot* was one of ten new steamers built for Nelson's River Plate service. The *Highland Scot* started her maiden voyage on 6 September 1910, from Glasgow.

Sailing from Buenos Aires to Rio de Janiero with a load of general cargo, the *Highland Scot* was wrecked at Maricas Island, Brazil, on 6 May 1918.

Valbanera
Pinillos, Izquierdo y Compañiá, Cadiz

Builders: C. Connell & Co, Glasgow, 1906.
Particulars: 5,099 gross tons, 400ft × 48ft.
Machinery: Triple-expansion engines, single screw, speed 12 knots.
Passengers: Over 1,000 in three classes.

Date of disaster: 12 September 1919.

The *Valbanera* was a typical Spanish steamer that plied between Spain and the continents of North and South America carrying emigrants, mails and cargo to the Spanish-speaking countries in the 'New World'.

On a voyage from Spain to New Orleans with 400 passengers and 88 crew, the *Valbanera* encountered a severe hurricane in the Caribbean. On arriving off Havana Habour, Cuba, Captain Ramos Martin decided to ride out the storm by heading back out to sea. At

Above Highland Scot *was one of ten ships designed by A.R.T. Woods* (World Ship Society Picture Library).

Below Highland Scot *breaking up on Maricas Island* (World Ship Society Picture Library).

1:15 pm on 12 September, weak radio signals were picked up in Havana and Key West from the *Valbanera* inquiring about weather conditions. Nothing more of the liner was heard of or seen — not lifeboats, floating debris or bodies.

On 19 September 1919, a US submarine chaser discovered a submerged wreck near Rebecca Shoals light, located about 46 miles west of Key West. The wreck was the *Valbanera* — in 40ft of water. Subsequent investigations by divers discovered the lifeboats intact and no structural damage. The only explanation was that the vessel went down suddenly, overwhelmed by the hurricane's wind and waves.

Chapter 3

Return to normality

The 1920s marked a return to normality in the world's shipping lanes. On the North Atlantic a new type of traveller — the American tourist — boarded the liners and sailed east. The Australia and New Zealand routes continued to be plied by ships carrying emigrants from England, while South American was favoured by the Spanish, Italian and German emigrants. Elsewhere, European nations strengthened their maritime connections with their distant colonies and protectorates in Africa, the Middle East, Asia and the West Indies by transporting administrative personnel, products and the mails.

All, however, was not smooth sailing: 21 ships met misfortune which ended their trading career. Eight liners were wrecked, six burned, two were involved in a collision, two had mechanical problems, two were overcome by adverse climatic conditions and one vessel was abandoned: all culminating in the deaths of 1,085 persons.

The most notable tragedy in this period was the storm-related sinking of the *Vestris,* followed by the *Celtic,* at one time the largest liner in the world.

Afrique
Compagnie des Chargeurs Rénuis, Marseille

Builders: Swan, Hunter & Wigham Richardson, Ltd, Newcastle, 1907.
Particulars: 5,404 gross tons, 391ft × 48ft.
Machinery: Triple-expansion engines, twin screw, speed 14.5 knots.

The Afrique *sailed between France and French West Africa* (Courtesy of the Steamship Historical Society collection/University of Baltimore Library).

Passengers: Data not available.

Date of disaster: 12 January 1920.

The *Afrique* was equipped with two masts and one funnel and was built to serve on the colonial route between France and her West African colonies.

During the night of Saturday, 12 January 1920, the *Afrique* was on a southbound voyage from Bordeaux to Dakar with 458 passengers and a crew of 127 under the command of Captain Le Du, when she developed engine trouble in the Bay of Biscay. Strong winds and a boisterous sea swept the hapless *Afrique* toward the swallow water covering the Roche-Bonne Reefs about fifty miles from La Rochelle. A wireless call for assistance was sent out and the *Ceylan,* also of Chargeurs Réunis, came to the rescue, but the *Ceylan* could do nothing but stand by and watch.

That evening, the SS *Lapland* arrived on the scene followed by the Belgian liner *Anversville.* Again, the weather prevented the ships from acting, but, two lifeboats from the *Afrique* were launched with great effort and their occupants reached the *Ceylan* safely. Finally at

about three o'clock in the morning of 13 January, the wireless messages from the *Afrique* ceased as she slipped off the shoal and sank in deep water. There were only 32 survivors, making this one of the worst French maritime disasters since the loss of the *La Bourgogne* in 1898.

Bohemian
Leyland Line, Liverpool

Builders: A. Stephens & Sons, Glasgow, 1900.
Particulars: 8,548 gross tons, 512ft × 58ft.
Machinery: Triple-expansion engines, single screw, speed 13 knots.
Passengers: 90 First Class.

Date of disaster: 1 March 1920.

The *Bohemian* was one of the last ships built for Leyland, a company with North Atlantic roots dating back to 1874. The *Bohemian* left

Leyland's Bohemian (Courtesy of the Steamship Historical Society collection/University of Baltimore Library).

on her maiden voyage from Liverpool on 8 September 1900 and remained in transatlantic service until 1920.

The *Bohemian* was wrecked on 1 March 1920 at Sambro, Nova Scotia. Only a general cargo was aboard: the crew took to the boats and rowed ashore safely.

Grampian
Allan Line, Glasgow

Builders: A. Stephens & Sons, Glasgow, 1907.
Particulars: 10,187 gross tons, 502ft × 60ft.
Machinery: Triple-expansion geared, twin screw, speed 15 knots.
Passengers: 210 First Class, 250 Second Class, 1,000 Third Class.

Date of disaster: 14 March 1921.

Launched on 25 July 1907, the *Grampian* was completed and commenced her maiden voyage from Glasgow to Boston on 7 December 1907. The *Grampian* was mainly employed on the Glasgow-Canada run. During 1914 and 1915, the *Grampian* made a few round voyages for Canadian Pacific between Liverpool and Canada. In 1918, her eastern terminus was extended to Antwerp.

During a refit at Antwerp on 14 March 1921, fire swept through the vessel. The *Grampian* was abandoned to underwriters as a total loss. In 1925, the remaining hulk was sold to F. Rijsdijk and scrapped at Hendrik-Ido-Ambacht.

Egypt
Peninsular & Oriental Steam Navigation Co, London

Builders: Caird & Co, Greenock, 1897.
Particulars: 7,912 gross tons, 500ft × 54ft.
Machinery: Triple-expansion engines, single screw, speed 16 knots.
Passengers: 460–500 in two classes.

Below *The* Grampian *at speed* (Frank O. Braynard collection).

Bottom *The* Egypt *sank off Ushant* (P & O Group).

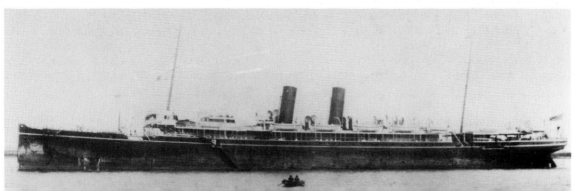

Date of disaster: 22 May 1922.

The *Egypt* was the last single screw passenger liner built for P & O. She was specifically constructed for the London-Bombay service. When demand warranted, the *Egypt* also undertook voyages to Australia. In 1910 she brought the Princess Royal home from Egypt, and in 1915 she became *Hospital Ship No 52* serving mainly in Mediterranean waters. She was released from duties and after a lengthy refit, re-entered service in 1921.

On 19 May 1922, the *Egypt* left Tilbury for Marseille and Bombay with 44 passengers and a crew of 294. In her holds was £1,054,000 in the form of gold and silver bars and coins. On 27 May at around 7:00 pm under dense fog conditions, 25 miles off Ushant, the *Egypt* was rammed on the port side by the French cargo steamer *Seine*. The *Egypt* heeled over after the impact and sank in about twenty minutes with the loss of fifteen passengers and 71 crew members. The *Seine* picked up the remaining survivors and returned them to Brest.

After many unsuccessful efforts, divers finally succeeded in 1935 in recovering over ninety per cent of the gold and silver bars and coins.

Wiltshire ***breaking up in Rosalie Bay*** (Arnold Kludas collection).

Wiltshire
Federal Steam Navigation Co, London

Builders: John Brown & Co, Clydebank, 1912.
Particulars: 10,390 gross tons, 544ft × 61ft.
Machinery: Quadruple-expansion engines, twin screw, speed 13.5 knots.
Passengers: 131 First Class.

Date of disaster: 31 May 1922.

Launched on 19 December 1911, the *Wiltshire* was completed and handed over to her owners on 15 February 1912. A month later, the *Wiltshire* entered the London-Brisbane trade. Besides her passenger and general cargo spaces, the *Wiltshire* had a refrigerated storage space of 375,000cu ft. This made her the largest meat carrier in the world. From 1914 to 1918 the *Wiltshire* was engaged as a troop transport. The *Wiltshire* was returned to service in 1918.

While approaching Auckland during stormy weather on 31 May 1922, the *Wiltshire* ran

aground in Rosalie Bay near the Great Barrier Island. Her wireless signal of distress was picked up by ships within a 300-mile radius and on land. The next day as the ship broke in two the crew clung to the fore part. They were later picked up by a party sent from Katoa. At the time the *Wiltshire* was not carrying passengers.

The troop transport Huron (Frank O. Braynard collection).

City of Honolulu *abandoned and listing in the Pacific* (Frank O. Braynard collection).

City of Honolulu
Los Angeles Steamship Co, Los Angeles
Previous names: *Friedrich der Grosse* (1896–1917), *Huron* (1917–22).

Builders: Vulcan, Stettin, 1896.
Particulars: 10,771 gross tons, 546ft × 60ft.
Machinery: Quadruple-expansion engines, twin screw, speed 15 knots.
Passengers: 244 First Class.

Date of disaster: 12 October 1922.

The *City of Honolulu* was completed on 11 November 1896, as North German Lloyd's *Friedrich der Grosse*. Under the German flag, she was utilized on the Australian and North Atlantic run. In August 1914, the *Friedrich der Grosse* was interned in New York. Seized by

the US Navy on 6 April 1917, the ship was renamed *Huron* and employed as a troop transport. In 1919, the *Huron* was handed over to the US Shipping Board, who in 1922 chartered her to the Los Angeles Steamship Company. Renamed *City of Honolulu*, she was extensively refitted for her new service between California and the Hawaiian Islands which she inaugurated on 11 September 1922.

On 12 October 1922, during the return portion of her first voyage, 670 miles south-west of San Pedro, the *City of Honolulu* was gutted by fire. An SOS was sent out and the 73 passengers and 145 crew were rescued by the freighter *West Faralon*. Five days later on 17 October, the burned-out *City of Honolulu* was sunk by gunfire from the US transport ship *Thomas*.

Monte Grappa
Navigazione Libera Triestina, Trieste

Builders: Stabilimento Technico Triestino, Trieste, 1921.
Particulars: 7,434 gross tons, 464ft × 57ft.
Machinery: Triple-expansion engines, single screw, speed 14 knots.
Passengers: 40 First Class.

Date of disaster: November 1922.

Navigazione was established at Trieste under the Austrian flag in 1906. The first four steamers carried only cargo to various parts of the world. After the First World War, the company came under the Italian flag. Passenger service was opened between Italy and New York/Philadelphia in 1921 by the *Monte Grappa,* Navigazione's first passenger ship. By 1923 Navigazione had 24 ships, of which five carried forty passengers each.

For unknown reasons, the *Monte Grappa* was abandoned in the North Atlantic by her crew during a voyage in November 1922.

Mossamedes
Empresa Nacional de Navegação, Lisbon
Previous names: *Sumatra* (1895–1914), unknown name (1914–16) in ownership of Arab SS Co of Bombay.

Builders: Alexander Stephen & Son Ltd, Glasgow, 1895.
Particulars: 4,615 gross tons, 400ft × 46ft.
Machinery: Triple-expansion engines, single

The ill-fated Monte Grappa — *note the unusual cargo derricks.* (Associazione Marinara Aldebaran of Trieste).

screw, speed 14 knots.
Passengers: 46 First Class, 48 Second Class.

Date of disaster: 23 April 1923.

As the *Sumatra* for P & O Lines, she carried 98 passengers in two classes between England and India. In 1914 she was sold to Arab Steamship Company. It is not known whether they renamed her. In 1916 the vessel was again sold, to the Portuguese, and renamed *Mossamedes*. ENN placed their new acquisition on the Portugal-Southern African route, touching at the Portuguese colonies of Angola and Mozambique.

The *Mossamedes* left Cape Town for Lisbon on 20 April, 1923 with 237 passengers and crew. On 24 April she sent out wireless signals stating she was ashore on the coast of Angola and needed assistance. When the liner *Port Victor* arrived, she found the *Mossamedes* high and dry and deserted. After searching the area and finding no one, the *Port Victor* continued her voyage to Cape Town. The people in the boats from the *Mossamedes* decided to make for Porto Alexandre and they voyaged in the open sea for nearly a week before being picked up by the French gunboat *Cassiopée* and the Portuguese gunboat *Salvador Correia* outside Porto Alexandre: 206 persons reached safety — the remaining 31 were believed drowned.

Marvale
Canadian Pacific, London
Previous name: *Corsican* (1907–15).

Builders: Barclay, Curle & Co, Glasgow, 1907.
Particulars: 11,439 gross tons, 516ft × 61ft.
Machinery: Triple expansion engines, twin screw, speed 16 knots.
Passengers: Approximately 1,300 in two classes.

Date of disaster: 21 May 1923.

Allan Line, a company engaged in the transatlantic business since 1854, built the 1,506-passenger *Corsican* to serve their Liverpool-St John route. On 12 August 1912, the *Corsican* collided with an iceberg near Belle Isle but sustained little damage. While serving as a troop transport, the *Corsican* was purchased by Canadian Pacific on 1 October 1915. Three years later on 24 August 1918, she resumed passenger service between England and Canada. In 1922 the *Corsican* was

The Mossamedes *connected Portugal with her African colonies* (Luis Miguel Correia collection).

Allan Line's Corsican *changed little when she became the* Marvale (Alex Duncan).

converted to a cabin-class ship at Liverpool. Renamed *Marvale* on 16 November 1922, she re-entered service in 1923 between Glasgow, Belfast, Quebec and Montreal.

Navigating through dense fog, the *Marvale,* under the command of Captain H. Lewis, stuck rocks at the entrance to Trepassy Bay, 25 miles west of Cape Race at 5:00 pm on 21 May 1923. Calm and order was maintained and within 25 minutes, 436 people (214 passengers and 222 crew) were transferred to the lifeboats without a single loss of life. The liner was then abandoned as a total loss.

Paparoa at anchor — note the rolled-up sails on the fore mast cross yards (De Mous collection/ Alexander Turnbull Library).

Paparoa
New Zealand Shipping, London

Builders: William Denny & Bros, Dumbarton, 1899.
Particulars: 6,563 gross tons, 430ft × 54ft.
Machinery: Triple-expansion engines, twin screw, speed 13 knots.
Passengers: 34 First Class, 45 Second Class, Steerage.

Date of disaster: 17 March 1926.

An improvement in trade between England and New Zealand at the turn of the century led New Zealand Shipping to initiate a building programme. The first of the new ships to arrive was the *Papanui* in 1898, followed by her sister-ship, the *Paparoa* in 1899, both vessels being square-rigged on the foremast in order to take advantage of the winds in the southern latitudes. The *Paparoa* embarked on her

maiden voyage from London to Cape Town, Auckland and Wellington on 9 November 1899. After serving in World War 1, she was returned to commercial service carrying only a general cargo and emigrants through the Panama Canal (first used by New Zealand Shipping in 1916).

The *Paparoa* caught fire in the South Atlantic while bound for Cape Town on 17 March 1926. The blaze could not be brought under control and the Captain sent out an SOS. The P & O steamer *Barrabool* arrived on the scene and took off all the *Paparoa's* passengers. How coincidental that her sistership *Papanui* had burned in the same general location fifteen years earlier.

Fontainebleau
Messageries Maritimes, Marseille

Builders: Ateliers et Chantiers de la Loire, St Nazaire, 1924.
Particulars: 10,015 gross tons, 501ft × 59ft.
Machinery: Geared turbines, twin screw, speed 15 knots.
Passengers: 130 First Class, 80 Second Class, 116 Third Class, 250 Steerage.

The Fontainebleau *was engaged in Messageries Maritime's Orient service* (Compagnie Générale Maritime).

Date of disaster: 12 July 1926.

Laid down as the *Islande* for the South American service of Chargeurs Réunis, the finished hull was sold to Messageries Maritimes in 1923. Completed in August 1924, the *Fontainebleau* was placed on the Marseille-Far East route.

En route to the Orient, at Djibouti on 12 July 1926, the *Fontainebleau* caught fire and was completely burnt out. The wreck was later sunk to form the foundations for a breakwater.

Persia
Lloyd Triestino, Trieste

Builders: Wigham Richardson & Company, Newcastle, 1903.
Particulars: 6,283 gross tons, 424ft × 53ft.
Machinery: Quadruple-expansion engines, single screw, speed 12 knots.
Passengers: 40 First Class.

Date of disaster: 24 August 1926.

The *Persia* was originally built for Lloyd Austriaco in 1903 and handed over to Lloyd Triestino in 1918 after the fall of the Austro-Hungarian Empire. She was employed in the African and Orient services of the company.

On 24 August 1926 on a voyage from Colombo to Karachi with a cargo of copra, the *Persia* was consumed by fire. She was towed to

Bombay, declared a total loss by her owners and subsequently broken up there.

Lloyd Triestino's Persia *regularly plied the oceans bordering Africa and Asia.* (Associazione Marinara Aldebaran of Trieste).

Braga
Fabre Line, Marseille
Previous names: *Laura* (1907–17), *Europa* (1917–19).

Builders: Russell & Co, Port Glasgow, 1907.
Particulars: 6,122 gross tons, 415ft × 50ft.
Machinery: Triple-expansion engines, twin screw, speed 16 knots.
Passengers: 130 Cabin Class, 1,350 Third Class.

Date of disaster: 16 November 1926.

The *Braga* sailed under the Austrian and Brazilian flags before joining the Fabre fleet in December 1919, as war reparation. She plied the Marseille-Naples-Palermo-New York route.

The *Braga* was wrecked on 16 November 1926, on Aspro Island, Greece.

Principessa Mafalda
Navigazione Generale Italiana Società Riunite Florio & Rubattino, Genoa

Builders: Società Esercizio Bacini, Riva Trigoso, 1909.
Particulars: 9,210 gross tons, 485ft × 56ft.
Machinery: Quadruple-expansion engines, twin screw, speed 16 knots.
Passengers: Approximately 1,700 in two classes.

Date of disaster: 25 October 1927.

Navigazion Generale Italiana (NGI) was created in 1881 with the merger of Florio Line and the Rubattino Line. NGI maintained regular services from Italy to points in the

Fabre's Braga (Frank O. Braynard collection).

Principipessa Mafalda *fully loaded at top speed* (Courtesy of the Steamship Historical Society collection/University of Baltimore Library).

Mediterranean, India, the Far East and the North and South American continents. The *Principessa Mafalda* was completed in 1909 and sailed from Genoa and Naples to Buenos Aires. When Lloyd Italiano was absorbed by NGI On 1 June 1918, the *Principessa Mafalda* continued in South American service.

With Captain S. Guli in command, the *Principessa Mafalda* left Cape Verde Island for Rio on 8 October 1927, with 971 passengers and a crew of 288. When nearing Abrolhos Island, off Brazil at around 5:00 pm on the 25th, the port propeller shaft broke. This resulted in water entering the boiler room causing them to explode. The passengers became frightened and panic ensued. As the *Principessa Mafalda* began to settle with a list to port, Captain Guli issued an SOS stating, 'Danger to engines'. In response to his call, the *Empire Star,* along with six other ships, rushed to the scene. After four and a half hours, the *Principessa Mafalda* capsized and sank taking 303 souls with her.

Cap Lay
Compagnie des Chargeurs Réunis, Marseille
Previous name: *Halgan* (1921–25).

Builders: Ateliers et Chantiers de la Loire, Nantes, 1921.
Particulars: 8,009 gross tons, 418ft × 55ft.
Machinery: Three steam turbines, single screw, speed 12 knots.
Passengers: 850 in three classes.

Date of disaster: 15 July 1928.

The *Halgan* was built as a freighter and converted to carry passengers in 1925. The change was accompanied by a new name. The *Cap Lay* was employed between France and the Far East.

The *Cap Lay* was lost in a typhoon in the Bay of Along on 15 July 1928.

Vestris
Lamport & Holt, Liverpool

Builders: Workman, Clark and Co, Belfast, 1912.
Particulars: 10,494 gross tons, 511ft × 61ft.
Machinery: Quadruple-expansion engines, twin screw, speed 15 knots.
Passengers: 280 First Class, 130 Second Class, 200 Third Class.

Date of disaster: 12 November 1928.

The *Vestris* was launched on 16 May, completed 3 September, and placed on

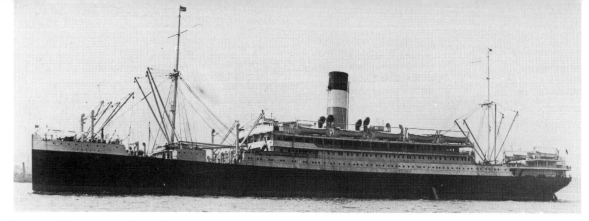

The Vestris *arriving at New York* (The Mariners' Museum).

Lamport's New York-La Plata service in 1912. In 1919 the *Vestris* was chartered to Cunard Line, of which service commenced 8 March 1919. After six round voyages, the last one 20 June 1921, the *Vestris* made one round voyage: New York-Cherbourg-Southampton-Hamburg on 20 May 1922, for Royal Mail Lines. After the voyage, the *Vestris* was returned to Lamport.

The *Vestris* left New York on 10 November 1928, for Barbados and Buenos Aires under the command of Captain W.J. Carey, with 129 passengers and a crew of 197. The *Vestris* encountered heavy weather resulting in a threatening list which grew worse due to shifting cargo and coal in the bunkers. The *Vestris* sent out an SOS that was answered by vessels in the area. In the meantime, the passengers and crew had to take to the lifeboats as the ship's list continued to increase. As evacuation proceeded, the vessel capsized and sank 300 miles off Hampton Roads: 68 passengers and 44 crew went down with the liner. The survivors were picked up from the *Vestris* lifeboats by the French tanker *Myriam,* the US battleship *Wyoming,* the US liner *American Shipper* and the North German Lloyd liner *Berlin.*

As a result of the adverse publicity and the subsequent depression in 1929, Lamport & Holt discontinued its passenger service from New York in 1930.

Celtic
White Star Line, Liverpool

Builders: Harland & Wolff, Belfast, 1901.
Particulars: 20,904 gross tons, 700ft × 75ft.

The four-masted Celtic *was at one time the largest liner in the world* (Frank O. Braynard collection).

Machinery: Quadruple-expansion engines geared to twin screw, speed 16 knots.
Passengers: 350 First Class, 250 Second Class, 1,000 Third Class.

Date of disaster: 10 December 1928.

The *Celtic* was the largest vessel in the world when she was completed and delivered on 11 July 1901; built expressly for White Star's Liverpool-New York route. On 20 October 1914, she was converted to an armed cruiser in the 10th Cruiser Squadron. In January 1916 the *Celtic* was laid-up, resuming commercial sailings between Liverpool and New York on 7 March 1916. On 15 February 1917, she hit a mine in the Irish Sea and had to be towed to Liverpool for repairs. In March 1918, the *Celtic* was torpedoed in the Irish Sea and limped to Belfast for repairs. Commercial service was resumed on 8 December 1918 from Liverpool. Passenger capacity was revised in 1920 from 347 First, 160 Second and 2,350 Steerage to 350 First, 250 Second and 1,000 Third; and again in 1926 to Cabin, Tourist and Third.

While making for the harbour entrance to Queenstown on 10 December 1928, during a 70 mph-gale, the *Celtic,* with 254 passengers, among them 25 survivors from the *Vestris* disaster, was hit with a violent gust of wind that swung her upon the rocks of Roche's Point. A gaping hole was smashed through the side of the engine room and soon water was flooding the ship. The *Celtic* was grounded and all passengers were transferred ashore by tenders. Valued at $1,150,000, the *Celtic* was declared a total loss. The wreck was sold to Petersen & Albeck of Copenhagen, who completed breaking-up in 1933.

Paul Lecat
Messageries Maritimes, Marseille

Builders: Constructions Navales, La Ciotat, 1911.
Particulars: 12,989 gross tons, 529ft × 58ft.
Machinery: Quadruple-expansion engines, twin screw, speed 15 knots.
Passengers: 194 First Class, 145 Second Class,

Top *The* Celtic *aground at Roche's Point* (Frank O. Braynard collection). **Above** *The* Celtic *minus her funnels and three of her masts* (Frank O. Braynard collection).

109 Third Class, 826 Steerage.

Date of disaster: 30 December 1928.

The *Paul Lecat* was completed in 1911 for Messageries Maritimes' Marseille-Far East colonial service. From 1915 to 1918 she served

Messageries Maritime's Paul Lecat *(Compagnie Générale Maritime).*

Paul Lecat *engulfed in smoke at Marseille* (Arnold Kludas collection).

as a troop transport, returning to commercial service in 1918.

On 30 December 1928, the *Paul Lecat* caught fire in Marseille harbour. She burned well into the next day. On 3 January 1929, she was declared a total loss and sold for scrap at La Spezia.

Highland Pride
Nelson Line, London

Builders: Russell & Co, Port Glasgow, 1910.

Particulars: 7,469 gross tons, 405ft × 56ft
Machinery: Triple-expansion engines, single screw, speed 13 knots.
Passengers: 80 First Class, 40 Second Class, 400 Third Class.

Date of disaster: 9 September 1929.

Like the *Warrior* and *Scot*, the *Pride* was part of the ten ships Woods designed. The *Highland Pride* was launched on 26 January 1910, and four months later, was sent on her maiden voyage from Glasgow to Buenos Aires.

Under the command of Captain Alford, the *Highland Pride* left Vigo on 8 September 1929 with 63 passengers, 83 crew members and some 3,000 tons of cargo. During the night of the 8th, in dense fog, she struck on the Roca Negra, a small group of islands near Vigo. In an orderly manner everyone took to the lifeboats and all were rescued by Spanish fishing boats. Lying on her keel, the crew managed to save some of the cargo and all the mails. On 10 September 1929, the *Highland Pride* broke in two.

The Highland Pride *of the Nelson Line* (Courtesy of the Steamship Historical Society collection/ University of Baltimore Library).

Manuka
Union Steam Ship Co of New Zealand Ltd, Wellington

Builders: William Denny & Bros, Dumbarton, 1903.
Particulars: 4,534 gross tons, 369ft × 47ft.
Machinery: Triple-expansion engines, twin screw, speed 15 knots.
Passengers: 222 First Class, 135 Second Class.

Date of disaster: 16 December 1929.

The *Manuka* was designed for the trans-Tasman service between New Zealand and Australia. After completing a five and one half week positioning trip, the *Manuka* started her maiden voyage from Melbourne to Wellington on 6 January 1904. When Union SS Co extended its transpacific service to Sydney, additional tonnage was required to maintain a balanced service and the *Manuka* was called upon. From May 1904 to April 1906 the *Manuka* called at Sydney, Wellington, Raratonga, Tahiti, and Vancouver. San Francisco served as the eastern terminus from April 1911 to 1914. After serving as a troopship, she was returned to her owners and entered the Wellington-Melbourne service.

The *Manuka* departed Melbourne at 10:00 am on 11 December with 218 passengers for Bluff, Dunedin, Lyttelton and Wellington. After disembarking 119 passengers at Bluff during the morning of 15 December the *Manuka* continued on to Wellington with 99 passengers and 1,089 tons of general cargo. During the evening of 16 December 1929, the *Manuka* encountered heavy fog and shortly before midnight a thunderous crash was heard, followed by a fearful roll. The *Manuka* was aground at Long Point, New Zealand, with a ruptured hull. There was no panic as passengers and crew took to the boats in the bitter cold night. However, as the ship took on a dangerous list, some passengers were knocked about by the unstable equilibrium of the vessel. The scantily-clad survivors eventually landed and were taken overland to Owaka, and then by special train to Dunedin. On 17 December, the abandoned *Manuka* broke apart and sank.

A court of inquiry later found the master, Captain Ross-Clark, guilty of negligence in failing to take all available precautions to ascertain his position before altering course at 10:30 pm and suspended his certificate along with that of the Third Officer.

Manuka spent her final days trading between New Zealand and Australia (Dickie collection/Alexander Turnbull Library).

Fort Victoria *sets sail for another voyage to Bermuda* (Frank O. Braynard collection).

Fort Victoria
Furness, Withy & Co, London
Previous name: *Willochra* (1913–19).

Builders: William Beardmore & Co, Glasgow, 1913.
Particulars: 7,784 gross tons, 412ft × 57ft.
Machinery: Quadruple-expansion engines, twin screw, speed 16 knots.
Passengers: 373 First Class, 56 Second Cabin.

Date of disaster: 18 December 1929.

The *Fort Victoria* first sailed as the *Willochra* between Australia, New Zealand and the United States. After serving as a troop transport, she was sold by Union SS Co to Furness in 1919. After a refit, Furness renamed their new ship *Fort Victoria* and placed her on the weekly New York-Bermuda run, one of the pioneers in cruises to Bermuda.

Under the command of Captain A.R. Francis, the *Fort Victoria* sailed from New York on 18 December 1929, with 171 cabin passengers and 35 Negro deck passengers. At four o'clock the *Fort Victoria* came to a halt at the entrance to Ambrose Channel. The moan of the sirens, the timed beat of melancholy bells and the sobbing blasts of whistle markers sounded on all sides. Suddenly, out of the gray clouds of fog, a tall sharp prow appeared. The Clyde liner, *Algonquin*, outbound for Galveston, cut a deep hole in the *Fort Victoria*, amidship on the port side. An emergency dynamo (wireless signal) was sent out by both ships, and police launches, coast guard vessels and tugs rushed to the scene. All passengers and crew from the *Fort Victoria* were quickly and safely evacuated, with Captain Francis being the last to leave. All were deposited safely in New York. At 7:30 pm the *Fort Victoria* slipped under the waves of the Atlantic.

Chapter 4

The flaming thirties

The early 1930s saw the introduction of the super liners: *Bremen, Europa, Empress of Britain, Rex, Conti de Savoia, Normandie* and *Queen Mary*, all employed on the North Atlantic between the Channel ports of northern Europe and New York. Only the *Queen Mary* made a profit. As the world slowly recovered from the Depression, Fascism and Nazism raised their ugly heads and helped curtail patronage on Italian and German ships. It was also the decade that witnessed the tragic end of 27 liners costing the lives of 336 people.

Of particular interest were the fires aboard many ships that were docked or near port at the time of tragedy. Especially vulnerable were French vessels. France was undergoing labour unrest during the '30s and labour unions threatened reprisals against French ships. The *L'Atlantique, Lafayette* and *Paris* were all victims of suspected sabotage. Malicious mischief may have also played a role in the fatal fires aboard the *Georges Philippar* and the *Reliance*. Other liners that were reduced to a sodden mass of steel were the *Asia, City of Honolulu, Bermuda, Pieter Corneliszoon Hooft, Ausonia, Berengaria* and the *Cabo San Antonio*.

The tragedy that shook America was the burning of the *Morro Castle*. Like the French liners, foul play was suspected. The crew's ineptitude and the lack of safety devices contributed to make this one of America's worst maritime disasters. Out of this tragedy grew a Senate investigation which led to new safety standards for American built and owned vessels.

Next in line to fires were strandings, which involved nine liners, most of them sailing in unfamiliar and uncharted seas. Radar, that new device for detecting other ships and objects in a ship's path, was still in its infancy with the French liner *Normandie* being the first and only liner in the late '30s to be fitted with the device.

Monte Cervantes
Hamburg-South America Line

Builders: Blohm & Voss, Hamburg, 1928.
Particulars: 13,913 gross tons, 524ft × 66ft.
Machinery: MAN-geared diesel, twin screw, speed 14 knots.
Passengers: 1,354 Tourist Class, 1,138 Steerage.

Date of disaster: 22 January 1930.

Hamburg-South America Line represented the German nation on the South Atlantic. A series of five sister ships were built between 1924 and 1931, of which the *Monte Cervantes* was one. Passenger accommodation was both austere and confining. In addition to the South America run, the *Monte Cervantes* was also engaged in cruising.

Top Monte Cervantes *sinking bow first around the Straits of Magellan (The Mariners's Museum).*
Above The Asia *which spent her last years on Fabre's various routes (Frank O. Braynard collection).*

During one such cruise from Buenos Aires on 22 January 1930, with 400 passengers abroad, the *Monte Cervantes* ran on to uncharted submerged rocks going around the Straits of Magellan. The liner was badly holed and started to sink. The passengers were ordered into the boats. The *Monte Cervantes* was then driven on to the Eclaireur Reef where she capsized on 24 January. The Captain went with his ship. It was not until 1951 that an attempt was made to raise the wreck but this was not accomplished until July 1954. However, during towing, the *Monte Cervantes* sank in deep water.

Asia
Fabre Line, Marseille
Previous name: *Alice* (1907–17).

Builders: Russell & Co, Port Glasgow, 1907.
Particulars: 6,122 gross tons, 415ft × 49ft.
Machinery: Triple-expansion engines, twin screw, speed 16 knots.
Passengers: 130 Cabin, 1,350 Third Class.

Date of disaster: 21 May 1930.

The *Alice* sailed for Unione Austriaca for ten years. She was seized in 1917 and renamed *Asia* for a Brazilian company. Like her sistership, the *Braga,* the *Asia* was awarded to France as war reparations. The *Asia* was placed on the Marseille-Lisbon-Providence-New York run in September 1920. Her last voyage on that route was undertaken in 1929. She was then switched to other shipping lanes maintained by Fabre.

About to sail with 1,500 pilgrims from Jeddah to Djibouti, the *Asia* caught fire on 21 May 1930, in the outer harbour. She burned to a hulk.

City of Honolulu
Los Angeles Steamship Company, Los Angeles
Previous names: *Kiautschou* (1900–1904), *Prinzess Alice* (1904–17), *Princess Matoika* (1917–22), *President Arthur* (1922–27).

Builders: A.G. Vulcan, Stettin, 1900.
Particulars: 10,860 gross tons, 540ft × 60ft.
Machinery: Quadruple-expansion engines, twin screw, speed 17 knots.
Passengers: 445 First Class, 50 Third Class.

Date of disaster: 25 May 1930.

As Hamburg America's *Kiautschou* and North German Lloyd's *Prinzess Alice,* the liner could accommodate 2,210 passengers on its Far East service. Interned in Manila, the *Prinzess Alice* was seized by the US Shipping Board on 6 April 1917 and renamed *Princess Matoika.* During the war the *Princess Matoika* served as a troop transport for the US Navy. Between 1921 and

Above *A beautiful view of the cruise liner* City of Honolulu (Frank O. Braynard collection).

Below City of Honolulu *ablaze at Honolulu* (Courtesy of the Steamship Historical Society collection/University of Baltimore Library).

1923 the ship sailed between New York and various European ports. Laid-up by the US Shipping Board in 1923, the vessel was sold in 1926 to the Los Angeles SS Co and extensively refitted at the Los Angeles Shipbuilding & Dry Dock Corp. In June 1927, she was renamed *City of Honolulu* and served on the company's California—Hawaii service.

While tied to a pier in Honolulu on 25 May 1930, a fire broke out aboard but after it was put out the gutted liner was able to return to Los Angeles under her own power. Los Angeles SS Co deemed the *City of Honolulu* beyond repair and laid the ship up until 1933 when she was purchased by Japanese shipbreakers.

Tahiti
*Union Steam Ship Co of New Zealand Ltd,
Wellington*
Previous name: *Port Kingston* (1904–11).

Builders: A. Stephens & Sons, Glasgow, 1904.
Particulars: 7,585 gross tons, 460ft × 55ft.
Machinery: Triple-expansion engines, twin
screw, speed 17 knots.
Passengers: 277 First Class, 97 Second Class,
141 Third Class.

Date of disaster: 15 August 1930.

The *Port Kingston* operated from Bristol to the
West Indies for Elder Dempster. When the
company lost the contract, the *Port Kingston*
was laid up. Purchased by Union Line in 1911,

The Tahiti *was engaged in Union Line's
transpacific service,* (Alexander Turnbull Library).

the vessel was given a paint job, renamed
Tahiti, and despatched from Sydney on 11
December to Wellington and San Francisco.
The *Tahiti* was requisitioned by the New
Zealand government on 13 August 1914, and
served as a troop transport until handed back
to Union Line at Auckland on 4 July 1919.
Following an extensive refit which included
conversion to burn oil fuel, the *Tahiti* was
returned to her Wellington-San Francisco
route. During 1923 she made a record passage
of sixteen and one half days between the two
ports. On 3 November 1927, the *Tahiti* sank
the Sydney Harbour ferry *Grecliffe,* resulting in
a heavy loss of life.

On 12 August 1930, the *Tahiti* left
Wellington bound for San Francisco under the
command of Captain A.T. Toten with a crew of
149, 103 passengers and 500 tons of general
cargo. Three days later, on 15 August, at
approximately 4:30 am, some 480 miles south-
west of Rarotonga, violent crashing noises
were heard from the direction of the starboard
main shaft tunnel. The tail shaft had fractured
and caused a puncture in the hull. As a result of

The Tahiti *sinking stern first into the Pacific Ocean*
(Frank O. Braynard collection).

Highland Hope *aground at Farilhoes Rocks* (Arnold Kludas collection).

the break the racing engine tore the base of the watertight bulkhead that divided the tunnel and No 3 hold. The engineers were quick to shut off the steam to the racing engines before more damage was done.

The Second Engineer in the engine room immediately reported the damage to the Captain, Chief Engineer and the other officers on the bridge. A gallant effort was now made by the crew to rig and man the pumps, and to prop up and support the bulkhead. In addition wireless messages announcing the danger were sent out. The Norwegian steamer *Penybryn*, which responded to the *Tahiti's* wireless SOS arrived at 10:19 pm on 16 August and stood by throughout the night. By 9:30 am on the 17th, the Chief Engineer reported that conditions were critical as the bulkhead gave in and the ship slowly began to settle stern first.

Captain Toten gave the order for passengers to abandon ship. They were lowered in lifeboats and picked up by the American steamer *Ventura*, which had also rushed to the *Tahiti's* SOS: the crew remained to fight on. By 1:30 pm on 17 August the crew could do no more and abandoned ship. The *Penybryn*, which assisted in the transfer of mails, luggage and bullion took on the exhausted crew from the *Tahiti*. At 2:30 pm the *Tahiti* disappeared stern first beneath the waves in to the South Pacific.

Later at the court of inquiry it was found that the *Tahiti* was '... a fine ship, well found, capably manned, with a clear course and fine weather'. The court continued, 'the ship's company on the *Tahiti*, from Commander down, rose magnificently to the occasion,' and then concluded by stating, '...the loss of the *Tahiti* was due to a peril of the sea which no reasonable care or foresight could have avoided'.

Highland Hope
Nelson Line, London

Builders: Harland & Wolff, Govan, 1930.
Particulars: 14,129 gross tons, 544ft × 69ft.
Machinery: Burmeister & Wain diesel, twin screw, speed 15 knots.
Passengers: 135 First Class, 66 Second class, 500 Third Class.

Date of disaster: 19 November 1930.

Completed on 18 January 1930, the *Highland Hope* shortly thereafter sailed on her regular route between London and South America. Unfortunately, the new ship did not survive the year.

The *Highland Hope* was headed for Vigo on a voyage to Buenos Aires with 150 passengers

under the command of Captain Thomas J. Jones, when on 19 November 1930, the liner ran into a bank of dense fog and at 5:00 am struck Farilhoes Rocks. Except for one person who jumped overboard (and later died from his injuries) all were safely taken off the grounded vessel. The *Highland Hope* was declared a total loss by the company and abandoned.

Malabar
Burns, Philip & Company Ltd, Sydney

Builders: Barclay, Curle & Co, Glasgow, 1925.
Particulars: 4,512 gross tons, 351ft × 49ft.
Machinery: Kincaid diesels, single screw, speed 12 knots.
Passengers: 165 First Class.

Date of disaster: 2 April 1931.

Burns Philip operated vessels on their major route between the east coast of Australia and Singapore. In November 1925, Burns took delivery of its first motorship, the *Malabar*. After her positioning trip to Sydney, she departed on 2 January 1926, on her maiden voyage to Java and Singapore. On this route passenger space was also provided for 32 Chinese passengers in separate quarters, and deck passengers were carried for short sectors in the East Indies.

On 2 April 1931, the *Malabar* was approaching Sydney harbour in a bank of fog. With visibility reduced, the Captain ordered the Malay helmsman to change course to five degrees starboard, away from the coast. The helmsman misunderstood the order and steered five degrees to port. Within minutes, the *Malabar* ran on to rocks inside Miranda Points and ripped huge holes in her bottom. The 28 passengers and most of her 108 crew evacuated the stricken liner in lifeboats.

Upon arrival of the pilot boat *Captain Cook* and trawler *Alfie Cam,* attempts were made by both to pull the *Malabar* off. The low tide made this impossible as the *Malabar* listed to starboard and rested on the bottom. The next day the tide came in accompanied by a gale that pounded the liner. On 5 April, the *Malabar* was broken into sections and sold. Today this suburb of Sydney is called Malabar.

Bermuda
Furness, Withy & Co, London

Builders: Workman, Clark & Co, Belfast, 1927.
Particulars: 19,086 gross tons, 547ft × 74ft.
Machinery: Doxford diesel, quadruple screw, speed 17 knots.
Passengers: 616 First Class, 72 Second Class.

Date of disaster: 17 June 1931.

The *Bermuda* was completed in 1927 and was one of the first ships built exclusively for cruising. She commenced her maiden voyage between New York and Hamilton on 14 January 1928, and proved so popular that Furness Withy made the *Bermuda* run a year round operation.

The *Bermuda* was not a lucky ship. On June 17 1931, while at her berth in Hamilton, a fire started at about 2:30 am in the aft section of the ship: it was quickly extinguished. Soon, another fire broke out in the forward section. The fire department was called and the engineroom abandoned at 4:45 pm, when the *Bermuda* took on a list. The passengers and all

Above Right *The* Bermuda *docking in Hamilton, Bermuda on her maiden voyage* (Frank O. Braynard collection). **Right** *The* Bermuda *burning at Hamilton Wharf* (Illustrated London News).

Georges Philippar *sporting the rather odd looking square funnels* (Compagnie Générale Maritime).

The Georges Philippar *almost burnt out thirty hours after the fire began* (Illustrated London News).

of the crew, except one who died in the engineroom, were put up in hotels in Hamilton. The damage was mostly confined to the superstructure and therefore the company's managers decided the *Bermuda* was worth repairing. The *Bermuda* was pumped out and in July sailed under her own power for Belfast.

On 19 November 1931, while undergoing rebuilding at Workman & Clark, another fire broke out, this time destroying the entire ship, causing her to sink. The wreck was raised by 24 December 1931. Declared a total loss, the intact engines were removed and the ship was towed to Rosyth to be scrapped. On the way, the wreck ran aground on the Badcall Islands in Eddrachilles Bay, Scotland and was lost.

Georges Philippar
Messageries Maritimes, Marseille

Builders: Ateliers et Chantiers de la Loire, St Nazaire, 1931.

Particulars: 17,539 gross tons, 567ft × 68ft
Machinery: Sulzer diesel, twin screw, speed
15 knots.
Passengers: 196 First Class, 110 Second Class,
83 Third Class, 650 Steerage.

Date of disaster: 16 May 1932.

After the *Paul Lecat* burned in 1929,
Messageries Maritimes replaced her with the
Georges Philippar. On 29 November 1930,
three weeks after being launched, the *Georges
Philippar* suffered a serious fire that caused
considerable damage to her unfinished interior
structures. Luckily most of her valuable fittings
were not yet installed. When the *Georges
Philippar* was completed in January 1932, her
interiors reminded her passengers of the
chateaux in the Loire Valley during the French
Renaissance. Prior to commencing her maiden
voyage, the French secret police warned
Messageries Maritimes of threats to destroy
their new ship. A thorough search was made by
authorities, but nothing was found.

The *Georges Philippar* departed Marseille on
her maiden voyage on 26 February 1932. She
arrived in Yokohama on 14 April. After a rather
quick turn around at Yokohama due to minor
civil unrest, she commenced her return
voyage. At Shanghai, the *Georges Philippar*
was forced to anchor in the harbour due to
threats by the Communists because she was
believed to be carrying munitions for the
Japanese forces fighting the Communists in
China. As the *Georges Philippar* sailed from
Colombo, she carried 518 passengers
(including Mr Herbert, Director of Justice in
French Indo-China and the journalist Albert
Londres who was covering a murder story) and
a crew of 347, of whom 184 were Chinese,
under the command of Captain Vieg. In the
holds were 5,500 tons of cargo including
bullion, kept in the storeroom. Twice during
the homeward voyage the alarm in the
storeroom went off without any apparent
reason.

At 2:10 am on 15 May, a short circuit caused
a fire in Cabin No 6 as the ship was approaching
the entrance to the Gulf of Aden. The Captain
was not immediately informed as the crew at

the scene tried to put out the fire. When the
flames started to spread and Captain Vieg was
notified, it was too late. He tried to increase
speed in order to beach his blazing ship at Aden
— but all that did was contribute to the
spreading of the fire. Captain Vieg realized this
was in vain and ordered everyone to abandon
ship, during which time he sent out an SOS.

Answering the *Georges Philippar's* call for
assistance were the Soviet tanker, *Sovietskaja
Helt* (which happened to have been in the
immediate vicinity of *Georges Philippar*), and
the British cargo ships *Contractor* and *Masilub.*
The Soviet tanker took aboard 400 survivors
and the British ships another 263. The number
of dead, including Albert Londres, differs with
each account probably because of the
embarking and disembarking of passengers,
particularly Steerage, among the rescue ships.
Three numbers obtained from my sources were
40, 54 and 90.

The *Georges Philippar* burnt for four days
and drifted some 160 miles. Finally, on 19 May,
the *Georges Philippar* sank 145 nautical miles
north-east of Cape Guardafui, becoming the
sixth Messageries Maritimes ship to be
destroyed by fire and the second liner to be lost
on its maiden voyage.

Pieter Corneliszoon Hooft
Nederland Line, Amsterdam

Builders: Ateliers et Chantiers de la Loire, St.
Nazaire, 1926.
Particulars: 14,729 gross tons, 549ft × 67ft.
Machinery: Sulzer diesel, twin screw, speed
17.5 knots.
Passengers: 205 First Class, 273 Second Class,
107 Third Class, 54 Fourth Class.

Date of disaster: 14 November 1932.

On 20 December, 1925, when the *Pieter
Corneliszoon Hooft* was almost completed, she
suffered a devastating fire that completely
destroyed her passenger accommodation. As a
result the French builders were unable to
adhere to a set date for the commencement of

Pieter Corneliszoon Hooft *plied between Holland and the Dutch East Indies* (Maritime Museum 'Prins Hendrik').

Pieter Corneliszoon Hooft *totally burned out* (Arnold Kludas collection).

trials. The *Pieter Corneliszoon Hooft* was moved to a yard in Amsterdam for repair and completion and not finally delivered to her owners until 27 August 1926. She sailed on her maiden voyage from Amsterdam to the Dutch East Indies in 1926. In 1931 the *Pieter Corneliszoon Hooft* was lengthened from 540ft to 549ft and was given new diesel engines. Her first voyage after rebuilding was in April 1931.

Another fire consumed the liner at the Sumatra Quay in Amsterdam on 14 November, 1932. She was immediately towed to another part of the harbour where efforts by firemen to save her failed. Totally destroyed, the *Pieter Corneliszoon Hooft* was towed to Hendrik Ido Ambacht to be scrapped.

L'Atlantique
Compagnie de Navigation Sud Atlantique, Bordeaux

Builders: Chantiers et Ateliers de St Nazaire, Penhoet, 1931.

Particulars: 42,512 gross tons, 744ft × 92ft.
Machinery: Geared steam turbines by Parson-Penhoet, quadruple screw, speed 21 knots.
Passengers: 414 First Class, 158 Second Class, 584 Third Class.

Date of disaster: 4 January 1933.

The *L'Atlantique* was the largest passenger ship ever built for the South American trade. The same standards of luxury found in French Line's North Atlantic liners were to be introduced on the South American route by the *L'Atlantique*. She sailed on her maiden voyage from Bordeaux to Buenos Aires via Lisbon, Rio and Montevideo on 29 September 1931.

On 4 January, 1933 under the command of Captain Schoofs, the *L'Atlantique* was on a trip from Bordeaux to Le Havre for her annual drydock. At 3:30 am a fire broke out in cabin 232 on E-Deck. The fire spread rapidly through the ship forcing the crew to abandon her. In the havoc, seventeen lives were lost. For two days the fire burned out of control and the ship

The French giant L'Atlantique (Chantier de l'Atlantique, Saint-Nazaire).

L'Atlantique *burning* (Author's collection).

drifted helplessly toward the Dorset coast off Portland Bill. Finally, on 6 January, the *L'Atlantique* was taken in tow to Cherbourg by French, Dutch and German tugs.

Lawsuits followed between the underwriters and Cie-Atlantique. The owners claimed the ship was a total constructive loss and claimed her value at £2 million. The underwriters claimed Harland & Wolff's estimate of the complete repair job was lower (£1,250,000) than the owner's claim. The company finally won its case. The *L'Atlantique* languished at Cherbourg until she was sold for scrap to Smith & Houston Ltd, Port Glasgow in 1936.

Guildford Castle
Union Castle Line, London

Builders: Barclay, Curle & Co, Glasgow, 1911.
Particulars: 8,001 gross tons, 452ft × 56ft.
Machinery: Quadruple-expansion engines, twin screw, speed 14.5 knots.

Passengers: 300.

Date of disaster: 1 June 1933.

The steamship *Guildford Castle* was an intermediate vessel engaged in the west coast service to South Africa. During World War 1 *Guildford Castle* was requisitioned as a hospital ship, after which she resumed her African service.

During a trip in the River Elbe, the *Guildford Castle* was sunk in a collision with the steamer *Stentor*, resulting in the loss of two lives on 1 June 1933.

Nicholas Paquet
Compagnie de Navigation Paquet, Marseille

Builders: Forges et Chantiers de la Méditerranée, La Seyne, 1928.
Particulars: 8,517 gross tons, 428ft × 57ft.
Machinery: Triple-expansion engines, twin screw, speed 16 knots.
Passengers: Approximately 1,100 in four classes.

Date of disaster: 6 July 1933.

The *Nicholas Paquet* had two masts, two funnels and a cruiser stern. As a colonial steamer she plied between France and the French colonies in West Africa.

The *Nicolas Paquet* was on a voyage from Marseille to Casablanca with a cargo of sugar when she was wrecked four miles off Cape Spartel, North Africa on 6 July 1933. She was declared a total constructive loss by the company.

Dresden
North German Lloyd, Bremen
Previous names: *Zeppelin* (1915–19), *Ormuz* (1920–27).

*L'Atlantique **on fire in the English Channel. Note that the funnels had been raised during her career** (Illustrated London News).*

Union Castle's intermediate steamer Guildford
Castle (Union Castle Line).

Builders: Bremer Vulkan, Vegasack, 1915.
Particulars: 14,690 gross tons, 570ft × 67ft.
Machinery: Quadruple-expansion engines,
twin screw, speed 15.5 knots.
Passengers: 399 Cabin Class, 288 Tourist
Class, 284 Third Class.

Date of disaster: 20 June 1934.

The *Zeppelin* was completed in 1915, and laid-
up. On 28 March 1919, the *Zeppelin* was
handed over to Great Britain and managed by
White Star Line. In 1920 she was sold to Orient
Line and renamed *Ormuz*. Refitted to carry 292
First Class and 882 Third Class passengers, the
Ormuz was despatched on the London-

Nicolas Paquet *was one of many liners Paquet built
for the West Africa service* (Courtesy of the
Steamship Historical Society collection/University of
Baltimore Library).

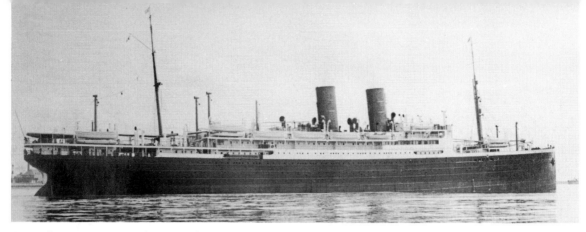

Australia route. In April 1927, the *Ormuz* was repurchased by North German Lloyd and named *Dresden*. After another refit the *Dresden* served on the Bremerhaven-New York route and cruising.

The *Dresden* was on a North Sea cruise with 980 passengers, all of whom were members of the German National Socialist organization 'Strength Through Joy'. At 7:30 pm on 20 June, 1934 the *Dresden* struck a submerged rock on Karmoe Island. The impact was so powerful that the liner shuddered from stem to stern. Passengers, many of whom had never sailed before, panicked, some jumping into the water. Four women lost their lives when their lifeboat struck the ship's propeller, throwing the occupants into the sea. The *Dresden* was beached, with some passengers and crew aboard, listing heavily. Water continued to pour into three holes and the stokehold, causing the *Dresden* to heel over and sink the

The Dresden *was one of many units in Germany's rebuilding programme* (Frank O. Braynard collection).

next day. The suvivors were landed at various nearby Norwegian coastal towns.

Morro Castle
New York & Cuba Mail Steamship Company, New York

Builders: Newport News Shipbuilding & Drydock Co, Newport News, 1930.
Particulars: 11,520 gross tons, 531ft × 70ft.
Machinery: Turbo-electric propulsion, twin screw, speed 20 knots.
Passengers: 430 First Class, 100 Tourist Class.

The fore-section of the Dresden *is all that remains* (Arnold Kludas collection).

The Morro Castle *departing New York City for Havana* (Courtesy of the Steamship Historical Society/University of Baltimore Library).

Date of disaster: 8 September 1934.

In the pre-Castro days, Cuba was a favourite holiday spot for American tourists. To meet demand Ward Line commissioned the *Morro Castle* and her sister-ship, *Oriente,* to offer fast and luxurious service between New York and Havana. The *Morro Castle* was launched on 5 March, completed on 8 August and sailed on her maiden voyage from New York on 23 August 1930.

On 8 September 1934, the *Morro Castle* was on the final leg of her homeward voyage with 316 passengers and a crew of 231 aboard. During the night of 7 September Captain Robert Wilmott died from an apparent heart attack. Taking over command was Chief Officer William Warms.

During the wee hours of the morning on 8 September, Daniel Campbell, a steward, entered the writing room. At 2:45 am he noticed smoke issuing from a locker used to store stationery and winter blankets. The crew on the scene tried to extinguish the flames, but when that proved to be of no avail they reported the fire to the bridge. Warms sounded the fire alarms, and split his officers and crew into two groups. One group was to fight the fire and another was to assist the passengers.

Fire fighting was hampered by the fact that Captain Wilmott had ordered the removal of

The hapless Morro Castle *drifting toward the New Jersey shore,* (National Archives, Washington, D.C.).

hoses from several hydrants on the Promende Deck (where the fire began), because a woman on a previous trip had slipped on the water from a leaky hydrant and sued the company. The crew therefore had to drag hoses from other areas to battle the flames. Fueling the flames were 40 mph north-easterly winds, which Warms failed to take account of by turning his ship westerly. Despite the growing inferno, Warms did not send out an SOS until 3:23 am. When the time arrived to evacuate the blazing liner, panic reigned.

Later, during testimony at United States District Court, all the passengers revealed that they 'saw no fire or boat drill and received no instructions at any time'. Many crew members were later also to testify that they did not receive training as to their duties in case of an emergency. Adding to the confusion was the reality that eight lifeboats were unlaunchable,

with crew incompetence reaching its apex. Though six miles off the New Jersey coast, the *Morro Castle* disaster claimed 137 lives. The blistering hulk drifted with the tides upon the shore of Asbury Park, New Jersey, where thousands of sightseers watched the final hours of the burning liner.

Ligitation of claimants seeking compensation for lost property, loved ones or injury were initiated in New York against New York & Cuba Mail SS Co. All claimants attested to the fact that there was no fire or lifeboat drill. Even Mrs Mathilda Wilmott, widow of Captain Wilmott, though not on that particular trip but a frequent traveller on the ship, stated in writing: 'While on the *Morro Castle* at no time did I see anyone don life preservers, either passengers or members of the crew'. The claimants also stated that the *Morro Castle* sailed from New York in an unseaworthy and unsafe condition,

Morro Castle *ashore at Asbury Park, New Jersey* (Courtesy of the Steamship Historical Society/ University of Baltimore Library).

being not only improperly equipped, designed and constructed with flammable materials everywhere, but also manned by insufficient, incompetent and inefficient ship personnel. The suit amounted to $13,512,261.11. In a final decree dated 26 February 1937 New York & Cuba Mail doled out the aggregate sum of $1,250,000.

The Senate launched its own investigation on maritime safety which eventually led to reforms and new regulations for US vessel construction and operation. Crew conditions, which at the time were very poor — leading to

The Orania *setting course for South America* (World Ship Society Picture Library).

White Star's Doric *sporting four large lifeboat davits* (Frank O. Braynard collection).

low morale and incompetence, were brought to light and addressed.

Orania
Royal Holland Lloyd, Amsterdam

Builders: Workman, Clark & Co Ltd, Belfast, 1922.
Particulars: 9,763 gross tons, 450ft × 59ft.
Machinery: Steam turbines, twin screw, speed 15 knots.
Passengers: 154 First Class, 68 Second Class, 120 Intermediate, 850 Third Class.

Date of disaster: 19 December 1934.

Royal Holland Lloyd was The Netherland's representative on the South America route. Their two last ships, *Orania* and *Flandria*, were both completed in 1922. The two-mast, two-funnel *Orania* started her maiden voyage from Amsterdam in 1922.

After waiting outside Leixoes Harbour for some time, the *Orania* steamed in and anchored. The Portuguese liner *Loanda* sailed into the harbour and ran down the earlier arrival. All 122 passengers and crew quickly evacuated the *Orania* which was sinking fast. She settled at the bottom with the tops of her funnels showing above the water.

Doric
White Star Line, Liverpool

Builders: Harland & Wolff, Belfast, 1923.
Particulars: 16,484 gross tons, 601ft × 68ft.
Machinery: Geared turbines, twin screw, speed 15 knots.
Passengers: 600 Cabin Class, 1,700 Third Class.

Date of disaster: 5 September 1935.

Neither ostentatious nor fast, the *Doric* served White Star as an intermediate liner on their secondary Liverpool-Montreal service. With a fall off of transatlantic business, the *Doric* was switched to cruising in 1933.

In fog off Cape Finisterre, the *Doric* collided with the 2,166-ton French steamer *Formigny* on 5 September 1935. The *Doric* was ripped open to the waterline on the starboard side: keeping her afloat were her watertight doors. All 735 passengers and crew managed to safely transfer to the British liners *Orion* and *Viceroy of India*. Listing, the *Doric* then proceeded to Vigo, where she underwent temporary repairs. From Vigo the *Doric* went to London where, after an inspection, Cunard-White Star decided it was uneconomic to fully repair the ship. Considered surplus, the *Doric* was sold to J. Cashmore and left for Newport on 7 October to be broken up. The *Doric* became the fifth

Doric *being abandoned after the collision* (Frank O. Braynard collection).

and final peacetime disaster for the unfortunate White Star Line.

Ausonia
Società Italiana di Servizi Maritimi, Rome

Builders: Ansaldo Spa, Sestri Ponente, 1928.
Particulars: 12,955 gross tons, 544ft × 66ft.
Machinery: Geared turbines, twin screw, speed 20 knots.
Passengers: 210 First Class, 120 Second Class, 60 Third Class.

Date of disaster: 18 October 1935.

The sleek *Ausonia* was built for the Genoa, Alexandria, Venice service, which she carried out with her sister-ship *Esperia*.

Within three quarters of an hour after entering Alexandria harbour from Haifa on 18 October 1935, a boiler room explosion started a flash fire that spread with great rapidity. Admiral Sir William Fisher, Commander-in-Chief of the Mediterranean Fleet ordered all boats, launches and pinnaces to stand by, and instructed the crews from three battleships in port to aid in the rescue effort. All 35 passengers were safely saved. Out of 240 crew, three were killed in the explosion and seven were seriously injured. The charred hulk was eventually towed to Trieste, where it was broken up in 1936.

Eubée
Compagnie des Chargeurs Réunis, Le Havre

Builders: Ateliers et Chantiers de France, Dunkirk, 1922.
Particulars: 9,645 gross tons, 483ft × 59ft.
Machinery: Triple-expansion engines, twin screw, speed 15 knots.
Passengers: 100 First Class, 40 Second Class, 85 Third Class.

Date of disaster: 14 August 1936.

The *Eubée* was Chargeurs' 36th vessel to enter their South American service. Launched on 17 December 1921, she commenced her maiden voyage a year later.

With 178 passengers on board and a general cargo, the *Eubée* commenced another voyage from Bordeaux to Buenos Aires. On 14 August 1936 during dense fog, ninety miles north of Rio Grande, the *Eubée* collided with the British steamer *Corinaldo*. Two days later the *Eubée* went down.

The yachtlike Ausonia (Courtesy of the Steamship Historical Society collection/University of Baltimore Library).

The charred Ausonia *outside Alexandria harbour* (Illustrated London News).

Spanish Line's transatlantic liner Cristobal Colon (Frank O. Braynard collection).

Cristobal Colon
Compañiá Transatlántica Española, SA, Barcelona

Builders: Soc Española de Construction Naval, Ferrol, 1923.
Particulars: 10,833 gross tons, 520ft × 61ft.
Machinery: Geared turbines, twin screw, speed 16 knots.
Passengers: 1,100 in three classes.

Date of disaster: 24 October 1936.

Completed in August 1923, the *Cristobal Colon* maintained the sea links between Bilboa and Central America. In 1927 New York was added as a port of call. Due to the outbreak of the Spanish Civil War, the *Cristobal Colon* received orders on 4 August 1936, to proceed to Southampton instead of Bilboa with her complement of 344 passengers. The authorities in England would not allow the Spaniards to disembark, so the *Cristobal Colon* sailed for Le Havre. Again the authorities would not allow

the passengers to land, therefore she then sailed on to St Nazaire to await orders.

On 15 August the *Cristobal Colon* was seized by Leftists. The ship sailed into Nantes where some passengers were allowed to land. Then it was back to St Nazaire. Between 20 and 30 August the ship was at sea. Finally, the *Cristobal Colon* steamed into Santander, Spain to a tremendous welcome.

In October, Franco sympathizers among the crew seized the ship. The *Cristobal Colon* left Spain that month for Mexico with a crew of 65. Way off course, the *Cristobal Colon* ran aground on a reef at East North Rock, eight miles north of Bermuda, at 12:30 am on 24 October 1936. Two powerful tugs were sent from St George to salvage the crippled liner. Their efforts were fruitless, as the *Cristobal Colon* was deemed a total loss.

President Hoover
Dollar Line, San Francisco

Builders: Newport News Shipbuilding &

President Hoover *entering Shanghai harbour* (Frank O. Braynard collection).

Drydock Co, Newport News, 1931.
Particulars: 21,936 gross tons, 654ft × 81ft.
Machinery: Steam turbo-electric engines, twin screw, speed 20 knots.
Passengers: 307 First Class, 133 Tourist Class, 170 Third Class, 378 Steerage.

Date of disaster: 10 December 1937.

The *President Hoover,* and her sister-ship, *President Coolidge* represented American interest across the Pacific. Completed and delivered in 1931, the *President Hoover* left New York for San Francisco and the Far East on 13 August 1931. First Class accommodation was both elegant and spacious. Tourist and third were not luxurious, but were comfortable and an improvement over the Japanese competition. The *President Hoover* was instrumental in the evacuation of refugees from war-torn Shanghai.

On a trip from Kobe to Manila, under the command of Captain George W. Yardley, the

President Hoover *aground and being abandoned on Hoishito Island* (Frank O. Braynard collection).

Above Guaruga *proved too slow for her original owners and was sold* (Courtesy of the Steamship Historical Society collection/University of Baltimore Library).

Below *French Line's intermediate liner* Lafayette (Compagnie Générale Maritime).

President Hoover, with over 1,000 passengers and crew members aboard, smashed into the rocky shoals off Japanese owned Hoishito Island, near Formosa (Taiwan) at 1:00 am on 10 December 1937. Passengers and crew had to abandon the liner and were landed at Hoishito Island. After several unsuccessful attempts to refloat the *President Hoover,* it was decided to sell her for scrap to a Japanese breaker in 1938.

Guaruja
Compagnie de Navigation France-Amerique, Marseille

Builders: Forges et Chantiers de la Méditerranée, La Seyne, 1921.
Particulars: 4,282 gross tons, 362ft × 46ft.
Machinery: Steam turbines & turbo electric, single screw, speed 13 knots.
Passengers: Data not available.

Date of disaster: 2 January 1938.

The small *Guaruja* was powered by two Ljunstrom turbines connected to two electric motors, however she proved too slow for SGTM's South American service. Therefore, in 1923 she was transferred to France-Amerique.

On 2 January 1938, near Punta Polacra, the *Guaruja* ran ashore and broke in two.

*The **Berengaria**, once the largest vessel of any kind afloat, was one of the most celebrated transatlantic passenger liners of the 1920s and '30s (F. W. Hawks).*

Berengaria
Cunard-White Star Line Ltd, Liverpool

Builders: Bremen Vulkan Shipyards, Hamburg, Germany, 1913.
Particulars: 52, 226 gross tons, 919ft × 98ft.
Machinery: Steam turbines, quadruple screw, speed 23 knots.
Passengers: 972 First Class, 630 Second Class, 606 Third Class, 515 Tourist Class.

Date of disaster: 3 March 1938.

Completed in April 1913 as the *Imperator* for Hamburg America Line's Hamburg-New York service, she was the largest ship afloat in 1913-14. She was laid up at Hamburg from 1914 to 1919, then handed over to the Allied powers as reparations, first to the United States (who sailed her as the USS *Imperator*), then to Great Britain. For the latter she was refitted and chartered to Cunard, who sailed her as *Imperator* from February 1920 until February 1921 on the Liverpool-New York route. She was sold outright to Cunard in the latter month and renamed *Berengaria*, thereafter running on the Southampton-New York service.

At 3 o'clock in the morning of 3 March 1938, while the *Berengaria* was berthed at Pier 90, Cunard's New York terminal, aged wiring started a fire that destroyed the main lounge. The US authorities revoked her sailing certificate, and with some of her passengers transferred to the smaller *Alaunia*, and others to the *Queen Mary* (sailing a week later), the *Berengaria* went empty to Southampton.

She was laid up there until November, when she was sold to breakers at Jarrow. She was scrapped down to the double bottom by the time war started in September 1939, and her remains were finally broken up at Rosyth in 1946.

MAY 22 1938

At the Left—A TRANSATLANTIC
LINER BURNS AT HER DOCK
IN FRANCE.
The hulk of the Lafayette after the
fire had burned itself out at the
wharf at Le Havre. The fire started
at midnight and spread so rapidly
that many of the crew narrowly
missed being trapped below decks.
The loss was estimated at
$10,000,000.

The totally destroyed **Lafayette** *at Le Havre* **(Frank O. Braynard collection).**

Lafayette
Compagnie Générale Transatlantique, Le Havre

Builders: Chantiers et Ateliers de St Nazaire, Pehoet, 1930.
Particulars: 25,178 gross tons, 613ft × 77ft.
Machinery: Four MAN diesels, quadruple screw, speed 17 knots.
Passengers: 583 First Class, 388 Tourist Class, 108 Third Class.

Date of disaster: 4 May 1938.

As an intermediate liner, the *Lafayette* was French Line's only motor vessel to be employed on the Le Havre-Plymouth-New York service. The *Lafayette* was an unlucky liner. While undergoing repairs in August 1933, a fire broke out in the cold storage room. During a departure from Le Havre on 16 January 1935, the *Lafayette* was rammed by a tug in her stern, loosening a plate below the waterline and forcing her to return to port. Within a year (31 August 1936) the *Lafayette* was involved in a collision in the St Lawrence River with a freighter of 1,200 tons, the *Benmaple*. Another fire broke out on board in October 1936 while she was at the repair dock.

The end of the *Lafayette* came on 4 May 1938, when the ship was in drydock for an overhaul. A fire started in the stockhold, around 9:15 pm, when an engineer attempted to light one of the vessel's oil burners. When the lighted oil blasted from the tank, it spread to the entire crude oil stores. By midnight, the vessel was a huge bonfire and the entire Le Havre fire department was called upon to combat the flames. The liner was completely gutted. The remaining hulk was sold to shipbreakers at Rotterdam.

Reliance
Hamburg American Line, Hamburg
Previous names: *Johann Heninrich Burchard* (1915-20), *Limburgia* (1920-22).

Builders: Joh C. Tecklenborg AG, Geestemünde, 1915.
Particulars: 19,618 gross tons, 615ft x 72ft.
Machinery: Triple-expansion engines, triple screw, speed 16 knots.
Passengers: 633 First Class, 186 Second Class.

Date of disaster: 7 August 1938.

Johann Heninrich Burchard was completed on 20 November, 1915, for Royal Holland Lloyd. After considerable debate, *Burchard* was

HAPAG's liner **Reliance** *(Author's collection).*

handed over to the Dutch. In February she was renamed *Limburgia,* left Bremerhaven for Amsterdam, and commenced service on the Amsterdam-La Plata route. The service proved unprofitable and the arguments persisted regarding the Dutch take-over of the ship.

In 1922 the disputed vessel was sold to United American Lines and refitted as the 19,582-ton *Reliance* to carry 290 First Class, 320 Second Class and 400 Third Class passengers between New York and Hamburg.

The Reliance *burning out of control at Hamburg* **(Arnold Kludas collection).**

***The* Paris *sailing past the skyline of lower New York City* (Compagnie Générale Maritime).**

She was bought back by Hamburg American Line on 27 July 1926 and kept on the same route. In 1928 the *Reliance* was used exclusively for cruising and her passenger capacity was reduced in 1934 to 500 First Class. Another refit followed in 1937 in which First and Second Class accommodation was provided for. The tonnages for the *Reliance* changed during the course of her career six times: 1915—19,980 GRT; 1922—19,582 GRT; 1923—16,798 GRT; 1926—19,527 GRT; 1928—19,802 GRT; 1937—19,618 GRT.

The *Reliance* was lying at her berth in Hamburg on 7 August 1938, preparing for a cruise to Scandinavia. A fire, said to have started in a paper store on the third deck, caused extensive damage. Hamburg American abandoned the *Reliance* as a total constructive loss and laid her up in Hamburg. In 1940 the charred hulk was sold to Krupp to be broken-up.

Paris
Compagnie Générale Transatlantique, Le Havre

Builders: Chantiers et Ateliers de St Nazaire, Penhoet, 1921.

Particulars: 34,569 gross tons, 764ft × 85ft.
Machinery: Steam turbines, quadruple screw, speed 21 knots.
Passengers: 563 First Class, 460 Second Class, 1,092 Third Class.

Date of disaster: 19 April 1939.

Construction started on the *Paris* in 1913. Work was suspended in 1914, but resumed with a launching on 16 September 1916, in order to free the slipway. When completed on 5 June 1921, the *Paris* was the largest liner built in France; and she was the flagship of French Line until 1927. Her maiden voyage from Le Havre to New York via Plymouth commenced on 15 June 1921. The interiors of the *Paris* were among the most beautiful and modern in the world. Art Nouveau was everywhere, with hints of what was to become Art Deco. The ambiance, personality and cuisine were definitely French and gave a hint to passengers of things to come when they disembarked in Le Havre.

In August 1929, while sitting at Le Havre, a fire completely destroyed the passenger accommodation of the *Paris,* putting her out of service until January 1930. The company took the opportunity to up-grade her accommodation, and when she re-entered service, the *Paris* had space for 560 First Class, 530 Second Class and 844 Third Class passengers.

On 19 April 1939, the *Paris* was again

consumed by flames. The fires were started simultaneously in the ship's bakery and on two higher decks. This time the fire was fatal. The *Paris* keeled over and sank at her berth in Le Havre. The probability of sabotage for both fires was not ruled out by police, since on both occasions the company was warned of plots against their ships. The partially exposed hull and superstructure remained in the harbour until 1946, when the *Liberté* broke her moorings and rammed into the wreck. When the *Liberté* was moved, the remains of the *Paris* were scrapped in 1947.

Athenia
Anchor-Donaldson Line, Glasgow

The Paris, *the ship that set the trend for others to follow, burns at Le Havre* (Frank O. Braynard collection).

Builders: Fairfield Shipbuilding & Engineering Co Ltd, Glasgow, 1923.

Particulars: 13,465 gross tons, 538ft x 66ft.
Machinery: Geared turbines, twin screw, speed 15 knots.
Passengers: 516 Cabin Class, 1,000 Third Class.

Date of disaster: 3 September 1939.

The *Athenia* and her sister-ship, *Letitia*, were built to replace similar vessels lost in the First World War. Both ships were intermediate cabin liners employed on the Glasgow-Liverpool run, with many voyages to Halifax and St John, New Brunswick. During the winter months, the *Athenia* was sent cruising to warmer climates. In 1927, her passenger complement was altered to 314 Cabin Class, 310 Tourist Class and 928 Third Class.

When the *Athenia* left Glasgow at noon on 1 September 1939, Hitler had attacked Poland, and England and France issued an ultimatum to Germany. The *Athenia* made calls at Liverpool and Belfast, then proceeded unescorted and unarmed across the Atlantic Ocean with 1,418 passengers aboard, including 311 Americans. When Hitler did not respond to the ultimatum, England and France declared war against Germany on 3 September 1939. Steaming at full speed, the *Athenia* was struck by two torpedoes from *U-30* at about 4:00 pm on 3 September 1939, 250 miles west of Inishtrahull, Northern Ireland. The *Athenia* went down in twenty minutes and 112 people died, including several Americans.

The *Athenia* was the first submarine victim of World War 2, despite an order to U-boat Captains that no action should be taken against passenger ships for the time being.

Right *The* Paris *heeled over and half submerged at Le Havre* (Arnold Kludas collection). Below *The first passenger ship casualty of World War 2 was the* Athenia (Frank O. Braynard collection).

Pegu *linked Britain with Burma* **(Courtesy of the Steamship Historical Society collection/University of Baltimore Library).**

Pegu
Burmah Steamship Co Ltd & British & Burmese SN Co Ltd.

Builders: William Denny & Bros Ltd, Dumbarton, 1921.
Particulars: 8,016 gross tons, 466ft × 59ft.
Machinery: Triple-expansion engines, single screw, speed 14 knots.
Passengers: 150 First Class.

Date of disaster: 26 November 1939.

Managed by Henderson Line, the *Pegu* sailed between Liverpool and Rangoon via the Suez Canal.

She was wrecked on the Liverpool revetment on 26 November 1939.

The **Cabo San Antonio** *on fire off the Canary Islands* **(Courtesy of the Steamship Historical Society collection/University of Baltimore Library).**

Cabo San Antonio
Ybarra Y Cia, Seville

Builders: Soc Española de Construction Naval, SA, Bilbao, 1930.
Particulars: 12,275 gross tons, 500ft × 63ft.
Machinery: MAN diesels, twin screw, speed 15 knots.
Passengers: 200 First Class, 50 Third Class.

Date of disaster: 29 December 1939.

Launched in January 1930 and completed in April 1930, the *Cabo San Antonio* entered Ybarra's Genoa-South American service.

On 29 December 1939, during a voyage from Buenos Aires to Genoa with 200 passengers aboard, a fire broke out in the galley and quickly spread through the ship. Her radio operator managed to get out distress calls before the room was consumed by flames. The Captain ordered everyone to abandon ship and in the process, five people lost their lives. The survivors were picked up by British, French and Portuguese vessels.

Chapter 5

The war years

Four ships came to a premature end in the 1940s. If wartime casualties were included, this section would be a book in itself.

The unknown of the group was the *President Quezon*. The exact date of her grounding is not known, since England was at war and Lloyds of London could not locate any record of her fate. Therefore to be safe, she is included in this work.

The British government found the *Niagara* financially important in her commercial service and exempted her from national service: she was also used to ferry war materials from New Zealand to England via the United States.

Once peace returned, many passenger vessels remained under government control doing repatriation work and while troops were sent to overseas colonies to re-establish colonial control. Beginning in 1947 the ships made a slow return to commercial service. To supplement the older tonnage and replace vessels lost during the global conflict, many

President Madison *in American Mail Line's markings, later became the* President Quezon (Courtesy of the Steamship Historical Society collection/University of Baltimore Library).

companies initiated a building programme. One of those new ships was the *Magdalena*, which became the third passenger ship to be lost on her maiden voyage.

It is truly surprising that in a four-year period only three liners were lost. Could it be that passenger ships under the various war administrations had better navigators and took better precautions against fire?

President Quezon
Philippine Mail Line, Manila
Previous names: *Bay State* (1920–22).
President Madison (1922–39).

Builders: New York Shipbuilding Corp, Camden, 1920.
Particulars: 14,187 gross tons, 533ft x 66ft.
Machinery: Geared turbines, twin screw, speed 17 knots.
Passengers: 560.

Date of disaster: January 1940.

Bay State was built as a combination passenger and cargo vessel and entered the Seattle-Yokohama service under the management of Admiral Oriental Line. In 1922 the vessel was renamed *President Madison*. During 1926 *President Madison* was sold to American Mail

Still smouldering, the Italian passenger ship Orazio *was photographed from the nearby* Conte Biancamano *on 21 January 1940* (Maurizio Eliseo).

Line and continued in the same service. On 24 March 1933, *President Madison* heeled over and sank at her pier in Seattle. The ship was raised in April, repaired, and returned to service in November. In 1939, the ship was purchased by Philippine Mail Lines and renamed *President Quezon*.

During 1940 *President Quezon* ran aground on the Riukiu Islands off Japan. The ship was raised and scrapped in Japan. No information can be ascertained as to whether she was engaged in commercial service or in government war service.

Orazio
'Italia'

Builders: Cantieri et Officine Meriodionali, Baia, Italy, 1927.
Particulars: 11,669 gross tons, 506ft x 61ft.
Machinery: B&W diesels, twin screw, speed 14 knots.
Passengers: 110 First Class, 190 Second Class, 340 Third Class.

Date of disaster: 21–22 January 1940.

Built for Navigazione Generale Italiana for its Genoa-West Coast of South America service, the *Orazio* was transferred to 'Italia' in 1932. While carrying 645 passengers and crew on a voyage from Genoa to Barcelona on 21 January 1940, she caught fire off the French coast. The blaze spread quickly and was soon out of control. Some French warships as well as the Italian liners *Colombo* and *Conte Biancamano* hurried to the scene, but bad weather made rescue efforts very difficult and 106 people perished when the ship finally sank on 22 January.

Niagara
Canadian-Australasian Line, London

Builders: John Brown & Co Ltd, Clydebank, 1913.
Particulars: 13,415 gross tons, 543ft x 66ft.
Machinery: Triple-expansion engines, triple screw, speed 17 knots.
Passengers: 290 First Class, 223 Second Class, 191 Third Class.

Date of disaster: 19 June 1940.

Union Steamship Company, the first owner of the vessel, broke with a tradition of selecting Maori names when it chose the name *Niagara* for its new flagship, the first large passenger liner to use oil fuel under a British Board of Trade certificate. Completed in Scotland, the *Niagara* made her

The Niagara *displaying her classic lines* (Richard Morse collection/Alex Duncan photograph).

delivery voyage from Clyde to Sydney on 12 March 1913. There, she commenced her maiden voyage on 5 May from Sydney to Vancouver. She was an instant success on this route and because of this she was not requisitioned for war service.

In 1932 the *Niagara* was handed over to Canadian-Australasian Line, a company formed by Canadian Pacific and Union SS Company to meet the growing American and Japanese competition on the Pacific. In 1935 the *Niagara* collided with the cargo ship *King Egbert* in the Strait of Juan de Fuca. Since both ships were only slightly damaged, they continued on their voyages. In September 1939, the British government again considered the *Niagara* too important on her commercial service to be requisitioned. Therefore, she continued her Pacific run.

Under the command of Captain W. Martin, the *Niagara* left Auckland on 18 June, 1940, for Suva, Honolulu and Vancouver with 136 passengers and a crew of 200. Also on board

was a valuable cargo consisting of £2,500,000 in gold and half the New Zealand stock of small arms ammunition for trans-shipment to Britain. During the early morning of 19 June, the liner ran into a minefield laid in Hauraki Gulf by the German raider *Orion*. Immediately the *Niagara* began to settle by the head and wireless calls for aid were sent out. The liner *Wangenella* and the British coaster *Kapiti* responded and, upon arrival, rescued all the passengers and crew. Later the *Niagara* sank to a depth of 500ft.

Salvage operations were begun in February 1942, resulting in the recovery of $2,379,000-worth of bullion. Later, in June 1953, 24 gold ingots valued at $120,000 were also recovered.

Magdalena
Royal Mail Line, London

Builders: Harland & Wolff, Belfast, 1949.
Particulars: 17,547 gross tons, 570ft x 73ft.

One of the few known pictures of the short-lived Magdalena (Furness, Withy Group).

Magdalena *aground and minus her fore-section on Tujucas Rocks* (Illustrated London News).

Machinery: Geared turbines, twin screw, speed 18 knots.
Passengers: 133 First Class, 346 Third Class.

Date of disaster: 25 April 1949.

The *Magdalena* was launched on 11 May 1948, and completed by February 1949. She departed on her maiden voyage from London to Buenos Aires on 9 March 1949. That was the first and last sailing of the *Magdalena* from London.

On the homeward portion of her maiden voyage, the *Magdalena* ran on to the Tujucas Rocks off Rio de Janeiro on 25 April 1949. Passengers and crew had to abandon the ship and rescue craft returned them to Rio. The next day the *Magdalena* was refloated and under tow to a naval drydock in Rio when the forepart broke off just forward of the superstructure and sank. The remainder of the hull was stranded and sold to a Brazilian firm in June for scrapping. The *Magdalena* became the third passenger ship in the century to be lost on her maiden voyage.

Chapter 6

To the rescue

The 1950s witnessed the greatest number of passengers carried across the oceans and seas with one of the lowest fatality rates — 157. Radar was refined during the war and was not available to passenger ships. Yet, despite the installation of the device, groundings, and collisions continued. Adding to the confusion were airport beacons. They were so new that the navigators of the *Champollion* mistook them for navigation buoys and plotted accordingly. The *Champollion* ended up on land.

After an absence of fifteen years, liner collisions with other steamers returned. The *Maipu* collided with a troop transport, and in one of the most famous maritime disasters, the *Andrea Doria* was sunk by a Swedish liner. Fog was the chief culprit, followed by speeding. The outbound *Stockholm* was increasing speed with her Captain retiring for the night, and the incoming *Andrea Doria* was one hour behind schedule because of a storm two days before. However, in all fairness to Captain Calamai, he did reduce speed from 23 knots, to 21 knots, took all the necessary precautions and remained on his bridge from mid-afternoon until rescued.

The three accidents following the *Andrea Doria* did not receive world-wide press coverage. The press did not get excited over a stranded British vessel, and appeared indifferent to the fate of a Greek liner striking a rock or an emigrant ship with a full complement burning in the Indian Ocean. However, the last maritime mishap did capture front page headlines. A new ship on its maiden voyage collided with an iceberg and sank.

Maipu
Cia Argentina de Nav Dodero, Buenos Aires.

Builders: De Schelde, Vlissingen, 1951.
Particulars: 11,515 gross tons, 520ft × 64ft.
Machinery: Sulzer diesel from builders, twin screw, speed 18 knots.
Passengers: 13 First Class, 740 Tourist Class.

Date of disaster: 4 November 1951.

Launched on 20 January 1951, the *Maipu* was completed in May 1951, and placed on the Buenos Aires-Hamburg route as a Tourist Class liner.

Travelling to Hamburg in thick fog, the *Maipu* collided with the US troopship *General M.L. Hersey,* north-west of the Weser lightship on 4 November 1951, at 7:32 am. The badly damaged *Maipu* started to sink. Captain Juan Marguez ordered the evacuation of his dying ship and all eighty passengers and 158 crew calmly proceeded to the lifeboats. They were picked up by the *General M.L. Hersey* and

German rescue craft. Three hours after the collision, at the age of six months, the *Maipu* sank.

Champollion
Messageries Maritimes, Marseille

Builders: Constructions Navales, La Ciotat, 1925.
Particulars: 12,546 gross tons, 550ft × 62ft.
Machinery: Triple-expansion engines, twin screw, speed 17.5 knots.
Passengers: 207 First Class, 142 Second Class, 150 Third Class.

The Argentine tourist liner Maipu (Courtesy of the B.V. Kon. Mij. 'De Schelde').

Date of disaster: 22 December 1952.

The *Champollion* was completed as a three-funnel liner and was employed in the Marseille-Alexandria service with passenger accommodation provided for 188 First Class, 133 Second Class, 128 Third Class and 500 Steerage. The liner was rebuilt in 1933: her

As originally built the Champollon *had three funnels. Here she is as she appeared after her 1950 refit.* (Compagnie Générale Maritime).

length was increased from 520ft to 550ft by the addition of a Maierform forepart and additional turbines were added. In 1940, the *Champollion* was laid up.

Between 1942 and 1946 the *Champollion* served as a troop transport for the Allies. Returned to Messageries Maritimes in 1946, *Champollion* ferried civil servants and troops between Marseilles and French Indochina. In 1950, the *Champollion* was modernized, emerging from the yard as a 12,546-ton one-funnel liner with space for 207 First Class, 142 Second Class, and 150 Third Class passengers.

In the early hours of 22 December 1952, the *Champollion* was approaching Beirut in very bad weather. By mistake, the ship's navigators set their course based on an airport beacon which happened to be working that night. As a result the *Champollion* ran aground on Elchat Elmalhoun reef. Buffeted by heavy breakers and a stiff westerly wind, the stranded liner was slowly cracked amidships with the terrified passengers still on board. Each successive wave enlarged the fissure. Two attempts by the crew to reach shore in their lifeboats failed, as one capsized and another was swamped by a wave. By the afternoon of 23 December, 313 persons were rescued by harbour and naval craft. Fifteen died in an effort to swim to shore. During the night, *Champollion* broke in two on the sand bar, three miles south of Beirut. The wreck was sold to a Lebanese firm for scrapping.

Klipfontein
United Netherlands Nav Co, The Hague

Builders: P. Smith Jr, Rotterdam, 1939.
Particulars: 10,544 gross tons, 520ft × 63ft.
Machinery: Burmeister & Wain diesel, twin screw, speed 17 knots.
Passengers: 106 First Class, 42 Tourist Class.

Date of disaster: 8 January 1953.

Holland's African service was represented by the cargo/passenger liner *Klipfontein* and her two sister-ships. The *Klipfontein* was launched and completed in 1939. In 1942 she became a troop transport under the US War Shipping Administration. On 1 February 1946, the *Klipfontein* was returned to her owners. Refitted, the *Klipfontein* resumed her sailing between Holland and Southern Africa.

During a voyage to Lourenco Marques (Maputo), Mozambique, the *Klipfontein* struck a submerged object five miles off Cape Barra.

Klipfontein *as a troop transport during the Second World War* (Frank O. Braynard collection).

The stern of the Klipfontein **rises in the air as she goes under** (Frank O. Braynard collection).

The forward bunker exploded and all 114 passengers and 119 crew safely abandoned the sinking liner. They were picked up by the Union Castle liner *Bloemfontein Castle*. The *Klipfontein* sank 45 minutes after the collision.

The Empress of Canada **connected Liverpool and Montreal** (Frank O. Braynard collection).

Empress of Canada
Canadian Pacific, London
Previous name: *Duchess of Richmond* (1928–47).

Builders: John Brown & Co Ltd, Clydebank, 1928.
Particulars: 20,325 gross tons, 600ft × 75ft.
Machinery: Geared turbines by Brown, twin screw, speed 18 knots.
Passengers: 400 First Class, 300 Tourist Class.

Date of disaster: 25 January 1953.

Originally, she sailed as the 20,022-ton *Duchess of Richmond* between Liverpool and St John, carrying 1,570 passengers in three classes. From January 1940 to May 1946, the *Duchess* served as a troopship. Returned to owners in 1946, the *Duchess* was overhauled and refitted. She emerged as the 20,325-ton *Empress of Canada*. Her first post-war sailing occurred on

16 July 1947, from Liverpool to Montreal.

While at Gladstone Drydock a severe fire broke out on 25 January 1953, causing the *Empress of Canada* to heel over and sink. The ship was refloated on 6 March 1954, and left for La Spezia to be scrapped on 1 September 1954, under the tow of the Dutch tug *Zwarte Zee*.

Altair
Rotterdam South America Line, Rotterdam

Builders: William Gray & Co, West Hartlepool, 1950.
Particulars: 6,410 gross tons, 440ft × 60ft.
Machinery: Two-stroke single-acting engines, single screw, speed 12 knots.
Passengers: 12 First Class, 80 Third Class.

Date of disaster: 15 April 1956.

This cargo liner catered for a small number of passengers on her South America voyages.

Along with the *Alioth,* they proved to be the last ships of Rotterdam South America Line to be completed with 'extensive' passenger accommodation.

During a voyage to South America, the *Altair* was wrecked on 15 April 1956, near the entrance to Vitoria, Brazil.

Andrea Doria
Italia-Società per Azioni di Navigazione, Genoa

Builders: Ansaldo SpA, Genoa, 1953.
Particulars: 29,083 gross tons, 700ft × 90ft.
Machinery: Six Parson geared steam turbines twin screw, speed 23 knots.
Passengers: 218 First Class, 320 Cabin Class, 703 Tourist Class.

Date of disaster: 25 July 1956.

The Andrea Doria *all dressed up and ready to sail* (Frank O. Braynard collection).

Pride of the Italian merchant marine, the Andrea Doria (Frank O. Braynard collection).

The *Andrea Doria* marked the rebirth of the Italian merchant marine and was the pride of Italian Line. The first of two sleek luxury liners, the *Andrea Doria* was placed on the fashionable Genoa-Cannes-Naples-Gibraltar-New York run. Under the command of Captain Calamai, the *Andrea Doria* set out on her maiden voyage from Genoa on 14 January 1953, bound for New York. The *Andrea Doria* boasted three outdoor swimming pools and 31 different public rooms, all decorated in a contemporary modern style predominated by simple furniture, wood paneling, indirect lighting and original art creations.

On 17 July 1956, the *Andrea Doria* departed Genoa on her 51st transatlantic voyage with Captain Calamai in command. After calls at Cannes, Naples and Gibraltar, the *Andrea Doria* had on board 190 First Class, 267 Cabin Class and 677 Tourist Class passengers and a crew of 572. In addition, the liner was carrying 401 tons of freight, nine automobiles, 522 pieces of baggage and 1,754 bags of mail.

On 25 July, the last day of the westward voyage, the *Andrea Doria* was racing at full speed toward Nantucket Lightship. By late afternoon thick, opaque fog had cut visibility down to only half a mile. The *Andrea Doria* reduced speed to 21 knots. At about 10:40 pm a pip was sighted on the radar scope. The officers in the wheelhouse monitored the pip, in the knowledge that if the other ship continued on course it should pass the *Andrea Doria's* starboard side. As the pip grew closer to the center of the scope, the captain ordered the ship's foghorn sounded every 100 seconds. In addition, he and his officers listened in the misty fog for the other ship. Nothing was heard, but lights were sighted coming directly at them. Two sharp blasts were sounded on the *Andrea Doria's* whistles and a hard turn ordered.

As the giant liner slowly began to respond to the helm, it happened. The *Stockholm,* steaming at 18 knots, ploughed her ice-strengthened razor-sharp bow almost 30ft within the *Andrea Doria's* starboard side, ripping the Italian liner open from her Upper Deck down to her double bottom tanks. The pivoting action of the two ships, upon impact

Above *A view of the rapidly sinking* Andrea Doria, *from the port side* (National Archives, Washington DC).

Below Andrea Doria *on 26 July listing to starboard* (National Archives, Washington DC).

and during the next couple of seconds, did additional underwater damage to the *Doria*. The *Stockholm* was finally able to reverse engines, disengage and temporarily disappear into the fog again. The *Andrea Doria* came to a stop and almost immediately took on a 18-degree list to starboard. The time was approximately 11:10 pm.

The list rendered the eight port-side lifeboats unlaunchable. There were now only eight lifeboats available with a capacity of 1,004. For fear of a stampede to the starboard boats, the Captain did not at first issue an abandon-ship alarm. He did, however, send out an SOS immediately. Ships in the area responded swiftly. One of the first to arrive was the French belle, *Ile de France*. In quick succession, she was followed by the destroyer escort *Allen*, freighter *Cape Ann*, and *PVT. William H. Thomas*. Together, along with the *Stockholm*, these ships rescued 1,663 persons. 47 people went down with the *Andrea Doria*, most in the collision area. By 5:30 am the *Andrea Doria* was completely abandoned. At 10:09 am on 26 July 1956, the youngest and fairest of the maidens was reported by the Coast Guard cutter *Evergreen* to have sunk 'in 225ft of water at 261409Z in position 40°29'4" North 69°50'5" West'.

Back in New York a court battle ensued, with each company blaming the other. Just before the *Andrea Doria's* engineering officers were to take the witness stand, Italian Line and Swedish American Line agreed, in January 1957, to settle out of court. What Italian Line feared was the revelation of a faulty watertight door, which they presumed caused her to sink, and/or improper ballasting.

Two and a half decades later, Peter Gimbel, adventurer, filmmaker and department store heir, led a series of salvage expeditions down to the *Andrea Doria*. He and his team not only recovered the safe from the *Andrea Doria*, which was opened on American television in August 1984, but Gimbel continued to search for the questionable missing or faulty watertight door. During one of their last dives they found the area. Peter and Ted, one of the other divers, came upon the '...edge of a huge hole in the bottom of the generator room... about 80ft of her hull was open to the sea'. The generator room itself was breached. The *Stockholm's* bow crushed the bulkhead where the watertight door was located. Whether the door was there or even faulty was inconsequential, as the area was destroyed upon impact leaving a puncture sufficiently large that nothing could have prevented the sea from pouring into and sealing the fate of the *Andrea Doria*.

Hildebrand
Booth Line, Liverpool

Builders: Cammell, Laird & Co Ltd, Birkenhead, 1951.
Particulars: 7,735 gross tons 421ft × 60ft.

Passenger-cargo liner Hilderbrand (Courtesy of the Steamship Historical Society collection/University of Baltimore Library).

Machinery: Steam turbines, single screw, speed 15 knots.
Passengers: 74 First Class, 96 Tourist Class.

Date of disaster: 25 September 1957.

The *Hildebrand* was a cargo passenger liner engaged on the Liverpool-Amazon River route. She started her maiden voyage on 28 December 1951.

Outward bound from Liverpool, the *Hildebrand,* under heavy fog conditions, was stranded near Cascais, near Lisbon, on 25 September 1957. Efforts to refloat her failed and she was abandoned by Booth Line.

Neptunia
Neptunia Shipping Co (Greek Line), Panama
Previous name: *Johan de Witt* (1920–48).

Builders: Nederlandsche Shipbuilding Co, Amsterdam, 1920.
Particulars: 10,519 gross tons, 523ft × 59ft.
Machinery: Triple-expansion engines, twin screw, speed 15 knots.
Passengers: 39 First Class, 748 Tourist Class.

Date of disaster: 2 November 1957.

The *Johan de Witt* was built for Nederland Royal Mail Line's Amsterdam-East Indies service with accommodation for 197 First Class, 120 Second Class and 36 Third Class passengers. Laid-up in December 1930 she returned to service in November 1932, to replace the *Pieter Corneliszoon.* The *Johan de Witt* was refitted and lengthened from 499ft to 523ft in April 1933. During the Second World War she served as a troop transport.

In 1945, the *Johan* was returned to Nederland Line and laid-up. Three years later, the vessel was sold to Greek Line and registered in the name of the Cia Mar del Este, company of Panama. Refitted with one funnel and renamed *Neptunia,* she was despatched in 1949 on the Piraeus-New York route. In April 1951, Greek Line switched her to New York-Bremerhaven sailings, then in April 1955, to Bremerhaven-Montreal voyages. Ownership changed to Neptunia Shipping Co in 1954.

On 2 November 1957 while entering Cobh, *Neptunia* struck Daunt's Rock, near the port and, with the assistance of the tug *Turmoil,* was beached. All 31 passengers aboard were safely taken off. The badly damaged ship was declared a total constructive loss and abandoned to underwriters. On 2 March 1958, after the leaking portions of the hulk were sealed, *Neptunia* was towed by the Dutch tug *Gele Zee* to Rotterdam for scrapping.

Skaubryn
I.M. Skaugen, Oslo

Builders: Gotaverken Shipyard, Gothenburg, 1951.
Particulars: 9,786 gross tons, 458ft × 57ft.
Machinery: Diesels geared to twin screw, speed 16.5 knots.

Greek Line's Neptunia (Luis Miguel Correia).

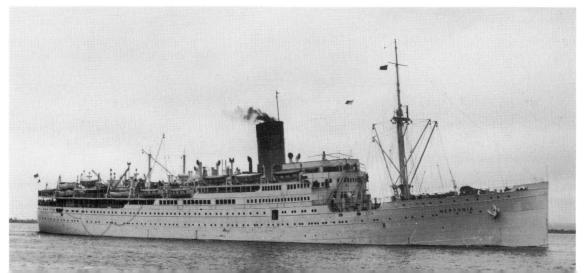

Skaubryn *at anchor* (Courtesy of the Steamship Historical Society collection/University of Baltimore Library).

Passengers: 16 First Class, 1,205 Tourist Class.

Date of disaster: 31 March 1958.

Originally laid down and launched as a cargo ship, the *Skaubryn* was shifted to Howaldtswerke A/G, Kiel and rebuilt as an emigrant ship. Completed in 1951, the *Skaubryn* was employed in the Europe-Australia immigrant service. In 1957, *Skaubryn* was charted by Greek Line and made four round-voyages between northern Europe (Liverpool and Bremerhaven) and Canada.

Skaubryn *ablaze in the Indian Ocean* (Courtesy of the Steamship Historical Society collection/University of Baltimore Library).

On 31 March 1958, between Bremerhaven and Australia with 1,300 persons aboard, the ship caught fire 300 miles south-east of Socotra Island in the Indian Ocean. Without loss of lives, *Skaubryn* was abandoned. All the survivors were picked up by the British freighter, *City of Sydney*. The charred hulk was taken in tow, but could not make it. The *Skaubryn* sank on 6 April.

Hans Hedtoft
Royal Greenland Trading Company, Copenhagen

Builders: Frederikshavns Vaerft & Flydedok, Frederikshavns, 1958.
Particulars: 2,875 gross tons, 383ft × 51ft.
Machinery: Diesel motor-ship, single screw, speed 13 knots.
Passengers: 55 One class.

Date of disaster: 30 January 1959.

During the mid-1950s there were deliberations in the Danish Parliament and in private circles regarding the feasibility of a year-round passenger service between Denmark and its overseas territory of Greenland. Aage Lynge, a Greenland representative in the Danish Parliament, warned that sailings undertaken in the months of January, February and March were the most dangerous because of icebergs and gales. Presenting the case for the service was Johannes Kjaerboel, Minister for Greenland, who believed that it was necessary to have a year-round passenger service to keep

Greenland traffic open. A decision was made in 1957 and construction began on a vessel. As the ship was being built, Lynge warned that in the event of an accident, 'there is no rescue to expect'.

The *Hans Hedtoft* was completed in December 1958, and delivered to her owners in January 1959. The *Hans Hedtoft* resembled a tanker with her living quarters and bridge aft and her cargo holds forward. Special features in her construction included a double bottom, seven watertight compartments and a highly reinforced bow. Fully equipped and filled to capacity, the *Hans Hedtoft* departed Copenhagen on her maiden voyage to Godthaab on 7 January 1959, under the command of Captain P.L. Rasmussen. She arrived there safely, discharged her cargo and passengers, reloaded and cast off on Thursday, 29 January, for Copenhagen with 55 passengers, including Aage Lynge, and a crew of forty.

On 30 January the *Hans Hedtoft* was steaming at 12 knots in a gale accompanied by thick snow squalls and 20ft waves. Thirty-seven miles south of Cape Farewell, the southernmost point of Greenland, at approximately 11:55 am, the *Hans Hedtoft* collided with an iceberg in position 59°5' North, 43°0' West. Captain Rasmussen immediately sent out a radio message for assistance. It was picked up by the US Coast Guard cutter *Campbell* and the German trawler *Johanna Kruess*. The *Campbell* relayed the message back to New York Coast Guard headquarters where the rescue effort was coordinated.

In the meantime, the *Johanna Kruess* which was in the vicinity, rushed to the help of the *Hans Hedtoft,* with the *Campbell* too setting course at full speed. When the *Johanna Kruess* arrived at the scene at 6:30 pm she reported, 'Nothing found or seen. No lights or lifeboats or ship. Plenty of ice from north-west...' The last message from the *Hans Hedtoft* was at 3:35 pm in which she reported, 'Slowly sinking and need immediate assistance.'

At noon on 31 January the *Campbell,* like the *Carpathia's* involvement in the *Titanic* disaster, arrived on the scene. However, unlike the *Carpathia,* which found lifeboats, the *Campbell* found nothing — not a lifeboat, life preserver or even debris. Three Danish ships, another German trawler and Air Force C-4 transports found nothing. For seven days the ships and planes combed the area, at many times hampered by poor visibility, rough seas and threatening icebergs. Finally on Saturday 7 February, the search was called off and the Coast Guard ordered the *Campbell* back to its normal station and the other ships to proceed on.

The plight of the *Hans Hedtoft* plunged Denmark into a state of mourning. All light radio programmes were cancelled, and special prayers were said in all the churches. The *Hans Hedtoft* became the second passenger vessel to collide with an iceberg on its maiden voyage and as a result the fourth passenger ship in the twentieth century to meet disaster on its maiden voyage.

The Hans Hedtoft *on sea trials* (Den Kongelige Gronlandske Handel).

Chapter 7

The transitional period

The 1960s marked a turning point for passenger liners. Colonies were obtaining their independence from Europe, thus eliminating the need for colonial mail steamers; international politics closed the Suez Canal, forcing many companies to either sail their ships two to three times the distance or cease operations; and jet aircraft were successfully competing against shipping on major routes.

Faced with the danger of bankruptcy, a few companies decided to enter into a new field — cruising — using surplus older tonnage. In addition, enterprising shipping entrepreneurs created new cruise lines. The results for some firms were disastrous. Many of the first cruise ships were running beyond their years and staffed by inexperienced crews. Consequently when misfortune struck panic ensued with a tremendous loss of life. In this category fell the *Lakonia* and *Yarmouth Castle* tragedies.

Fires on board ships shifted from cabins and other superstructure locations to include engineroom explosions. Engineroom fires and explosions were not common before the 1960s, begging the question, 'Why now the engineroom fires?' There does not seem to be any particular reason beyond chance or ill fortune. Then there were storms which caused two ferry disasters that left 292 people dead, and eventually put their respective owners out of business.

A new danger, terrorism, took to the seas and claimed the British mail vessel *Dara*. Who was responsible for this act has remained a mystery. All told, this was not a progressive period in passenger shipping. There were 20 ship disasters that took the lives of 1,024 people. Part of the blame must lie with poor maintenance and worn parts, looked after by inexperienced personnel.

Alcoa Corsair
Alcoa Steamship Co, New York

Builders: Oregon Shipbuilding Corporation, Portland, Oregon, 1947.
Particulars: 8,481 gross tons, 455ft × 62ft.
Machinery: Steam turbines, single screw, speed 16.5 knots.
Passengers: 98 First Class.

Date of disaster: 22 October 1960.

Originally laid down as the USS *Iredell,* an 'Attack Transport' intended to fly the pennant 'APA 242', construction was halted when the war in the Pacific ended, producing a surplus of ships. The shipyard sold the partly completed hull, along with two other ships of similar design to Alcoa, which redesigned them as passenger/cargo vessels for the West Indies trade.

Renamed *Alcoa Corsair,* accommodation

was provided for 98 passengers housed in an aluminium superstructure, the beginning of a new trend in shipbuilding. The other vessels were named *Alcoa Cavalier* and *Alcoa Clipper*. The *Alcoa Corsair* was despatched on 21-day round voyages from New Orleans to the Caribbean in April 1947. Southbound general cargo was carried and northbound bauxite. Though very popular with travellers (an average of sixty passengers were carried per sailing) the advent of the jet aircraft and the resurgence of travel to Europe necessitated the withdrawal of Alcoa's passenger service.

The first to go was the *Alcoa Corsair*. On 21 October 1960, the *Alcoa Corsair* departed New Orleans on her last voyage with fifty passengers. During the early morning of 22 October, in the Mississippi River, off Empire, Louisiana, the *Alcoa Corsair* collided with the Italian motor vessel *Lorenzo Marcello*. A 150ft gash on the starboard side was sustained by the *Alcoa Corsair*, ripping apart passenger and crew accommodation and killing five passengers and five crewmen. In addition, her

shell plating was ripped open and three holds began to flood. To prevent the *Alcoa Corsair* from sinking, her Captain beached her. The voyage was cancelled, the ship refloated, patched up, then laid up.

In March 1961 the *Alcoa Corsair* was sold at public auction 'as lies' to American Bulk Carriers Inc of New York. She sailed as a freighter with the name *Alcoa* until March 1962, when it was changed to *Rye*. After experiencing boiler trouble in the summer months of 1963, she was sold in September 1963 to Japanese shipbreakers.

Tarsus
Denizcilik Bankasi TAO (Turkish Maritime Lines), Istanbul
Previous names: *Exochorda* (1931–40), *Harry Lee* (1940–46).

Builders: New York Shipbuilding Co, Camden, New Jersey, 1931.
Particulars: 9,451 gross tons, 475ft × 62ft.
Machinery: Steam turbines, single screw, speed 16 knots.

Alcoa Corsair *showing where she was rammed* (Alcoa Steamship Company Inc).

Passengers: 189 First Class, 66 Second Class, 210 Third Class.

Date of disaster: 14 December 1960.

The long and varied career of the *Tarsus* started in 1931 under the houseflag of American Export Lines. As their *Exochorda*, she plied the New York-Mediterranean run for ten years. In 1940 the *Exochorda* was acquired by the US Navy and sailed as the transport *Harry Lee*. Declared surplus after the war, she was returned to American Export who renamed her *Exochorda*. American Export quickly sold her to the Turkish government in 1946. Renamed *Tarsus,* she disappeared from the maritime world for three years.

After an extensive refit at Bethlehem Steel Company's yard at Baltimore during 1949–50, that saw her passenger capacity increase from 140 to 465, the *Tarsus* was ready to resume her pre-war sailings between New York and Istanbul, but under the houseflag of Turkish Maritime Lines. Only three round voyages were made, the first in 1950, the second in 1954 and the third in 1955. It can only be presumed that her transatlantic activities were not financially successful: after the third she was confined to

trading in the Mediterranean.

The Yugoslav tanker, *Peter Zoranic* was sailing through the Bosphorus laded with gasoline and kerosene. About midway through, she crashed into the empty Greek tanker, *World Harmony* sailing from the Sea of Marmara to the Black Sea. A tremendous fire broke out on the *Peter Zoranic* and several explosions occurred aboard the Greek tanker. After the collision the Yugoslav tanker, burning fiercely and out of control, started to drift with the current across the Strait. The *Peter Zoranic* collided with *Tarsus* which was anchored outside a drydock awaiting repairs. The fire spread from the tanker to the *Tarsus* and she was completely destroyed.

Dara
British India Steam Navigating Co, London

Builders: Barclay, Curle & Co, 1948.
Particulars: 5,030 gross tons, 399ft × 55ft.
Machinery: Doxford oil engines, twin screw, speed 14 knots.
Passengers: 80 First Class, 30 'A' Second Class, 24 'B' Second Class, 1,377 Deck.

Above *The British colonial steamer* Dara (P & O Group).

Left *The* Tarsus, *a ship which was at the wrong place at the wrong time* (Courtesy of the Steamship Historical Society collection/University of Baltimore Library).

Below *The burned out* Dara *in the Persian Gulf* (P & O Group).

Date of disaster: 7 April 1961.

Delivered on 30 June 1948, the *Dara* was the third 'D' Class ship delivered to BI after the war for the India/Gulf run, where she spent her whole career.

On 7 April, 1961 the *Dara* was loading cargo and embarking and disembarking passengers at her anchorage in Dubai. A sudden storm blew up and Captain Elsan found it impossible to continue work. He decided to move his ship out of the harbour into open water to avoid being blown aground. During the night, at approximately 4:40 am, a large explosion between decks started a flash fire throughout the vessel. Many frightened passengers and crew members jumped into the warm water of the Persian Gulf.

An SOS was sent and the British frigates *Loch Ruthven, Loch Alvie* and *Loch Fyne* rushed to the scene and extinguished the blaze. Later, an attempt was made to tow the burnt ship to Bahrain. On 10 April while under tow of the tug *Ocean Salvor,* the *Dara* sunk in 60ft of water. Of the reported 819 persons aboard the *Dara,* 581 survived.

Save
Companhia Colonial de Navegação, Lisbon

Builders: Grangemouth Dockyard Company Ltd, Grangemouth, 1951.

Particulars: 2,037 gross tons, 259ft × 42ft.
Machinery: Two oil engines, twin screw, speed 12 knots.
Passengers: Data not available.

Date of disaster: 8 July 1961.

The *Save* was a small Portuguese motor vessel that plied along the coast of the Portuguese African possessions of Mozambique, Angola and Portuguese Guinea. During the first half of 1961, the Portuguese were using the *Save*, along with other steamers, as troop transports, ferrying paratroopers from Portugal to their African possessions to forestall demands for independence.

On 6 July 1961 the *Save* left Beira for Quelemane, both ports in Mozambique, with 495 passengers (200 were African and the rest labourers), a crew of 54 and a load of cargo. During a heavy storm, on 7 July the tiny *Save* took shelter by anchoring in the mouth of the River Linde, ten miles south of Quelemane. As the storm progressed the *Save* broke loose and ran on to a sandbar. The *Save* managed to free herself the next day but a fire broke out on 9 July and she was driven ashore again by the

The Portuguese steamer Save (Luis Miguel Correia).

heavy seas. Shortly after the second grounding a series of heavy explosions occurred in the forward hold, believed to have been caused by the munitions and fuel aboard. The *Save* was completely destroyed, taking with her sixteen crew members and 243 passengers.

Bianca C
Costa Armatori SpA, Genoa
Previous names: *Maréchal Petain* (1944–46), *La Marseillaise* (1946–57), *Arosa Sky* (1957–58)

Builders: Constructions Navales, La Ciotat, 1944.
Particulars: 18,427 gross tons, 592ft × 75ft.
Machinery: Sulzer diesels, triple screw, speed 20 knots.
Passengers: 200 First Class, 1,030 Tourist Class.

Date of disaster: 22 October 1961.

The *Maréchal Petain* was christened and launched by the Vichy government on 16 June 1944. The ship was then towed to Port de Bouc where she remained in an incomplete state. When the Germans withdrew from France, the *Maréchal Petain* was scuttled by the retreating troops. In 1946 the vessel was renamed *La Marseillaise,* refloated and towed to Toulon, and later back to La Ciotat for completion. The flagship of Messageries Maritimes set out on her maiden voyage on the Marseille-Yokohama route on 18 August 1949.

In 1957 the liner was sold to Arosa Line who renamed her *Arosa Sky.* Placed on the Bremerhaven-New York route, accommodation was provided for 202 First Class and 1,030 Tourist Class passengers. When Arosa Line was threatened with bankruptcy, the ship was sold to Costa in October 1958. Renamed *Bianca C,* she emerged in 1959 at 18,427 tons for the Naples-Genoa-La Guaira service.

While anchored off St George, Grenada, on an intermediate stop on 22 October 1961, an explosion in the engineroom touched off a fire which quickly spread throughout the ship. The 400 passengers and 273 crew were quickly and safely evacuated by the ship's boats and various harbour craft. Not all survived. The Chief Engineer and two passengers later died from burns and one crew member was never found. The British frigate, *Londonderry,* secured a towing cable to the still burning wreck and attempted to beach the ship. The attempt failed as the hull sprang a leak and sank in deep water.

*Bianca C *sailing past the Statue of Liberty in New York* (R. Scozzafava/Richard Morse collection).

The two-funnel De Grasse *in French Line colours*
(Author's collection/Steamship Historical Society of
America).

Venezula
*Sicuia Oceanica Società per Azioni, (Siosa),
Palermo*
Previous names: *De Grasse* (1924–53),
Empress of Australia (1953–56).

Builders: Cammell Laird & Co, Birkenhead,
1924.
Particulars: 18,769 gross tons, 641ft × 71ft.
Machinery: Parsons geared turbines, twin
screw, speed 16 knots.

Siosa's Venezuela *before her refit* (Courtesy of the
Steamship Historical Society collection/University of
Baltimore Library).

Passengers: 180 First Class, 500 Tourist Class,
800 Third Class.

Date of disaster: 17 March 1962.

The *Venezula* began her long career as French
Line's two-funnel intermediate cabin liner *De
Grasse,* carrying 2,111 passengers in two
classes between Le Havre and New York. In
1940 the *De Grasse* was used by the German
occupation forces at Bordeaux as an accommodation ship. On 30 August 1944, the evacuating
German troops sunk the *De Grasse.* Raised 30
August 1945, the liner was given an overhaul,
then sent on her first post-war sailing on 12 July
1947. With the arrival of the *Flandre* in 1953,
the *De Grasse* was transferred to the West
Indies service.

On 26 March 1953, the vessel was purchased
by Canadian Pacific who renamed her *Empress
of Australia,* and reconditioned her to 19,379
tons with a passenger capacity for 220 First
Class and 444 Tourist Class. Sold again on 15
February 1956, to Siosa Line who renamed her
Venezula, the liner was placed immediately on
the Naples-La Guaira service. In 1960 the
Venezula received a major refit in which she
was lengthened and passenger capacity
increased to the above figures.

High winds drove the *Venezula* against the
rocks off Iles de Lerins (ten miles off Cannes)
about midnight 17 March 1962. A hole was torn
in the hull and after Captain Michele Petro's
crew failed to stop the water pouring in, he

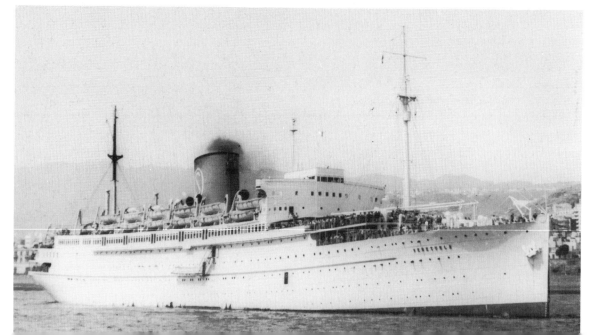

decided it was best to beach his ship. The beaching enabled the Captain and his crew to safely land the 510 passengers. The ship was refloated on 16 April and given a thorough inspection. The company decided that repairs would be uneconomical and sold the *Venezula* to La Spezia on 26 August 1962.

Speculation surrounded the accident of the *Venezula*. Before she sailed from Genoa, Italian police received an anonymous message stating that a robbery would be attempted aboard a ship carrying gold. On board the *Venezula* were gold ingots, worth $2,862,500. When she struck the rocks her radar (believed to have been thrown out of action by radio-interference) was not working. It has been suggested that even in high winds, had the radar not been sabotaged the *Venzula* could have avoided the rocks. The gold, however, was recovered.

Venezuela *after being refloated — note the new bow and grounding marks along the hull* (Antonio Scrimali).

Chandris Lines' Brittany *burning outside Skaramanga harbour. (Author's collection).*

Brittany
Chandris Lines, Piraeus
Previous name: *Bretagne* (1952–61).

Builders: Chantiers et Ateliers de St Nazaire, Penhoet, 1952.
Particulars: 16,644 gross tons, 581ft × 73ft.
Machinery: Parsons geared turbines, twin screw, speed 18 knots.
Passengers: 150 First Class, 1,050 Tourist Class.

Date of disaster: 8 April 1963.

The *Brittany* was originally built as the four-class 1,290-passenger liner *Bretagne* for SGTM's Marseille-Buenos Aires service. On 18 November 1960, the *Bretagne* was chartered to Chandris Lines. After a refit, Chandris despatched her on the lucrative Australian emigrant trade from Piraeus, the first sailing occurring on 3 May 1961. Four months later, in September, Chandris purchased the vessel. In 1962 Chandris renamed her *Brittany* and switched her European terminus to Southampton.

Outbound on a voyage to Sydney, the *Brittany* was forced to return to port due to engine trouble. While undergoing engine

Chandris Line's Brittany *(Alex Duncan).*

repairs in Hellenic Shipyards at Skaramanga, the *Brittany* caught fire on 28 March 1963, and was completely destroyed. The wreck was beached in Vasilika Bay on 9 April, raised 10 May, and laid-up. The *Brittany* was towed to La Spezia, where she arrived on 31 March 1964, to be scrapped.

Lakonia *as a cruise liner (Alex Duncan/Richard Morse collection).*

Lakonia
Greek Line, Piraeus
Previous name: *Johan van Oldenbarnevelt* (1930–62).

Builders: Nederlandsche Shipbuilding, Amsterdam, 1930.
Particulars: 20,314 gross tons, 608ft × 75ft.
Machinery: Sulzer diesel engines, twin screw, speed 17 knots.
Passengers: 700 one class.

Date of disaster: 22 December 1963.

When the *Johan van Oldenbarnevelt* was completed in 1930, she was the largest vessel built for Nederland Royal Mail Line. Designed to carry 770 passengers in four classes, the *'JVO'* was commissioned in May 1930, to serve Amsterdam and the Dutch East Indies via the Suez Canal. Between 1940 and 1945 she was requisitioned and served as a troop transport. The *'JVO'* re-entered commercial service on her old route in 1946, but was switched to the Australian trade in 1950 upon the independence of Indonesia.

To take advantage of the booming Australian emigrant trade, the *'JVO'* was refitted in 1951 to carry 1,414 passengers. Another refit followed in 1959, which saw her tonnage increased from 19,787 to 20,314 tons and her

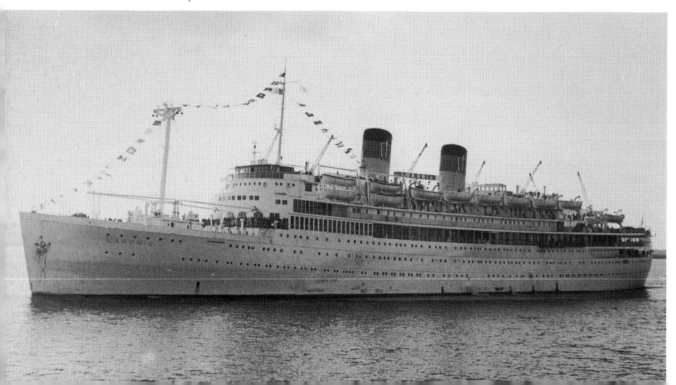

passenger capacity reduced to 1,210. She was then sent on round-the-world sailings. In 1962 *Johan van Oldenbarnevelt* was sold to Greek Line, overhauled at Genoa, and on 8 March 1963 renamed *Lakonia*. Greek Line placed her on cruise service between Southampton and the Canary Islands in April 1963.

The *Lakonia* departed Southampton on 19 December 1963, on an eleven-day Christmas cruise to the Canary Islands under the command of Captain M.N. Zarbis. On board were 651 passengers and a crew of 385. Three days later on 22 December a fire broke out in the hairdresser's salon as the liner was cruising 180 miles north of Madeira. A large bang was later heard and black smoke quickly spread in the liner. Confusion started to reign as passengers went to their cabins to fetch life jackets but were given no further instructions by the crew over the ship's loudspeaker system.

The information that was available was through word of mouth, passengers being told either to stay below or assemble in the dining room. Those that managed to ascend to the Boat Deck witnessed the confused state and ineffectiveness of the crew trying to launch the lifeboats. Partly due to that factor, 131 people died — 89 in the disaster and 42 persons unaccounted for.

Lakonia *undergoing refitting at Genoa* (G. Ghiglion/Antonio Scrimali collection).

A distress call was sent out and ships in the area rushed to the scene. One of the first to arrive was the Argentinian liner, *Salta*. She was followed by the *Centaur, Montcalm, Export Aide* and *Charlesville*. Together, the ships rescued 905 persons. Still burning, the *Lakonia*

Lakonia *burning north of Madeira* (The Mariners' Museum).

was taken in tow by the Norwegian salvage tug *Herkules* on 24 December. Five days later, 29 December, the *Lakonia* heeled over and sank 250 nautical miles west of Gibraltar in position 35°56' N, 10°00' W.

Rio de la Plata
Flota Mercante del Estado, Buenos Aires

Builders: Ansaldo, Sestri-Ponente, 1950.
Particulars: 11,317 gross tons, 550ft × 66ft.
Machinery: FIAT diesels, twin screw, speed 18.5 knots.
Passengers: 372 Tourist Class.

Date of disaster: 19 November 1964.

The *Rio de la Plata* was employed in the Buenos Aires-New York service. In 1962 Flota Mercante del Estado and FANU amalgamated to form Espresa Lineas Maritimes Argentinas (ELMA). At the end of 1962 New York service was suspended. Refitted in 1963 at Hamburg, passenger capacity was increased from 116 First Class to 372 Tourist Class. After renovation, the *Rio de la Plata* was placed on the Buenos Aires-Hamburg run.

While refitting at Demarchi yards in Buenos Aires on 19 November 1964, the *Rio de la Plata* was gutted by fire. The hulk was finally broken up at Buenos Aires in 1968.

Yarmouth Castle
Yarmouth Cruise Lines, Miami
Previous name: *Evangeline* (1927–63).

Builders: William Cramp & Sons, Philadelphia, 1927.

Rio de la Plata *arriving in New York* (Frank O. Braynard collection).

Particulars: 5,002 gross tons, 380ft ×
57ft.
Machinery: Steam geared turbines, twin
screw, speed 18 knots.
Passengers: 350 one class.

Date of disaster: 13 November 1965.

The *Evangeline* was constructed as a hurricane
decker for the Eastern Steamship Line who
employed her between Boston and Yarmouth
during the summers, and in winters to the
Caribbean from New York. After serving in the
US War Department form 1942 to 1945, she
was returned to her owners. In 1954 the
Evangeline was switched to Liberian registry,
with Volusia Steamship Company listed as
operator, and later concluded her last sailing
between Yarmouth and Boston on 19
September 1954. In December 1954 the

Evangeline commenced cruises from Miami.

In 1963 the aging liner was sold to Yarmouth
Cruises. The following summer saw her
limping into New York as the *Yarmouth Castle*
to undertake a series of seven-day cruises to
Nassau under the charter of Caribbean Cruise
Line. The poor 'liner' was running fifteen hours
late on each strip due to faulty engines. The
Yarmouth Castle was placed in drydock and
the remaining cruises scrubbed amidst charges
and counter-charges by CCL and Chadade SS
Co, actual owners of the vessel. Hundreds of
angry passengers were left stranded in New
York. With no northern home base, Yarmouth
Cruises placed their vessel on the Miami-Nassau
run.

On a cruise to Nassau with 371 passengers
aboard, the *Yarmouth Castle,* under the helm
of young Greek Captain Byron Voutsinas and

One of the pioneers in cruising out of Miami was the Yarmouth Castle *(Courtesy of the Steamship Historical
Society collection/University of Baltimore Library).*

his crew of 174, was involved in one of the worst marine disasters in American waters. During the night (around 12:45 am) of 13 November 1965, a fire was discovered in Cabin 610, which at the time was being utilized for storage. Despite attempts by the crew to put it out, the flames leaped out of the cabin and spread along the wooden companionways and up ladders to the decks above. It took twenty-five minutes for the news to reach the bridge and when Captain Voutsinas, who went to investigate the fire, returned to his bridge, he did not order his operator to send out an SOS.

Instead, forty minutes passed from the start of the fire to his sounding the abandon-ship signal on the whistle, which many passengers claimed they never heard. Could it be because those below could not hear due to the flames, smoke and confusion? An hour after the discovery no messages could be sent since flames consumed the bridge, radio shack and half her lifeboats. Panic among the passengers broke out as a few members of an inexperienced crew tried to help them find life preservers, life rings and their boat station.

An officer on the *Bahama Star* sighted an orange glow five miles ahead, and informed his master, Captain Brown, who, without hesitation, raced to the *Yarmouth Castle*. Standing by already was the freighter, *Finnpulp*. The first lifeboat from the burning liner to reach the *Finnpulp* was occupied by Captain Voutsinas, two senior officers, the bosun and a few passengers. The Captain of the *Finnpulp* was so incensed by the lack of seamanship that he refused to let Captain Voutsinas board his vessel, and instead, ordered him to return to his dying ship. The two rescue ships eventually succeeded in saving 458 persons, many of whom were plucked from the sea. At 6:00 am, the blazing hulk rolled over and by 6:15 am the *Yarmouth Castle* disappeared beneath the Caribbean Sea thirteen miles from Great Stirrup Bay.

Like previous tragedies near United States waters carrying American citizens, this disaster led not only to an investigation by the United States Coast Guard, but to the passage of 'HR 10327' on 6 November 1966 by the House of Representatives. Such equipment and practices like improved alarms, electric lifeboats winches, approved sprinkler systems, bi-weekly drills at sea and continuous radio watch henceforth became standard features on ships sailing out of American ports.

Viking Princess
A/S Berge Sigval Bergesen, Oslo
Previous names: *Lavoisier* (1950–61), *Rivera Prima* (1961–64).

Builders: Ateliers et Chantiers de la Loire, St Nazaire, 1950.
Particulars: 12,812 gross tons, 537ft × 64ft.
Machinery: Sulzer diesels, twin screw, speed 17 knots.
Passengers: 657 First Class.

Date of disaster: 8 April 1966.

The 11,968-ton *Lavoisier* was employed on Chargeurs Réunis' Hamburg-Le Havre-Buenos Aires service. Declining revenue forced the company to sell the *Lavoisier* in 1961 to Commerciale Marittime Petroli, Palermo. The ship was rebuilt for cruising, entering service in that role in 1962 as the *Rivera Prima*. Two years later, the *Rivera Prima* was sold to A/S Berge Sigval Bergesen and renamed *Viking Princess*. The company based their cruise liner out of New York in the spring, summer and autumn and Miami in the winter.

Returning to Miami from a seven-day cruise with 239 passengers aboard, the engineroom of the *Viking Princess* exploded into flames sixty miles south-east of Guantanamo Bay, Cuba, on 8 April 1966. Captain Otto Thoreson and his crew ordered the passengers to their boat stations and, in an orderly manner, the passengers proceeded into the lifeboats. During the lifeboat drill a few days earlier, the Captain told one passenger, 'You had better listen to this boat drill because the next time it might be the real thing'. As the fire raged out of control, the Captain gave the order for the crew to abandon the ship. All persons were picked up by the German *Cap Norte*, the Chinese

Chunking Victory and the Liberian *Navigator*. The latter vessel then towed the *Viking Princess* to Port Royal, Jamaica. Beyond repair, the owners sold the burnt-out hulk to breakers in Bilbao. Out of 498 passengers and crew, 496 survived and two were known dead.

Hanseatic
Hamburg-Atlantic Line, Hamburg
Previous names: *Empress of Japan* (1930–42), *Empress of Scotland* (1942–58).

Right *The cruise liner* Viking Princess *(Alex Duncan)*.

Below *The abandoned and burned out* Viking Princess *in the Caribbean (Author's collection)*.

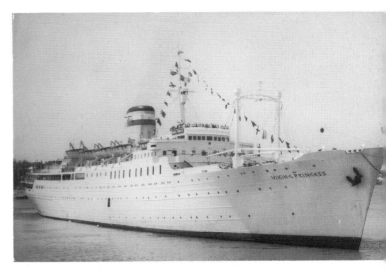

Canadian Pacific's Empress of Scotland *passing Bayonne Naval Yard* (Canadian Pacific).

Builders: Fairfield Shipbuilding & Engineering, Glasgow, 1930.
Particulars: 30,030 gross tons, 673ft × 84ft.
Machinery: Geared turbines, twin screw, speed 21 knots.
Passengers: 85 First Class, 1,167 Tourist Class.

Date of disaster: 7 September 1966.

The 1,173-passenger *Empress of Japan* was the fastest liner on the Vancouver-Yokohama route. On 26 November 1939 she became a troop transport, and on 16 October 1942 was renamed *Empress of Scotland*. Released from duties in 1948, and after an overhaul and refit, she resumed Canadian Pacific service between Liverpool and Quebec. In January 1958 the vessel was sold to Hamburg-Atlantic Line and

briefly renamed *Scotland* for the voyage to Hamburg.

After being refitted and modernized the ship was named *Hanseatic*. Her first voyage left Cuxhaven for New York on 19 July 1958. Besides being engaged in transatlantic service, the *Hanseatic* was also employed in winter cruising and was one of the pioneers in making Florida (Port Everglades) a cruise port.

At 7:30 am on 7 September 1966, a fire started in the engineroom when diesel oil leaking from a ruptured fuel line or a faulty

After a seven-month refit the Hanseatic *emerged with two funnels* (Author's collection).

gasket reached the ship's hot engines. Flames quickly engulfed the two enginerooms and spread upward undetected through hidden vents to five passenger decks. Only three of the 425 passengers were on board the vessel, which was scheduled to depart at 11:30 am. The sailing was cancelled and the damage assessed. Too costly to repair, the *Hanseatic* was first laid-up in New York, then towed to Hamburg where she was sold on 2 December 1966 to Eisen & Metall AG to be broken up.

Heraklion
Typaldos Lines, Piraeus
Previous name: *Leicestershire* (1949–65).

Builders: Fairfield Shipbuilding & Engineering Co Ltd, Glasgow, 1949.
Particulars: 8,922 gross tons, 498ft × 60ft.
Machinery: Steam geared turbines, single screw, speed 15.5 knots.
Passengers: 300 one class.

Date of disaster: 12 December 1966.

As built for the Bibby Line's UK-Burma trade, the *Leicestershire* had accommodation for 76 First Class passengers and also space for a considerable amount of cargo. For some while, the *Leicestershire* was chartered out to British India to supplement its sailings between London and East Africa. In 1964 she was sold to Typaldos and arrived in Piraeus the following March for a refit. Renamed *Heraklion* and

registered under the Aegean Steam Navigation, the *Heraklion* operated the ferry service between Piraeus and Heraklion, Crete.

The *Heraklion* sailed from Crete into the stormy Aegean Sea for Piraeus on Wednesday 7 December 1966 with a complement of 288 persons. The gale-lashed Aegean shook the poorly-secured trucks and cars loose in the hold until finally one sixteen-ton refrigerated trailer slammed open a bow door, letting in the gale-driven waters. Half-way through the trip at two o'clock in the morning on 8 December, the *Heraklion* radioed that she was in danger of sinking in heavy seas off the rocky islet of Falconcra in the Cyclades. The Greek Air Force, Greek Navy, the British minesweepers *Ashton* and *Leverton* and other ships hurried to the scene. One vessel that reached the area within thirty minutes of the call found nothing of the vessel. All that was evident of a tragedy was the debris floating around and a great quantity of oranges and tangerines that had been aboard. Eventually 47 survivors were found clinging to the rocks on the island of Falconcra.

The Greek government immediately launched an investigation and found the owners guilty of negligence because there was no drill for abandoning ship, the call for assistance was sent out too late and none of the ship's officers had organized rescue work. The company was also charged with manslaughter and faking public documents. The owner, Haralamos Typaldos, and general manager, Panssyotis Kokkinos, were given jail sentences in 1968. In addition, twelve out of Typaldos's fifteen ships failed Greek safety standards.

The Typaldos Line's ferry Heraklion (Alex Duncan).

The Elisabethville, *one of many ships that connected Belgium with Africa* (Compagnie Maritime Belge).

The *Elisabethville* was one of five ships the Belgians employed to maintain links with their African possessions. The *Elisabethville* commenced her maiden voyage from Antwerp on 18 January 1949 to Matadi, Congo and Angola.

On 20 March 1968 the *Elisabethville* was gutted by fire at her pier in Antwerp. The company decided she was not worth repairing and sold the ship to the breakers.

As a result, the company lost patronage right after the disaster which forced it to cancel its 1967 cruise programme. Finally with the owner in jail, the company ceased all operations, bringing to an unhappy end one of the oldest Greek coastal line businesses and one of the pioneers in Greek inter-island cruising.

Elisabethville
Compagnie Maritime Belge, Antwerp

Builders: John Cockerill SA, Hoboken, 1948.
Particulars: 10,901 gross tons, 504ft × 64ft
Machinery: Burmeister & Wain diesels, single screw, speed 15.5 knots.
Passengers: 179 one class.

Date of disaster: 20 March 1968.

The damaged Elisabethville *after the fire* (Arnold Kludas collection).

Wahine
Union Steamship Co of New Zealand, Wellington

Builders: Fairfields Ltd, Glasgow, 1966.
Particulars: 8,948 gross tons, 489ft × 73ft.
Machinery: Steam turbines, twin screw, speed 22 knots.
Passengers: 924 berthed.

Date of disaster: 11 April 1968.

The *Wahine* was an inter-island passenger and car ferry which ran between the capital of Wellington on the North Island and Lyttelton on the South Island of New Zealand. In that service she normally made six overnight trips between the two ports each week.

In the worst weather in New Zealand's recorded history, the *Wahine* was approaching Wellington during a screaming gale with gusts reaching 123 mph and visibility reduced to zero. The *Wahine* became unresponsive to her helm and virtually out of control. At 6:41 am the *Wahine* was flung upon Barretts Reef at the

harbour entrance. The *Wahine* mananged to free herself, but in the process badly holed her hull and severed her starboard propeller causing engine damage as water began to enter the engineroom. An attempt was made to bring the ship into a safe haven, but again the strong winds blew her aground, this time at the eastern entrance to Chaffers Passage.

As water rushed into the ruptured hull, the *Wahine* lurched over on her starboard side. At 1:30 pm the order was given to abandon ship. Panic seized the 750 passengers and crewmen as they scrambled to the starboard lifeboats, the only ones launchable owing to the ship's list. Miraculously, as the ship was being abandoned, the howling winds stopped. However, the heavy seas continued to menance lifeboats. Later, 46 bodies were recovered from the sea and five people were listed as missing. The *Wahine* was declared a total constructive loss and later refloated and sold for scrap.

It was not until 1972 that Union replaced the *Wahine* with the *Rangatira*. However, by then it was too late. New Zealanders lost trust in the company and found other ways of getting to Lyttelton and beyond. Therefore, eight years after the *Wahine* disaster and in financial difficulties, Union Steamship Company, founded in 1875, ceased operation.

Rio Jachal
Flota Mercante del Estado, Buenos Aires

Builders: Ansaldo, Sestri-Ponente, 1950.
Particulars: 11,342 gross tons, 550ft × 66ft.
Machinery: Fiat diesels, twin screw, speed 18.5 knots.
Passengers: 116 First Class.

The New Zealand ferry Wahine (Alex Duncan/ Richard Morse collection).

The remains of the Wahine (The Evening Post/Alexander Turnbull Library).

Argentine State Line's Rio Jachal (R. Scozzafava/Richard Morse collection).

Date of disaster: 17 April 1968.

The *Rio Jachal* was one of three Argentine sister-ships built to carry on trade between Buenos Aires and New York. In 1962 Flota Mercante del Estado and FANU amalgamated to form Empresa Lineas Maritimas Argentinas (ELMA).

The *Rio Jachal* was seriously damaged by fire in New York on 28 September 1962, and laid-up there. Two years later, in April 1964, the *Rio Jachal* sailed to Buenos Aires and was repaired, after which she was laid-up again. Another fire consumed the *Rio Jachal* in Buenos Aires on 17 April 1968. This time there were no repairs. The ship was sold for breaking up in 1969 and the work commenced in 1970 at Buenos Aires.

Fred Olsen's North Sea ferry Blenheim (Courtesy of the Steamship Historical Society collection/ University of Baltimore Library).

Blenheim
Fred Olsen & Co, Oslo

Builders: Akers M.V, Oslo, 1951.
Particulars: 4,766 gross tons, 374ft × 53ft.
Machinery: Burmeister & Wain type diesels, single screw, speed 16.5 knots.
Passengers: 243 one class.

Date of disaster: 21 May 1968.

The *Blenheim* was built in two different shipyards: her hull subcontracted out to Thornycroft, Southampton, then the super-structure and interior fittings carried out at Oslo. She sailed as a ferry between Newcastle, England and Oslo, Norway, and in that capacity had space in her forward hold for forty vehicles.

The *Blenheim* sustained heavy damage to her accommodation on A-Deck, salons, bars and bridge area when a fire broke out on 21 May 1968, while she was on a run between Newcastle and Oslo. The *Blenheim* was abandoned by her passengers and crew, and later on 23 May, towed into Kristiansand for

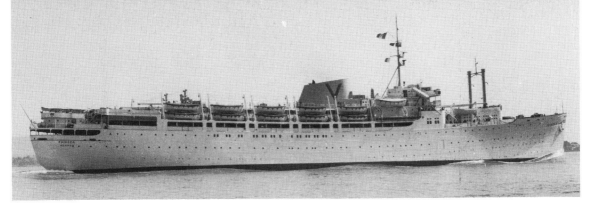

examination. Repairs were thought uneconomical and she was sold in December 1968 to Uglands Rederi and the hull was converted into a bulk/car carrier.

Fairsea
Alvion Steamship Corp, Panama
Previous name: *Charger* (1942–49).

Builders: Sun Shipbuilding and Drydock Co, Chester, 1942.
Particulars: 13,317 gross tons, 482ft × 70ft.
Machinery: Doxford geared diesels, single screw, speed 16 knots.
Passengers: 1, 212 Tourist Class.

Date of disaster: 24 January 1969.

On 1 March 1941, the *Rio de la Plata* was launched as a Moore-McCormack C3 cargo and passenger vessel. She was altered while fitting out to an auxiliary aircraft carrier and completed on 3 March 1942, with the name *Charger*. Bought in 1949 by Alvion SS Corp, a subsidiary of the Sitmar group, the *Charger* was rebuilt as the passenger ship *Fairsea* for 1,800 immigrants and placed on Bremerhaven-Sydney service. Refitted and modernized in 1957–58 she emerged at 13,432 tons with accommodation for 1,460 passengers. Another refit followed in the early '60s in which the passenger complement was reduced to 1,212. However, fittings continued to be austere and conditions a bit crowded.

On 24 January 1969, during a voyage from Sydney to Southampton, the *Fairsea* was disabled by a fire that started in her engineroom while some 900 miles west of Balboa. The *Fairsea* was taken in tow by the

The Australian emigrant carrier Fairsea (Luis Miguel Correia).

American vessel *Louise Lykes* to Balboa which they reached on 12 February. There her passengers disembarked. Laid-up, the *Fairsea* was sold 'as is' for $300,000 in 1969 to Spezia. She arrived in tow on 6 August and was shortly thereafter broken up.

Caribia
Universal Line S/A, Panama
Previous names: *Caronia* (1948–68), *Columbia* (1968).

Builders: John Brown & Co, Clydebank, 1948.
Particulars: 34,274 gross tons, 715ft × 91ft.
Machinery: Six steam turbines, twin screw, speed 22 knots.
Passengers: 860 First Class.

The site where the Caribia *committed the 'parking' offence* (Theodore W. Scull).

Caribia *being pounded by the waves at Guam* (Courtesy of the Steamship Historical Society collection/University of Baltimore Library).

Date of disaster: 5 March 1969.

The *Caronia* was affectionately known as either the 'Green Goddess' or the 'millionaire's yacht'. She was launched and named by Her Royal Highness Princess Elizabeth on 30 October 1947, completed in December 1948, and sent on her maiden voyage on 4 January 1949, from Southampton to New York. To give her a distinctive look, Cunard painted her three shades of green. Besides transatlantic crossings in which she carried 932 passengers in two classes, Cunard saw the potential in cruising and despatched the *Caronia* on cruises worldwide in which she catered to no more than 500 fortunate souls at a time. Her world cruises every January were an annual event.

A refit was ordered in 1965 and work started in October. Three months later, the *Caronia* emerged with a new lido deck and completely redecorated and refurnished rooms but jet aircraft, modern tonnage and a new younger breed of traveller sealed the fate of the *Caronia*. In November 1967, she was laid-up. In 1968 she was sold to Star Line, Panama, renamed *Columbia* and taken to Piraeus for a refit. There, the company changed its name to Universal Line, S/A, Panama and renamed the ship *Caribia*. The *Caribia* returned to New York in 1969 to start a series of seven and fourteen-day cruises.

The *Caribia* left New York on her second Caribbean cruise on 28 February 1969, with 325 passengers. On 5 March 1969, a steam line exploded in the engineroom killing one crew member. A fire resulted which knocked out the *Caribia's* electrical system. The liner drifted out of control, unable to manoeuvre, for one

day. She was finally towed to St Thomas where the passengers were allowed to disembark. The *Caribia* arrived under tow in New York on 25 March 1969. Later in 1969 she was purchased by Andrew Kostantinidis.

The *Caribia* remained at anchorage at Gravesend Bay, then moved in the autumn of 1969 to a pier in Brooklyn. In the spring of 1970 New York City refused Kostantinidis permission to berth his ship. The *Caribia* was then towed back to Gravesend Bay. Threatened with losing his insurance coverage if the ship was not berthed, Kostantinidis decided to move the *Caribia* between Piers 84 and 86 on West 45th Street. The city retaliated by ordering the police to give the *Caribia* a parking ticket. The summons described the 'vehicle' as follows: 'Boat — SS *Caribia*. Year 1949. Make — John Brown, Hull [sic]. Color — white. Offense — Berthing, no permit.' In early '71, the city relented and gave permission for Kostantinidis to berth his ship at Pier 56 in Manhattan.

Various schemes to get the *Caribia* sailing fell through. At a cost of $50,000 a month for maintenance and an anticipated fuel bill of $7 million, the *Caribia* was draining her owner's resources. With an offer of $3.5 million from Taiwan breakers, Kostantinidis sold his prize possession and on 25 April 1974, the *Caribia* left New York under the tow of the German tug, *Hamburg*. On her way to Taiwan, nasty weather forced the *Hamburg* to put into

The passenger-cargo liner Paraguay Star (Richard Morse collection).

Guam. As the tug and *Caribia* approached the entrance to the harbour on 13 August 1974, the *Caribia* stuck the breakwater, impaled herself, heeled over and broke into three sections. The remains were later dismantled at the site.

Paraguay Star
Blue Star Line, London

Builders: Cammell Laird & Co, Birkenhead, 1948.

Paraguay Star *on fire at London docks* (Illustrated London News).

Particulars: 10,722 gross tons, 503ft × 68ft.
Machinery: Parsons geared turbines, single screw, speed 16 knots.
Passengers: 47 First Class.

Date of disaster: 12 August 1969.

The *Paraguay Star* was built as a combination passenger-cargo vessel for the London-Buenos Aires service, in which she commenced sailing in November 1948.

On 12 August 1969, while at her dock in London, the *Paraguay Star* was badly damaged by a fire that started in the engineroom. Not worth repairing, the ship was sold to Eckardt & Co in Hamburg for scrapping. The *Paraguay Star* arrived in Hamburg in September 1969.

Chapter 8

The burning seventies

The transition from line voyages to cruising continued. Most of the vessels that met misfortune in this decade were either cruise ships, liners confined to trade in the Mediterranean or pilgrim ships.

Fire, that four letter word, continued to menace liners, destroying seventeen ships. It is interesting to note that with the exception of six ships, sixteen sailed for previous owners. Particularly newsworthy were the fires aboard the *Fulvia*, the *Heleanna* – which was carrying more people than she was licensed to transport – the *Seawise University*, the former *Queen Elizabeth*, and the *Angelina Lauro*.

The *Antilles* ran aground, bringing an end to French Line's West Indies passenger service, the Spanish cargo liner *Monte Udala* sprang a leak and the *Caribia*'s engines failed.

There were 21 ships involved in tragedies, costing 167 lives. This low figure for the number of ships involved could be attributed in part to the vessels' proximity to land when disaster struck and the new safety standards imposed after the disasters in the 1960s.

Fulvia
Costa Armatoria SpA, Genoa
Previous name: *Oslofjord* (1949–69).

Builders: Nederlandsche Shipbuilding, Amsterdam, 1949.

Particulars: 16,923 gross tons, 577ft × 72ft.
Machinery: Stork-type diesel, twin screw, speed 20 knots.
Passengers: 690 First Class.

Date of disaster: 20 July 1970.

The *Oslofjord* commenced her maiden voyage from Oslo to New York on 26 November 1949. Thereafter, she was engaged principally on this route via Copenhagen and Kristiansand, with occasional calls at Stavanger and Bergen. The *Oslofjord* was fitted with motion stabilizers in November 1957 and in November 1963 she was given a three-month major refit in Holland. In 1969 the *Oslofjord* was chartered for three years to Costa Cruises and in December renamed *Fulvia*.

With Captain C. B. Fasting in command, the *Fulvia* departed Genoa on 14 July 1970, on a ten-day Atlantic Island and Morocco cruise with 447 passengers. Between Funchal and Tenerife, 100 miles north of the Canary Islands, a fire broke out in the No 2 engineroom at approximately 1:00 am on Sunday morning, 19 July. The crew tried to contain the fire, but several minor explosions spread the flames, and the blaze got out of control. The flames, heat and smoke engulfed the entire liner from stem to stern. However, passengers and crew managed to use the ship's lifeboats to safely dismembark from the fiery liner. The French liner *Ancerville,* which was in the vicinity, answered the call for assistance and picked up all the *Fulvia's* passengers and crew: 36 hours later the *Fulvia* sank in position 29° 57'N,16° 30'W during an attempt to tow her to Teneriffe.

Antilles
Compagnie Générale Transatlantique, Le Havre

Builders: Arsenal de Brest, Brest, 1953.
Particulars: 19,828 gross tons, 598ft × 80ft.
Machinery: Steam turbines, twin screw, speed 23 knots.
Passengers: 424 First Class, 284 Cabin Class, 111 Tourist Class.

Date of disaster: 8 January, 1971.

The *Antilles* was the last liner built for French Line's West Indies service. Following two cruises in Europe, the *Antilles* was sent on her maiden voyage from Le Havre to the Caribbean in May 1953. At the end of her career, she did a few cruises from San Juan during January and February.

The *Antilles* departed San Juan on a nine-day

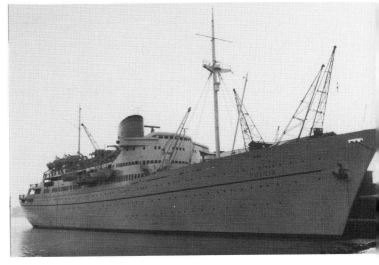

Costa's new cruise ship Fulvia (Alex Duncan).

cruise with 340 passengers aboard. In command was Captain Kerverdo and his crew of 350. On 8 January 1971, while navigating through a shallow reef-filled area, the *Antilles* struck an unmarked underwater reef off the

The last French Line vessel in the Caribbean was the Antilles (Compagnie Générale Maritime).

The converted tanker and former passenger ferry Heleanna *(G. Ghiglion/Antonio Scrimali collection).*

island of Mustique. The reef ruptured the fuel tanks and the escaping fuel caught fire, triggering explosions in the engine room. Captain Kerverdo sent out a distress call and ordered his passengers and crew to take to the lifeboats.

An hour after the grounding, the *Antilles* was fully abandoned. The 690 people were picked up by the *Queen Elizabeth 2*, the *Suffren, Point Allegre* and by small ships from Mustique. The next day the still burning *Antilles* capsized. Ten days after hitting rocks, on 18 January, the *Antilles* broke into three pieces, was abandoned and today has mostly disappeared from view.

Heleanna
C.S. Efthymiadis, Piraeus
Previous name: *Munkedal* (1954–66).

Builders: AB Gotaverken, Gothenburg, 1954.
Particulars: 11,674 gross tons, 549ft × 66ft.
Machinery: Diesels from builders, single screw, speed 15 knots.
Passengers: 620 one class. 220 vehicles.

Date of disaster: 28 August 1971.

The *Munkedal* sailed as an oil tanker for the Swedish concern of Munkedals A/B. Purchased

by Efthymiadis in 1966, the Greeks renamed the vessel *Heleanna* and fitted her with passenger accommodation. In 1967 the *Heleanna* sailed as the world's largest passenger and car ferry between Patras, Greece, and Ancona, Italy.

On a voyage from Patras to Ancona, disaster befell the *Heleanna* during the early morning hours of 28 August 1971, when a gas cylinder exploded in the kitchen 25 miles from Brindisi. The stern of the ship was quickly engulfed in flames. As the fire and smoke spread, more than 1,000 passengers and crew began to panic, many jumping into the Ionian Sea. Four rescue tugs raced to the smouldering vessel and sprayed foam and water on to the burning ship. When all was over 24 people had died, and the ship was towed to Brindisi.

At Brindisi, Italian authorities issued a warrant for the arrest of Captain Demetrios Antypas on the following charges: multiple homicide; embarking more passengers than the ship was licensed to carry; not having adequate fire-fighting equipment on board; and failing to provide proper aid to passengers when it became apparent that the fire was a serious one. The Captain was apprehended while trying to board another Greek ferry.

The wreck of the *Heleanna* was sold in February 1974, to Italian shipbreakers. They in turn resold the wreck in late '74 and it was converted to a barge at Toulon.

Again, safety standards on board passenger vessels were tightened as a result of tragedy. No longer would a ship be allowed to sail with more passengers than it was licensed to carry. Furthermore, fire fighting equipment was to be conveniently placed and clearly marked.

Monte Udala
Naviera Aznar, Bilbao

Builders: Cia Euskalduna, Bilbao, 1948.
Particulars: 10,170 gross tons, 487ft × 63ft.
Machinery: Sulzer diesels, single screw, speed 16.5 knots.
Passengers: 62 First Class, 40 Second Class, 290 Third Class.

Aznar's Monte Udala (Courtesy of the Steamship Historical Society collection/University of Baltimore Library).

Date of disaster: 8 September 1971.

The *Monte Udala* was a cargo passenger liner employed on the Italy, Spain, South American run, that commenced in August 1948.

During a voyage from Buenos Aires to Genoa the *Monte Udala* developed a leak in her engineroom and was abandoned by passengers and crew. She later sank seventy nautical miles off Ilheus in position 15° 02'S, 36°W.

Seawise University
C. Y. Tung, Hong Kong
Previous name: *Queen Elizabeth* (1940–68).

Builders: John Brown & Co, Clydebank, 1940.

Queen Elizabeth *arriving at New York (Cunard Line).*

Queen Elizabeth *departing for Europe* (Author's photograph).

Particulars: 83,673 gross tons, 1,031ft × 119ft.
Machinery: 16 steam turbines, quadruple screw, speed 28.5 knots.
Passengers: 2,288 one class.

Date of disaster: 9 January 1972.

The *Queen Elizabeth* was the largest passenger liner ever built. The *Queen* was laid down in December 1936, launched 27 September 1938, and on 2 March 1940 sailed secretly, incomplete, for New York. Between 1940 and 1946 the *Queen* steamed 500,000 miles and carried 800,000 passengers world-wide as a troop transport. Released from service, the *Queen Elizabeth* was overhauled and refitted to carry 823 First Class, 662 Cabin Class and 798 Tourist Class passengers. She departed Southampton

Seawise University *on fire in Hong Kong Harbour* (South China Morning Post).

for New York on her first commercial voyage on 16 October 1946. When the *Queen Elizabeth* was joined back in commercial service in July 1947 by her running mate *Queen Mary,* the century-old goal of a weekly luxury express steamer service between the United States and England was finally achieved.

In March 1955 the *Queen Elizabeth* was fitted with twin stabilizers. Further modernization was carried out in 1965 to make her more suitable for cruising. The *Queen* emerged from an autumn facelift at 82,998 tons, completely air-conditioned and with a new lido deck. The refit was not sufficient. The *Queen* was too grand and too old. Maintenance was costly, passengers were few and her size placed a limit to the number of cruise ports she could visit. Therefore, with losses soaring, Cunard decided to retire the famous vessel. She departed New York on her last commercial sailing on 30 October 1968.

The *Queen Elizabeth* sailed from Southampton on 29 November 1968 for Port Everglades where she was to be converted to a convention centre and tourist attraction. The *Queen* languished in Port Everglades for two years, as two companies, Elizabeth Corporation and later, The Queen Limited, ran into financial difficulties. Finally in 1970, the *Queen Elizabeth* was purchased by C.Y. Tung. He renamed her *Seawise University* and prepared the ship for her voyage to Hong Kong, where she would be refitted as a floating university and cruise liner at a cost of $4.5 million. The *Seawise University* sailed from Port Everglades on 10 February 1971, and arrived in Hong Kong via Aruba, Curaçao, Cape Town and Singapore on 16 July. This was truly a slow boat to China, as the *Seawise* experienced boiler trouble throughout the trip.

During final fitting out in Hong Kong harbour on 9 January 1972, fire seemed to have erupted everywhere aboard the *Seawise University*. A helicopter circled overhead and

Seawise University **burning fiercely with the blaze out of control** (South China Morning Post).

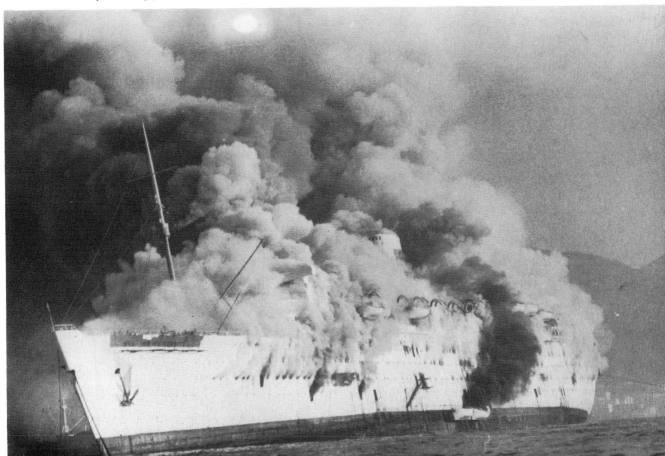

The end of the Seawise University *(South China Morning Post).*

at around 10:30 am reported the blaze to harbour officials. The onboard elaborate fire precaution system was useless. As the flames worked their way through five of the ship's eleven decks, more than 200 workers aboard scurried to safety. The raging inferno was fed by the contents of a subsidiary diesel oil tank which had exploded. By the time Hong Kong fireboats and more that 100 fire fighters arrived, 80 per cent of the *Seawise University's* superstructure was ablaze. By late afternoon, fire fighting efforts ceased due to the intense heat and a 17-degree list developed. A silent vigil was now kept over the dying *'Queen'*. At

daybreak the fire exhausted itself except for small pockets in the fore section.

Twenty-four hours after the start of the blaze, the *Seawise University* gave up, rolled over and sank in some 43ft of water at an 80-degree list. Removal of the wreck was started in 1974.

Marmara
Denizcilik Bankasi TAO (Turkish Maritime Lines), Istanbul

Builders: A. G. Weser (Seebeck yards), Bremerhaven, 1956.

The Marmara *was employed in Mediterranean or Black Sea service* (Courtesy of the Steamship Historical Society collection/University of Baltimore Library).

Particulars: 6,042 gross tons, 402ft × 54ft.
Machinery: MAN diesels, single screw, speed 14 knots.
Passengers: 68 First Class, 74 Second Class, 448 Tourist Class.

Date of disaster: 5 March 1972.

The *Marmara* was the last of a trio of German-built liners for Turkish Maritime Lines. The *Marmara* was employed either on the Istanbul, Greece and Italy route or between Istanbul and Black Sea ports. To meet the seasonal traffic of workers or pilgrims, some 320 unberthed passengers could be carried in the 'tween decks.

While undergoing repairs at the Gold Horn on 5 March 1972, a fire broke out which completely gutted the liner, causing her to sink.

Oriental Warrior
United Overseas Export Line, Taiwan
Previous name: *Hamburg* (1954–67).

Builders: Bremer Vulkan, Bremen-Vegesack, 1954.
Particulars: 8,269 gross tons, 538ft × 64ft.
Machinery: Two MAN-type diesels, single screw, speed 16.5 knots.
Passengers: 84 First Class.

Date of disaster: 25 May 1972.

The *Hamburg* and her other two sister-ships, the *Hannover* and *Frankfurt,* were the first to be called 'combi'-vessels, passenger and cargo ships. The *Hamburg* achieved distinction when she became the first Hamburg-American Line ship to visit Southampton in over fourteen years. Amenities for passengers included all of the shipboard fittings found on larger liners, plus private facilities in every cabin, still a unique feature in the mid-'50s.

With profits dwindling, the Germans withdrew her from service and placed her up for sale. In 1967 Orient Overseas Line purchased the vessel, painted her white and renamed her *Oriental Warrior*. Overhauled, she was placed on the New York, Gulf Coast, Far East service. In 1971 the *Oriental Warrior* was sold to Malaysia Overseas Line, then in 1972 to United Overseas Export Lines, both companies registered in Monrovia.

Travelling from New York to Hong Kong, an engineroom explosion followed by a fire overwhelmed the *Oriental Warrior* forty miles north-east of Daytona Beach on 25 May 1972.

Oriental Warrior *in Orient Overseas colours* (Alex Duncan/William H. Miller Jr collection).

Two days later, she arrived in Jacksonville and there settled on the bottom. Refloated by 25 September she was found to be damaged beyond economic repair and was towed out to position 30°23'N, 79°23'W and scuttled on 1 October.

Caribia

Sicula Oceanica Società per Azioni (Siosa), Palermo

Previous name: *Vulcania* (1928–65).

Builders: Cantiere Navale Triestino, Monfalcone, 1928.
Particulars: 24,496 gross tons, 631ft × 80ft.
Machinery: Fiat 28,000 SHP diesel engines, twin screw, speed 21 knots.
Passengers: 337 First Class, 368 Cabin Class, 732 Tourist Class.

Date of disaster: 23 September 1972.

The *Vulcania* was built for Cosulich Line's Trieste-Naples-New York service. The *Vulcania* formally joined 'Italia', created by Mussolini in 1932 to consolidate Italy's North Atlantic service under one financial umbrella, and she was fully integrated into their fleet by 1937. During the early months of 1935 the *Vulcania* undertook some trooping voyages to the East, after which she was given an extensive refit starting in May.

She returned to service in December 1935 with an increase of tonnage from 23,970 to 24,469 and with new Fiat diesel engines replacing the slower Burmeister & Wain diesel engines. Her ornate First Class public rooms were not touched. World War 2 saw the *Vulcania* first serving as an Italian troop transport to Tripoli, then in 1942 as an International Red Cross ship evacuating troops, prisoners and refugees out of East Africa, and finally in 1943, after Italy's capitulation, a US Army transport plying (mainly) the Atlantic.

At the conclusion of hostilities, the *Vulcania* was chartered to American Export Lines and undertook six round voyages from New York to Naples and Alexandria in 1946. Returned to 'Italia' in November 1946, the *Vulcania* was given a refit, then resumed commercial service in July 1947, by making one sailing to South America, before returning to the Italy-USA route in September. With the imminent arrival of 'Italia's' twin super liners *Michelangelo* and *Raffaello,* the *Vulcania* became redundant and after completing her last sailing from New York on 21 April 1965, she was laid up in Italy. Within a few months she was purchased by Siosa Line and renamed *Caribia*.

Caribia *before being painted white for cruising* (Alex Duncan).

Refitted with revised accommodation for 1,437 passengers, the *Caribia* was despatched on Siosa's Southampton-West Indies service in February 1966. In December the *Caribia* returned to the shipyard for a white coat of paint and an extension to her funnel. As passenger fare revenues began to dry up in the West Indies trade, Siosa looked to other means of employing their ships. The answer was in cruising. The *Caribia* took over the highly popular 'Seven Mediterranean Pearls' cruises, first inaugurated by Siosa's *Ascania* in 1966. These were seven-day cruises from Genoa to ports in France, Spain, Tunis and islands off Italy. This took care of *Caribia's* summers, and during the winters she was sent south on cruises out of Tenerife or Dakar to West African ports — quite a novel destination.

It was at the beginning of the *Caribia's* last 'Pearl' cruise of the season that disaster struck. The *Caribia* departed Genoa on 23 September, and after a quick call at Nice to embark additional passengers, the *Caribia* set sail for Barcelona. During the evening of 23 September, the *Caribia's* starboard diesel engine failed, causing her to drift, which resulted in her striking submerged rocks in Cannes Bay. The 880 passengers aboard were taken ashore by boats after water entered her engine compartment. The cruise was cancelled, and the *Caribia* proceeded to La Spezia where she was laid up on 29 September, after it was determined that her old engines were beyond economic repair. The *Caribia* was sold to Spanish shipbreakers and arrived in tow at Barcelona in September 1973. The *Caribia* was subsequently resold and departed Barcelona on 15 March 1974, in tow for Kaohsiung for scrapping. However, on arrival at the entrance to the harbour on 20 July she sank before she could reach the scrappers' berth. Later pumped out, she was finally scrapped.

Though Siosa had planned to retire the 44-year-old *Caribia* at the conclusion of her 23 September voyage, the fact that the cruise was not completed merits her entry in this work.

Knossos
C.S. Efthymiadis Line, Piraeus
Previous name: *La Bourdonnais* (1953–68).

Builders: Arsenal de Lorient, Lorient, 1953.
Particulars: 10,886 gross tons, 493ft × 64ft.
Machinery: Burmeister & Wain type diesels, twin screw, speed 17 knots.
Passengers: 346 First Class.

Date of disaster: 3 May 1973.

From 1953 to 1968 Messageries Maritimes

Scrapping of the Knossos (Antonio Scrimali).

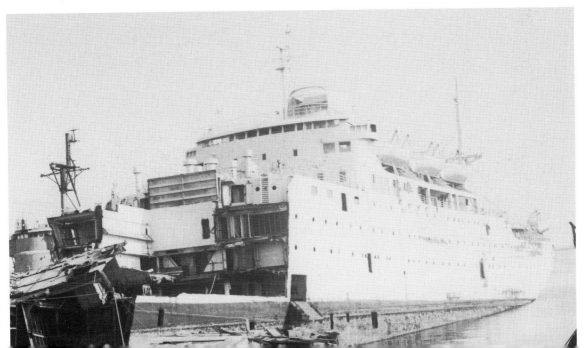

Pilgrim liner Saudi. (James Shaw).

engaged *La Bourdonnais* on their Marseille-Mauritius service, in which she carried 402 passengers in four classes. Dwindling passenger and cargo revenues coupled with raising operating costs, led Messageries Maritimes to sell *La Bourdonnais* in 1968 to C. S. Efthymiadis, who renamed their new ship *Knossos*. She was employed out of Piraeus to Mediterranean ports and on the inter-island trade.

On 3 May 1973, on a voyage from Piraeus to Limassol, leaking fuel oil spilled on to the generator causing a fire that did considerable damage to her main switchboard. The 186 passengers and some crew members were transferred to Adriatica's *Stelvio* by lifeboat without incident. The *Knossos* was later towed back to Piraeus, where she was laid-up. Three years later, she was sold to Spanish shipbreakers.

Saudi
Mongul Line Ltd, Bombay

Builders: Lithows Ltd, Port Glasgow, 1956.
Particulars: 5,973 gross tons, 426ft × 57ft.
Machinery: Triple-expansion engines, single screw, speed 13.5 knots.
Passengers: 4 De Luxe, 8 First Class, 987 Deck.

Date of disaster: 26 June 1973.

Pilgrim liner Saudi. (James Shaw).

The *Saudi* was built to carry twelve passengers and general cargo between India and the Red Sea ports during the off season, and deck passengers between India, Sri Lanka and Jeddah during the pilgrim season.

On 26 June 1973, the *Saudi* sank off Cape Guardafui in position 11°34'N, 51°25'E after she had capsized in heavy monsoon seas during a voyage from Port Sudan to Bombay, resulting in the loss of 41 people.

Satrustegui
Compañiá Trasatlántica Española, SA, Barcelona
Previous name: *Explorador Iradier*
(1948–52).

Builders: Union Naval de Levante, Valencia, 1948.
Particulars: 6,615 gross tons, 401ft × 55ft.
Machinery: Burmeister & Wain type diesels, twin screw, speed 16 knots.
Passengers: 44 First Class, 192 Tourist Class.

Date of disaster: 30 June 1973.

Originally built for Empresa Nacional Elcano de la Marina Mercante, the *Sastrustegui* was subsequently bought by Trasatlántica Española. As the *Explorador Iradier* and later the *Satrustegui*,

The Satrustegui *arriving at La Guaira* (**Author's photograph**).

she sailed between Spain and Central America. In 1973 she was sold to Cia Trasmediterránea SA and was to be renamed *Isla de Cabrera*.

On 30 June 1973, while undergoing repairs in drydock at Barcelona, the *Satrustegui* was extensively damaged by a fire on board. As a result of the damage she was sold to Spanish shipbreakers and arrived at Castellon on 2 February 1974.

Homeric
Home Lines, Panama
Previous name: *Mariposa* (1931–53).

Builders: Bethlehem Shipbuilding Corp, Quincy, 1931.

The Satrustegui, *thoroughly burned out and laid up at Barcelona in 1973* (**William H. Miller Jr**).

Particulars: 18,563 gross tons, 641ft × 79ft.
Machinery: Geared steam turbines, twin screw, speed 20.5 knots.
Passengers: 147 First Class, 1,096 Tourist Class, 723 Cruising.

Date of disaster: 1 July 1973.

Launched on 18 July, completed on 10 December, and delivered on 14 December 1931, the 704-passenger liner *Mariposa* ran on Matson Lines San Francisco-Honolulu-Sydney service. After serving as a US Navy transport from 1941 to 1946 she was laid-up. In 1953 the vessel was sold to Home Lines and renamed *Homeric*. After an engine overhaul at Alameda by Todd Shipyards *Homeric* sailed to Trieste for interior work. The *Homeric*'s tonnage was increased from 18,017 to 18,563 and she was lengthened from 632ft to 641ft. The *Homeric* departed from Venice on her first voyage to

New York on 24 January 1955. From May 1955 to 1957 she was engaged on the Southampton-New York trade, then in 1957 switched to the Canadian-European route. From 1963 onwards the *Homeric* was employed exclusively on West Indies cruises from New York. Starting in the winter months of 1972, the *Homeric* inaugurated Home Line's cruises from Port Everglades.

The *Homeric* departed New York on 30 June

Home Line's popular Homeric (Antonio Scrimali).

1973, on a fourteen-day cruise with 640 passengers aboard. The next morning at 4:00 am, a fire broke out in the galley. The blaze was confined to the galley, but smoke and water caused slight damage to the enginerooms and

The pilgrim liner Malaysia Kita (Airfoto, Malaysia).

Close-up of the extensive fire damage on the Malaysia Kita (Airfoto, Malaysia).

boiler room. While the crew was extinguishing the fire, the passengers were instructed to don their life preservers and report to the Boat Deck as a precautionary measure. In addition, Home Line's *Oceanic* was standing by, ferrying breakfast and other supplies to the *Homeric*. By mid-afternoon, the *Homeric* sailed back for New York, arriving at 8:00 am on 2 July.

After inspection by Home Lines and the underwriters, the *Homeric* sailed for Genoa on 16 July. There, she was inspected again. The first damage was more extensive than Home Lines anticipated and when presented with an estimated repair bill, the company decided to settle on the insurance money, which was more than the repair cost. The *Homeric* was sold to Nan Feng Steel Enterprises, and left Genoa under her own power on 11 December 1973. She arrived in Kaohsuing on 29 January 1974 and was there scrapped.

Malaysia Kita
Fir Line, Malaysia
Previous names: *Viet Nam* (1952–67), *Pacifique* (1967–70), *Princess Abeto* (1970–71), *Malaysia Baru* (1971–72).

Builders: Chantiers Navales de La Ciotat, 1952.
Particulars: 11,792 gross tons, 532ft × 72ft.
Machinery: Parsons geared turbines, twin screw, speed 21 knots.
Passengers: Approximately 1,612.

Date of disaster: 12 May 1974.

As originally completed, the 539-passenger *Viet Nam* sailed on Messageries Maritimes' Marseille-Yokohama service. In 1967, owing to the Vietnamese War, the company changed her name to *Pacifique*. Dwindling revenue forced Messageries to sell *Pacifique* in 1970 to Cia de Nav Abeto, who tripled her capacity and renamed her *Princess Abeto*. The liner was despatched on pilgrim service. In 1971 she was again sold, this time to Fir Line and renamed *Malaysia Baru*. As such she was used on pilgrim voyages between Malaysia and Jeddah and on regular runs between Malaysia, Singapore and India. In 1972 her name was changed to *Malaysia Kita*.

A fire broke out on board on 12 May 1974, while the ship was lying at Singapore for repairs. The *Malaysia Kita* was towed out of the harbour, where the fire was allowed to burn for several days. Gutted, the charred vessel sank in shallow water. The wreck was raised on 26 June 1975, and on 22 April 1976, the remains of the ship were towed to Kaohsiung to be scrapped.

Cunard Ambassador
Cunard Line, Southampton

Builders: P. Smit Jr, Rotterdam, 1972.
Particulars: 14,160 gross tons, 484ft × 71ft.
Machinery: Stork-Werkspoor geared diesels,
twin screw, speed 22 knots.
Passengers: 831 First Class.

Date of disaster: 12 September 1974.

The *Cunard Ambassador* was the second
Cunard liner built exclusively for cruising and
saw service from various North American East
Coast ports to the Caribbean.

The Cunard Ambassador *was the second Cunard
vessel built for cruising* (Cunard Line).

On a positioning trip from Miami to New
Orleans, a fire broke out from a ruptured fuel
tank at 7:15 am on 12 September 1974. An SOS
was sent and the Coast Guard responded. The
ship's crew and the Coast Guard tried to put
out the fire, but when it knocked out the
Cunard Ambassador's emergency power, the

The livestock carrier Linda Clausen (Fremantle Port
Authority).

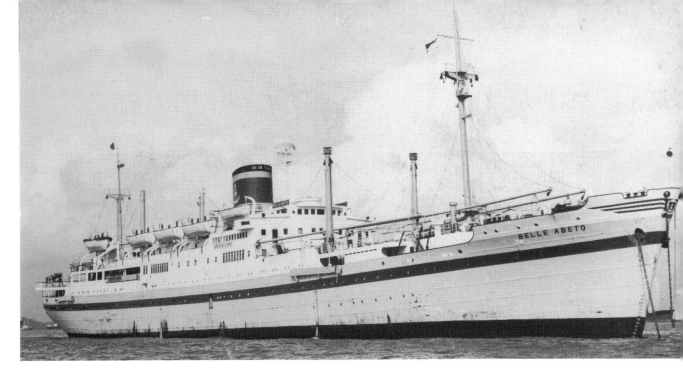

The Indonesian pilgrim liner Belle Abeto (Alex Duncan).

Captain and the remaining fire fighters had to abandon the liner. On 15 September, the *Cunard Ambassador* was towed to Key West by the salvage tug *Cable*. Cunard declared the ship a total loss and sold her to the Danish concern of C. Clausen D/S A/S.

Renamed *Linda Clausen,* the liner was towed to Landskrona to be converted to a livestock transport for service between Australia and the Persian Gulf. In 1980 the vessel's name was changed to *Procyon*. In 1983 the vessel was sold to the country of Qatar and they renamed her *Raslan*. On 11 July 1983 the vessel again suffered a fatal fire, and this time she was laid up. Finally she was sold in 1985 to Taiwan breakers.

Belle Abeto
Compañiá de Navigation Abeto SA, Panama
Previous name: *Laennec* (1951–66).

Builders: Ateliers et Chantiers de la Loire, St Nazaire, 1951.
Particulars: 12,177 gross tons, 538ft × 64ft.

Machinery: Sulzer diesels, twin screw, speed 17 knots.
Passengers: 100 cabin passengers, 1,352 pilgrims.

Date of disaster: 30 July 1976.

The *Laennec* operated as Cie Sudatlantique's 436-passenger liner between Northern European Channel ports and South America. In attempts to trim its fleet, the French government considered the *Laennec* redundant and sold her to Indonesian interests in 1966. Renamed *Belle Abeto*, she was refitted to carry pilgrims between Indonesia and Jeddah.

On 30 July 1976, at Sasebo anchorage, the *Belle Abeto* was gutted by fire that started in her engineroom. The next day she sank at the anchorage.

Malaysia Raya
Fir Line, Malaysia
Previous names: *Laos* (1954–70), *Empress Abeto* (1970–71).

Builders: Chantiers Navales de La Ciotat, 1954.
Particulars: 11,792 gross tons, 532ft × 72ft.
Machinery: Parsons geared turbines, twin

The one-time French liner now pilgrim ship **Malaysia Raya** (Airfoto, Malaysia).

screw, speed 21 knots.
Passengers: 1,696 one class.

Date of disaster: 23 August 1976.

The *Laos* sailed on Messageries Maritimes' Marseille-Yokohama route. Under that name she was registered at 13,212 tons and carried 539 passengers in three classes. Lack of passengers and cargo, coupled with the expenses of sailing via the Panama Canal or round Cape Horn, eventually made the *Laos* uneconomic to operate. Therefore, she was sold in 1970 to Cia de Nav Abeto and rebuilt as the *Empress Abeto,* an 11,792-ton pilgrim ship. In 1971 she was sold to Fir Line, renamed *Malaysia Raya* and employed in the Malaysia-Jeddah pilgrim service and passenger runs

between Malaysia-Singapore-India.

While lying at anchor off Port Kelang, the *Malaysia Raya* was completely destroyed by fire on 23 August 1976. The wreck was beached the next day and declared a total loss.

Blue Sea
Ahmed Mohammed Baaboud, Jeddah
Previous name: *Europa* (1952–76).

Builders: Ansaldo SpA, La Spezia, 1952.
Particulars: 11,340 gross tons, 521ft × 68ft.
Machinery: Fiat diesels from builders, twin screw, speed 19.5 knots.
Passengers: 446 one class (cabins).

Date of disaster: 12 November 1976.

Completed in October 1952, the *Europa* offered comfortable accommodation on Lloyd Triestino's Trieste-Cape Town/East Africa service. Jet aircraft competition caused the *Europa* to be sold in September 1976, to Baabound who renamed her *Blue Sea*.

Lying at Jeddah on 12 November 1976, a fire broke out aboard the vessel. Her pilgrim passengers were all safely disembarked, and during the night of 14 November, she sank.

Mecca
Orri Navigation Lines, Jeddah
Previous name: *Gullfoss* (1950–74).

The completely destroyed **Malaysia Raya** (Airfoto, Malaysia).

Builders: Burmeister & Wain, Copenhagen, 1950.
Particulars: 3,858 gross tons, 355ft × 48ft.
Machinery: Burmeister & Wain diesels, single screw, speed 15.5 knots.
Passengers: 209 (Lloyds 76/77).

Date of disaster: 18 December 1976.

The *Gullfoss* was one of the main links between Copenhagen, Leith and Reykjavik. Newer vessels and jet competition accelerated Iceland Steamship Company's decision to sell her in 1974. Purchased by the Saudi Arabian interests, she was renamed *Mecca* after the holy city, and spent most of her trading activity in pilgrim voyages.

During a voyage from Jeddah to Port Sudan with 1,100 pilgrims, the *Mecca* caught fire when she was about seventeen miles from Jeddah on 18 December 1976. She was safely abandoned by her passengers and crew, and then went aground the next day. During that night she heeled over and sank.

Top *Lloyds Triestino's* Europa *which later became the* Blue Sea (Courtesy of the Steamship Historical Society collection/University of Baltimore Library).

Above *The ferry* Gullfoss *which later became the* Mecca (Courtesy of the Steamship Historical Society collection/University of Baltimore Library).

Below *The Danish ferry* Kronprins Frederik *that ended her career as the* Patra (Alex Duncan).

Patra
Arab Navigators, Alexandria
Previous name: *Kronprins Frederik* (1941–76).

Builders: Elisinore Shipbuilding & Engineering Co, Elsinore, 1941.
Particulars: 3,920 gross tons, 378ft × 50ft.

The cruise liner Rasa Sayang *burning in the Straits of Malacca* (Airfoto, Malaysia).

Machinery: Burmeister & Wain type diesels, twin screw, speed 20 knots.
Passengers: 324 one class.

Date of disaster: 25 December 1976.

Completed in 1941, the *Kronprins Frederick* did not make her commercial debut for DFDS, a Danish concern, until 1946. Employed as a ferry between Harwich, England and Esbjerg, Denmark, the *Kronprins Frederick* introduced new standards of comfort, appearance and speed — reducing the 24-hour passage to nineteen hours. In June 1964 she was switched to the Newcastle-Esbjerg run, which she maintained until newer tonnage necessitated her sale in 1976. Purchased by Arab Navigators, the vessel was renamed *Patra* and immediately despatched on the Suez-Jeddah route as a drive-on drive-off ferry.

The remains of the Rasa Sayang *outside Pireaus harbour* (Antonio Scrimali).

The *Patra* departed Jeddah on 25 December 1976 with a full load of passengers returning home to Suez from a pilgrimage to Jeddah and Mecca. Five hours out of Jeddah a gas leak from an engine led to a fire, according to a government investigative committee. The ship was soon engulfed in flames and fumes. Captain Mohammed Shaaban ordered a distress signal to be sent out and sounded the abandon ship alarm. An explosion was heard that further panicked the 387 passengers. Later, Captain Shaaban said that he had to chase passengers off the vessel with axes, since many of them did not want to abandon the ship without their belongings. The Soviet tanker *Lenino* reported to the scene and rescued 201 persons assisted by half-a-dozen other craft. The *Patra* sank fifty miles from Jeddah, taking with her around 100 souls.

Rasa Sayang
Michaelis Stroubakis (owner), Piraeus
Previous names: *Bergensfjord* (1956–71), *De Grasse* (1971–73), *Rasa Sayang* (1973–78), *Golden Moon* (1978–80).

Builders: Swan Hunter and Wigham Richardson, Newcastle, 1956.
Particulars: 18,739 gross tons, 578ft × 72ft.
Machinery: Stork-type diesels, twin screw, speed 20 knots.
Passengers: 878 one class.

Dates of disasters: 2 June 1977 and 27 August 1980.

Launched on 18 July 1955, the *Bergensfjord* was completed in May 1956, and handed over

Nederland Royal Mail liner, Oranje **(Author's collection).**

to Norwegian American Line who placed her on the Oslo-New York route. In 1971 French Line purchased her to replace the *Antilles*. Renamed *De Grasse*, French Line deployed her on the Le Havre-West Indies service and cruising. A proposed sale to Home Lines and Coral Rivera Ltd in 1973 fell through but the *De Grasse* was sold in that year to Thoresen & Co Ltd, Singapore. After modernization, as the *Rasa Sayang*, she inaugurated fourteen-day cruises from Singapore to Indonesia.

On 2 June 1977, 653 passengers had to abandon the burning *Rasa Sayang* in the Strait of Malacca. The fire started in the forward section of the upper deck but was brought under control twelve hours later, having cost the lives of two crewmen. The *Rasa Sayang* was towed to Singapore and repaired. The vessel was laid-up on 18 June 1978 and offered for sale. Purchased by Sunlit Cruises Ltd, a Cypriot business concern, the *Rasa Sayang* sailed to Piraeus, arriving on 11 December 1978.

After being renamed *Golden Moon* the liner was immediately laid-up at Perama. Finally in July 1980, the liner was sold to Michaelis Stroubakis, who had planned to charter the ship out to CTC Lines of London for cruises out of Sydney. In preparation for that activity, the *Golden Moon* was given her earlier name, *Rasa Sayang*. On 27 August 1980, while undergoing a refit at Perama, an engineroom fire consumed the ship. The *Rasa Sayang* was towed to Kynosoura where she sank in shallow water.

Angelina Lauro
Achille Lauro, Rome

Previous names: *Oranje* (1939-64), *Angelina Lauro* (1964–79)

Builders: Nederlandsche Shipbuilding Co, Amsterdam, 1939.
Particulars: 24,377 gross tons, 674ft × 83ft.
Machinery: Sulzer diesels, triple screw, speed 21 knots.
Passengers: 1,510 First and Second Class, 800 on cruises.

Date of Disaster: 30 March 1979

The *Oranje* was the largest passenger ship ever built and owned by Nederland Royal Mail Line. The *Oranje* introduced new levels of comfort and luxury on the Dutch East Indies route, which she commenced in September 1939. Her commercial activity ceased in December 1939, when she was laid-up. Remaining under the Dutch flag, the *Oranje* entered war service as a

Angelina Lauro *with Costa's funnel colours* **(Luis Miguel Correia).**

The burned out **Angelina Lauro** *in St Thomas with a 25 degree list* **(Courtesy of the** *Steamship* **Historical Society collection/University of Baltimore Library).**

hospital ship in the Royal Australian Navy on 30 July 1941. Returned to Nederland on 19 July 1946, the *Oranje* was given a brief refit then re-entered Amsterdam-Indonesia service.

In 1959, the *Oranje* was thoroughly refitted. Her tonnage was increased from 20,017 to 20,551 and her passenger accommodation restyled to 323 First Class and 626 Tourist Class. On 4 September 1964, Mr Achille Lauro purchased the *Oranje* and had her extensively refitted at Cant del Tierreno, Genoa. During rebuilding, on 24–26 August 1965, six people lost their lives in a large fire. Mr Lauro named his ship, *Angelina Lauro*, and she left the yard at 24,377 tons, lengthened from 656ft to 674ft and with a passenger complement of 189 First Class and 1,427 Tourist Class. Like the *Brittany* and *Fairsea*, the *Angelina Lauro* was placed on the profitable Southampton-Sydney trade in March 1966.

With the implementation of tighter Australian immigration controls, passenger numbers started to decline. In response, Lauro Lines assigned the *Angelina Lauro* to cruising from European and North American ports. To increase her visibility in the American market,

the *Angelina Lauro* was chartered to Costa Armatora SpA in October 1977 for a three-year period. To successfully promote her for the American market Costa marketed her as the *Angelina*.

While in St Thomas on a seven-day cruise, the *Angelina Lauro* was gutted by fire which started in the galley on 30 March 1979. The *Angelina Lauro* took on a 25 degree list to port, causing her hull to settle in 30ft of water alongside the pier. Luckily, most of her 675 passengers were out sightseeing and shopping but the ship was declared a total loss. On 6 July 1979, the *Angelina Lauro* was refloated and, later, was taken under tow by the Japanese tug *Nippon Maru* to Kaohsiung for scrapping. On the way to Kaohsiung, however, on 24 September 1979, the *Angelina Lauro* sank in the Pacific Ocean.

Chapter 9

The sinking eighties

By 1980 the transition from line voyages to cruising was practically complete. The only way to cross now was by jet aircraft.

Despite the advances of modern technology in ship construction, maintenance and navigation, 19 liners met a premature end during this decade. The first ship to ring the bell at Lloyd's was the *Leonardo Da Vinci*. Next was the *Ernesto Anastasio*, followed by the *Prinsendam* on a long, leisurely cruise to the Orient by way of Alaska. Fires, still a plague to ships, brought an end to the *Reina Del Mar, Atlantis, Mediterranean Star, Turkmenia, Priamurye* and *Lavia*. The only ship that was engaged on a line voyage year round was the *Chidambaram*; she suffered a fatal fire, claiming the lives of 40 people.

Terrorism returned to end the trading career of the *Arion*. Groundings, a frequent occurrence during the first 20 years of this century, claimed the *Columbus C, Mikhail Lermontov* and *Logos,* the *Jupiter* sank following a collision, and human error appeared to be the cause of the capsizing of the ferry *Herald of Free Enterprise* off Zeebrugge.

Leonardo Da Vinci
Italia-Società per Azioni di Navigazione, Genoa.

Builders: Ansaldo SpA, Genoa, 1960.

***The well proportioned* Leonardo da Vinci *at anchor in St Thomas* (Author's photograph).**

Above *Showing a little rust, the* Leonardo da Vinci *arrives in New York* (Author's photograph).

Left *The capsized* Leonardo da Vinci (Antonio Scrimali).

Below left *Raised but with her bridge caved in, the* Leonardo da Vinci *awaits demolition* (Antonio Scrimali).

Particulars: 33,340 gross tons, 767ft × 92ft.
Machinery: Four steam turbines geared to twin screws, speed 23 knots.
Passengers: 413 First Class, 342 Cabin Class, 571 Tourist Class.

Date of disaster: 3 July 1980.

The *Leonardo Da Vinci* was built as a replacement for the *Andrea Doria*. The keel was laid on 23 June 1957 with launch occurring on 7 December 1958. After a brief five-day Mediterranean cruise, the sleek and graceful *Leonardo Da Vinci* departed Genoa on 30 June 1960 on her maiden voyage to New York. Passengers were able to enjoy the five open swimming pools on her neatly-terraced after decks and the thirty public rooms done in modern Italian decor. Italy's maritime pride and presence on the Atlantic was again re-established.

Beside her regular transatlantic service between Genoa, Cannes, Naples, Gibraltar and New York, the *Leonardo Da Vinci* was also employed in cruising. To make her more suitable for that role and to match her with her larger running mates, the *Michelangelo* and *Raffaello,* the *Leonardo* was given a white hull. Four unusual cruises made by the *Leonardo Da Vinci* were: a January 1970 31-day Rio cruise, a February 1970 41-day Hawaiian cruise, a January 1972 49-day African Safari cruise and a July 1975 23-day North Cape cruise.

In 1974 the *Leonardo Da Vinci* was switched from a three-class vessel carrying 1,326 passengers to two classes carrying 1,284. In June 1976 the *Leonardo Da Vinci* made the last Italian Line departure from New York when she left at 11:30 am on the 27th for Naples. In July 1977 the ship was transferred to Italian Line Cruises International for three- and four-day Port Everglades-Nassau cruises. Unsuccessful out of Port Everglades, the *Leonardo Da Vinci* returned to Italy and was laid-up at La Spezia on 23 September 1978 and offered for sale.

On 3 July 1980 fire broke out in the chapel, which quickly swept through the entire liner. *Leonardo Da Vinci* was towed outside La Spezia where the fire was allowed to burn itself out. The unfortunate ship eventually heeled over on her port side with a 60 degree list. The charred liner was raised by 3 March 1981,

minus her bridge, and on 1 January 1982 scrapping commenced.

Ernesto Anastasio
Compania Transmediterránea SA, Madrid

Builders: Union Naval de Levante, Valencia, 1955.
Particulars: 7,295 gross tons, 413ft x 55ft.
Machinery: Burmeister & Wain type diesels, twin screw, speed 18 knots.
Passengers: 113 First Class, 60 Second Class, 60 Third Class.

Date of disaster: 24 April 1980.

The *Ernesto Anastasio* was designed for the express service between Spain and the Canary Islands.

Shortly after leaving Pasajes for Villagareia on 24 April 1980, the *Ernesto Anastasio* ran aground. Upon arrival and examination in Bilbao, she was cited beyond economic repair and was sold for scrap.

Prinsendam
Holland America Cruises, Rotterdam

Builders: De Merwede Shipyards, Hardinxveld, 1973.
Particulars: 8,566 gross tons, 427ft x 62ft.
Machinery: Werkspor-type diesels, twin screw, speed 21 knots.
Passengers: 375 First Class.

Date of disaster: 4 October 1980.

Transmediterránea's Ernesto Anastasio (Courtesy of the Steamship Historical Society collection/ University of Baltimore Library).

***The* Prinsendam *was built specifically for the Indonesian cruise trade* (Holland America Cruises).**

This mini cruise liner was the first ship to be built with the Indonesian cruise service in mind. Launched on 7 July 1972, the *Prinsendam* suffered a fatal fire on 24 April 1973 when a blaze destroyed her passenger accommodation and most of her superstructure. Following repairs, Holland America took delivery of their new ship on 12 November 1973. The *Prinsendam* departed Rotterdam for Singapore, her new home base, on 30 November 1973, and embarked on her first cruise around the Indonesian archipelago on 14 January 1974. The *Prinsendam*'s first year of operation, particularly the summer season, was not successful and HAC

***The fire damaged* Prinsendam *in the Gulf of Alaska* (US Coast Guard).**

switched the *Prinsendam* to the more profitable Alaskan summer cruise trade out of Vancouver. For the next five years, the *Prinsendam* was based out of Singapore in the winters and Vancouver in the summers.

In the late autumn of 1980, 320 passengers boarded the *Prinsendam* in Vancouver for a 29-day positioning cruise to Singapore which the company's brochure described as '...the cruising adventure you're likely to remember the longest'. On 4 October 1980, in the Gulf of Alaska, fire broke out in one of the *Prinsendam*'s main engines around 12:30 am. The crew sealed the area and sprayed carbon dioxide into the flames, but when the crew opened the area, the fire was found to be spreading. A radio message was sent out at 1:08 am, and a rescue team was quickly assembled and despatched to the scene: included were helicopters, units of the United

States Coast Guard and the supertanker, *Williamsburgh*.

Passengers were asked to assemble in the lounge, while firefighting efforts continued below. When these efforts failed and the fire eliminated electrical power, water pressure and all firefighting capabilities, Captain Cornelius Wabeke gave the order at 5:15 am to abandon ship. All passengers and the majority of the crew calmly boarded the lifeboats, from which they were later rescued by the *Williamsburgh* and US Coast Guard vessels. Fifty crew members volunteered to remain with the Captain in a further attempt to save their ship but by 4:00 pm the fire was raging out of control and the remaining crew also abandoned the vessel. The survivors were landed along Alaska's coastal towns.

Attention now turned to salvaging the burning hulk. An attempt to tow the *Prinsendam* to Portland, Oregon was made on 7 October by the tug, *Commodore Straits*. As the days progressed, the situation of the *Prinsendam* grew worse. On 9 October she was listing 15 degrees, taking on water and rolling. Winds of 25 knots did not aid rescue efforts. By 10 October the deck fires were extinguished, but the fire was still raging deep inside the vessel. In addition, the list increased to 35 degrees with the bow going under. The *Commodore Straits* cut her tow off, and on the next morning at 8:35 am, the *Prinsendam* sank 79 miles west of Sitka in position 55°53' N, 136°27' W.

Reina Del Mar
Dolphi (Hellas) Shipping, Piraeus
Previous names: *Ocean Monarch* (1951–67), *Varna* (1967–78)

Builders: Vickers-Armstrong Ltd, Newcastle, 1951.
Particulars: 13,581 gross tons, 516ft × 73ft.

Completely abandoned, the **Prinsendam** *is left to nature* (**US Coast Guard**).

Machinery: Parsons geared turbines, twin screw, speed 18 knots.
Passengers: 600 one class.

Date of disaster: 28 May 1981.

The *Ocean Monarch* was specifically designed and built for Furness Withy's New York to Bermuda service, which she started on 3 May 1951. In September 1966, the *Ocean Monarch* was laid-up on the River Fal. Within a year, in August 1967, the ship was sold to Balkanturist, a Bulgarian company, and renamed *Varna*. As the *Varna* she was chartered to SS Gala Cruises in 1970 for Saguenay Summer cruises from Montreal. The liner was subsequently chartered to March Shipping for the 1971 and '72 summer

Reina Del Mar *gets up steam on 27 May 1981* (**James Shaw**).

Reina Del Mar *burns off Salamina Island on 28 May 1981* (James Shaw).

seasons on the same cruises. The *Varna* changed charterers in 1973 to Sovereign Cruises for a series of cruises, but only two were made. The ship was then laid-up.

In 1978 the *Varna* was purchased by Dolphin Shipping who intended to rename her *Rivera*. They scheduled her first cruise for 19 July 1979. The deal fell through and the ship languished until spring 1981, when it was announced by Dolphin that they would rename her *Reina Del Mar* and despatch her on a series of Mediterranean cruises in 1981.

During renovations in preparation for her upcoming cruises, a fire started in the boiler room and quickly spread to the engineroom and to her passenger accommodation. The blaze totally destroyed the *Reina Del Mar* off the ship repair yard at Perama on 28 May 1981. Completely gutted, with her superstructure caved in, the *Reina Del Mar* was towed near the burnt out *Rasa Sayang*, where she rolled over and sank on 31 May.

An attempt is made to tow the burning **Reina Del Mar** *from the rocks* (James Shaw).

Syria
Egyptian Navigation Company Ltd, Alexandria

Builders: Deutsche Werft AG, Hamburg, 1962.
Particulars: 4,423 gross tons, 354ft x 55ft.
Machinery: MAN diesels, single screw, speed 15.5 knots.
Passengers: 30 First Class, 108 Second Class, 400 Third (Deck) Class.

Date of disaster: 20 August 1981.

The *Syria* and her sister-ship, the *Algazayer,* were built for Egypt's Mediterranean service between Alexandria, Beirut, Piraeus and Venice. The *Syria* was equipped with a swimming pool, and Third Class was accommodated in four dormitories.

During a voyage from Piraeus to Alexandria, the *Syria* was stranded on the north-east coast of Crete on 20 August 1981. Her 300 passengers were evacuated, and the ship was relocated eight days later. She sustained extensive hull damage and was withdrawn from service. Within a year, the company ceased its passenger service in the Mediterranean.

The Egyptian liner Syria (James Shaw).

Arion
Maritime Company of Lesvos, Mytilini
Previous names: *Nili* (1965–67), *Jamaica Queen* (1967-69), *Nili* (1969–75).

Builders: Fairfield Shipbuilding & Engineering Co Ltd, Glasgow, 1965.
Particulars: 6,400 gross tons, 450ft x 62ft.
Machinery: Sulzer diesels, twin screw, speed 20 knots.
Passengers: 544 one class, 120 vehicles.

Date of disaster: 20 December 1981.

The *Nili* was originally built for the Societé Mercantile of Financière SA (Switzerland), but was handed over to Somerfin Passenger Lines, an Israeli firm, during the early phase of construction. Within two years she was sold to Zim Lines, another Israeli firm, who retained her name and kept her on the Israel, Greece and Italy run. In September 1967, she was sold for $6.4 million to AG Weston Enterprises and renamed *Jamaica Queen* for the cruise trade between Miami and Jamaica, under the American representative of Continental Cruise Lines. She was returned to Zim Lines in 1969 and resumed her old route with her original name. Zim Lines left the passenger business and sold the ship to Maritime Company of Lesvos. They

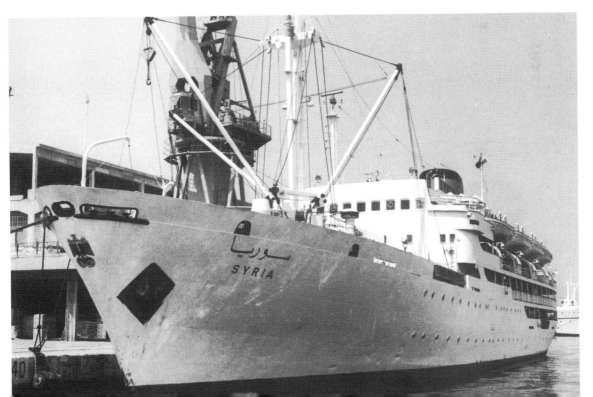

Continental Cruise Lines' **Jamaica Queen** (Author's collection).

in turn changed her name to *Arion* and placed her on the Piraeus-Haifa route.

On approaching Haifa from Limassol on 20 December 1981, an explosion in one of her cabins was followed by a fire. The *Arion* managed to berth at the new quay outside the harbour to disembark her passengers; then she was towed away from the berth and beached so the fire could burn itself out. Gutted, she heeled over onto her side and settled at a 33 degree list to starboard. The *Arion* was refloated on 13 January and towed into the harbour to discharge the cars still on board. Abandoned by her owners, the *Arion* was moved to Haifa on 20

The charred superstructure of the **Arion** *at Piraeus* (Antonio Scrimali).

March 1983. It is heavily suspected that the cause of the initial explosion was a terrorist bomb.

Mediterranean Star
Karageogris Lines, Piraeus

Previous names: *Bloemfontein Castle* (1950–59), *Patris* (1959–79), *Mediterranean Island* (1979–81).

Builders: Harland & Wolff, Belfast, 1950.
Particulars: 16,259 gross tons, 595ft x 77ft.
Machinery: Burmeister & Wain diesels, twin screw, speed 18.5 knots.
Passengers: 1,403 one class, 250 vehicles.

Date of disaster: 28 August 1982.

The *Bloemfontein Castle* was one of many post-war units built by Union Castle for their London-Beira service. Considered surplus, Union Castle sold her in 1959 to Chandris Line. Renamed *Patris*, the ship was refitted as an emigrant carrier for the Australian service, with berths for 1,403 passengers. Out of 473 cabins, only one had private facilities. The first voyage commenced from Piraeus on 14 December 1959.

As immigration to Australia declined, the *Patris* was switched to cruising from Australian ports. A tropical storm devastated Darwin in 1975 and the *Patris* was chosen to serve as an

accommodation ship from February to November. In 1979 the *Patris* was sold to Karageogris Lines who refitted her and renamed her *Mediterranean Island*. She was renamed again by Karageogris in 1981 to *Mediterranean Star*, and was employed on the Greece-Italy ferry service.

On 28 August 1982, en route from Patras, Greece, to Ancona, Italy, with some 1,000 passengers aboard, the *Mediterranean Star* suffered a serious fire in the engineroom. All passengers and some of the crew swiftly and safely abandoned the liner. The remaining crew stayed on board to extinguish the flames. The ship subsequently sailed on her own power to Perama. Over-capacity on the route and her age forced the company to hold off repairs. For some years considered a loss, she returned to service in July 1986 under charter to the Egyptians. Sold to Pakistani scrappers in 1987, she was delivered to Gadani Beach that October as the *Terra*.

Atlantis
K-Hellenic Lines, Piraeus
Previous name: *Adonis* (1965–76)

Builders: Cantiers Ruiniti dell' Adricatico, Monfalcone, 1965.
Particulars: 4,505 gross tons, 318ft x 52ft.
Machinery: Sulzer-type diesels, twin screw, speed 17 knots.

The former emigrant carrier, then ferry, Mediterranean Star (Antonio Scrimali).

Passengers: 332 Cruising.

Date of disaster: 7 March 1983.

The *Adonis* was one of three ships built for the Greek inter-island trade being first chartered to Nomikos Lines, then transferred in 1966 to K-Hellenic. In 1976 the *Adonis* underwent extensive refitting and emerged as the cruise ship *Atlantis* employed from Piraeus on cruises to the Greek Isles and Turkey.

At around 5:30 pm on 7 March 1983, when the *Atlantis* was undergoing outfitting at Xaveri Dock in Piraeus in preparation for her summer season, a fire broke out in her passenger accommodation. The *Atlantis* was towed out of the harbour to an anchorage where the fire was allowed to burn itself out. The liner was subsequently laid-up, then sold to Greek shipbreakers in July 1983.

Columbus C
Costa Armatori, Genoa
Previous name: *Kungsholm* (1953–64), *Europa* (1964–81)

Builders: 'De Schelde', NV, Koninklijke Mij, Vlissingen, 1953.
Particulars: 16,317 gross tons, 600ft x 77ft.

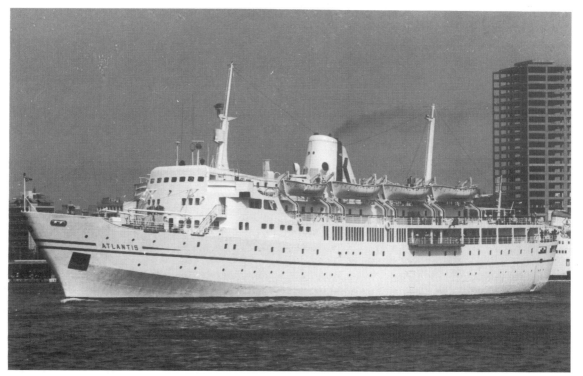

Atlantis *sailing from Piraeus* **(Luis Miguel Correia).**

Machinery: Burmeister & Wain diesels, twin screw, speed 19 knots.
Passengers: 785 First Class.

Date of disaster: 29 July 1984.

The *Columbus C* sailed for two distinguished companies before joining the Costa family. As

The burned out Atlantis *is laid up pending disposal* **(Antonio Scrimali).**

the *Kungsholm* she plied the Atlantic for Swedish America Line, as well as cruising the world. In 1964 the *Kungsholm* was sold to North German Lloyd, who took delivery on 16 October 1965. Three months later, on 9 January 1966, she sailed from Bremerhaven to New York as the *Europa*. Summers were spent on the transatlantic run and winters on cruises, but lack of transatlantic voyagers eventually led Hapag-Lloyd to use the *Europa* solely for cruises. In anticipation of the delivery of a new luxury cruise ship, Hapag sold the *Europa* to Costa. That company too employed her as a cruise liner, under the new name of *Columbus C*.

Nearing the end of a Mediterranean cruise that originated from Genoa, the *Columbus C* holed herself when she was blown against an underwater breakwater spur while docking at Cádiz, Spain on 29 July 1984. She made it to the dock and disembarked her 620 passengers but subsequently, with her engineroom flooded, she settled at the dock with a 25 degree list to starboard. Refloated on 2 November 1984, the *Columbus C* was returned to her owners five

days later. She lay waiting at Cadiz until March 1985 when Costa decided to sell her, after which the *Columbus C* departed under tow for Spanish shipbreakers.

Chidambaram
Shipping Corporation of India, Bombay
Previous name: *Pasteur* (1966–72).

Builders: Ateliers et Chantiers de Dunkirk et Bordeaux, Dunkirk, 1966.
Particulars: 17,226 gross tons, 571ft x 79ft.
Machinery: Sulzer diesels, twin screw, speed 20 knots.

Costa's **Columbus C** *entering Lisbon* (Luis Miguel Correia).

Passengers: 152 First Class, 1,526 in dormitories (three grades).

Date of disaster: 12 February 1985.

The *Pasteur* was the last passenger ship built for the one-time giant firm of Messageries Maritimes. Originally she was ordered in 1963 for M M Australian service and given the

The **Columbus C,** *minus her aft mast, settled on the bottom at Cadiz* (William H. Miller Jr).

Chidambaram *docked at Singapore* (Author's photograph).

tentative name of *Australien*. However, she was renamed before launching and upon completion, placed on the Europe–South American run. The *Pasteur* could not match the speed of jet aircraft, and once the French government decided to sink all its funds into the airlines (Air France and UTA, with the former introducing Concorde service from Paris to Rio), M M had no choice but to withdraw the *Pasteur* from service.

Placed on the selling block, she was purchased in 1972 by the Shipping Corporation of India, who sailed her to Amsterdam for a refit. She left the shipyard with the name *Chidambaram*, one of the pioneers in India's maritime development, in March 1973, and made her first voyage on her new route from Madras to Singapore in April 1973. There were no changes made in the First Class accommodation, but dormitory accommodation was introduced in lieu of other classes. This consisted of three grades: grade one being four, six and eight-berth cabins; grade two consisting of cubicles for ten persons each with attached shower; and bunk, a large compartment housing between 50–100 people. Westerners were not allowed to book passage in the last two grades.

During the afternoon of Tuesday, 12 February 1985, some 300 miles east of Madras, a fire in her B-Deck galley broke out and spread rapidly to C-Deck dormitory quarters while the *Chidambaram* was en route from Singapore to Madras with 702 passengers aboard and a crew of 186. After a sixteen-hour battle the blaze was brought under control, and the ship limped into

Madras on 14 February. The dazed passengers (half were quartered in the area of the blaze) and crew streamed ashore, among them 100 injured. Forty persons did not survive the ordeal and were carried ashore covered in white sheets. It is interesting to note that the *Chidambaram* was described in the newspapers as a 'cruise ship'.

It was disclosed that the *Chidambaram* was to be retired in June 1985, due to high operating costs, and replaced with another vessel. This fire obviously sealed her fate, and she became the last ship to have performed a year-round line voyage. She was delivered to scrappers in Bombay in April 1985.

Mikhail Lermontov
Baltic Shipping Co, Leningrad

Builders: V.E.B. Mathias-Thesen Werft, Wismar, East Germany, 1972.
Particulars: 20,027 gross tons, 577ft x 77ft.
Machinery: Sulzer diesels, twin screw, speed 21 knots.
Passengers: 700 one class.

Date of disaster: 16 February 1986.

The *Mikhail Lermontov* was the last of a quintet of Soviet 19,000 ton liners delivered between 1965 and 1972, designed for both cruise service and line voyages. Completed in February 1972, the *Mikhail Lermontov* was sent cruising from Europe in the spring, before embarking on a summer programme of transatlantic summer voyages between Leningrad and Montreal. On 28 May 1973 *Mikhail Lermontov* departed Leningrad, and after calls at Bremerhaven, London and Le Havre, she proceeded to New York, arriving on 11 June, becoming the first Soviet liner to call there in 25 years. The *Mikhail Lermontov* continued to serve New York during the summers, with winters spent cruising out of European ports. In 1980 President Reagan retaliated against the Soviets for their invasion of Afghanistan. This resulted in a banning of all Soviet ships entering US waters and the *Mikhail Lermontov* was switched to cruising out of Europe.

Considering the date when the *Mikhail*

Lermontov was completed, more than half her cabins were without modern facilities. To make her more suitable for cruising the Soviets spent $15 million on her in 1982 to bring her up to a competitive standard. All cabins were fitted with private facilities, all public rooms and spaces were renovated, and the exterior was painted white.

Under the command of Captain Vladislav Vorobyev, the *Mikhail Lermontov* departed Wellington, New Zealand with 409 passengers for a South Pacific cruise. On Sunday night, 16 February 1986 in stormy seas, the *Mikhail Lermontov* struck a rock in Cook Strait, off Port Gore in New Zealand and tore a hole in her hull. The crippled liner took on a 12° list and drifted into Port Gore harbour where Captain Vorobyev tried to beach his ship. However, the *Mikhail Lermontov* then drifted back offshore and sank in about 100 feet of water. All passengers and 229 members of the crew were rescued. One crew member was listed as missing and presumed to have drowned.

The Soviets blamed the New Zealand pilot, Captain Don Jamison for taking a route where there were no indications of depth shown on the chart. The New Zealand government counter-charged that the charts were more than adequate and that Captain Jamison returned control of the ship to Captain Vorobyev well before it hit the rock.

The Mikhail Lermontov *departing New York* (Author's photograph).

Uganda
British India Steam Navigation Co Ltd, London

Builders: Barclay Curle & Company Ltd, Glasgow, Scotland, 1952.
Particulars: 16,907 gross tons, 540ft x 71ft.
Machinery: Steam turbines, twin screw, speed 16 knots.
Passengers: 306 adults, 920 students.

Date of disaster: 22 August 1986.

Even the very end of a final voyage can be tragic, and so it was for the 16,907-ton *Uganda*.

The Uganda, *the last of Britain's educational cruise ships, laid up in the River Fal* (P&O Group).

Notably, she was Britain's last colonial passenger ship as well as one of the most beloved and popular cruise ships. Built at Glasgow and completed in August 1952, the *Uganda* was designed especially for the London-East Africa run — London via Gibraltar or Naples, Port Said and Aden to Mombasa, Tanga, Zanzibar, Dar-es-Salaam, Beira and Durban — carrying 299 passengers (190 in First Class, 109 in Tourist) and considerable freight. She and a sister, the *Kenya* (this ship having a noticeably smaller funnel), ran the service until the mid-'60s, but by then their trade had fallen away — the passengers mostly to aircraft, the freight to new container ships and emergent Third World tonnage. The *Uganda* was retired first, in the spring of 1967.

After extensive rebuilding at Hamburg she resumed sailing, but as a schools' cruise ship, carrying 306 adults in cabins and 920 students in large dormitories. British India had restarted its pre-Second World War educational cruising with two smaller passenger ships, the *Dunera* and the *Devonia,* so, together with the newer, larger *Nevasa* (a former troopship), the *Uganda* would strengthen this service. Mostly she made two-week cruises from various British ports to Scandinavia, Northern Europe, the Scottish isles, Iberia and the Mediterranean. She became a huge success, loved by students and teachers as well as the older, adult passengers.

The *Uganda* was hurriedly called to Government duty during the Falklands War in May 1982, and was fitted out at the Royal Navy's Dockyard at Gibraltar as an all-white-painted, Red Cross-marked hospital ship. Then in September, after heroic service in South Atlantic waters, she resumed cruising. However, economic realities were increasingly harsh towards this ageing ship and her dwindling clientele.

She resumed British Government service in June 1983 and ran supply sailings between Ascension Island and the Falklands. Once this two-year charter was completed, the scarred, rusted, well-worn ship was decommissioned and sent to lay up in Cornwall's River Fal to await her fate. A preservationist group was formed with hopes of saving her as a museum, but again the economics wielded a decisive blow.

As expected she was sold to Taiwanese scrappers, but through an intermediary firm who renamed her *Triton* for the final voyage from Falmouth out to the East. She reached Kaohsiung, but then, on 22 August 1986, while awaiting a slip at the breaker's yard, she was lashed by typhoon 'Wayne' and capsized. Since broken in half, she lies on her side to this day — a sad reminder of one of Britain's finest passenger ships.

Admiral Nakhimov
Black Sea Shipping Company
Previous name: *Berlin* 1925–49

Builders: Bremer Vulkan, Vegesack, 1925.
Particulars: 17,053 gross tons, 572ft x 69ft.
Machinery: Triple-expansion engines, twin screw, speed 16 knots.
Passengers: 870 one class.

Date of disaster: 31 August 1986.

Completed in 1925 for North German Lloyd's Bremen-Southampton-New York service, the *Berlin* was capable of carrying 1,122 passengers in three classes. This figure was reduced in 1929 to 879. The *Berlin* remained on the North Atlantic until she was laid up at Bremerhaven in 1938. During one crossing in 1928 she was present to rescue 23 survivors from the sinking *Vestris*.

In May 1939 she undertook two cruises for the 'Kraft durch Freude' ('Strength through Joy'), then on 17 July 1939 she suffered a boiler explosion off Swinemunde in which seventeen men were killed. She was taken over by the German Navy in 1939 and fitted out as a naval hospital ship at Hamburg. In 1944 she became an accommodation ship, and as such was sunk after hitting a mine off Swinemunde on 1 February 1945.

The *Berlin* was seized by the Soviets, raised in 1949 and named *Admiral Nakhimov*, after a Czarist naval commander who was killed in the Crimean War in 1855. The 'Admiral' was towed to Warnow yard at Warnemunde where she was rebuilt. After eight years of work, a rather long time for any ship, the *Admiral Nakhimov* was handed over to the Black Sea Shipping Company to operate between Odessa, her home port, and Batumi. Her ports of call were Sevastapol, Yalta, Novorossisk, Sochi, Sukhumi and Batumi. Up until the 1970s anyone could book passage but once new Soviet ships appeared, the *Admiral Nakhimov* became off limits to non-Soviet citizens. One Western eye-witness who visited the ship in 1981 said her interiors fittings were restored to their original state, and that inside and out she was meticulously maintained.

The *Admiral Nakhimov* was on a voyage between Odessa and Batumi, as part of a cruise for 'good' Soviet citizens, when misfortune struck on 31 August 1986. The *Admiral Nakhimov* departed Novorossisk at 11:30 that night with 888 passengers and a crew of 346. In command was Captain Vadim G. Marko. Forty-five minutes later, the '*Admiral*' was rammed on the starboard side by the Soviet bulk carrier *Pyotr Vasev*, which had failed to heed warnings of an imminent collision. The impact ripped open a gash between the engine and boiler rooms, and the *Admiral Nakhimov* took on a list and started to sink. Fifteen minutes later, the venerable liner was under the sea. Survivors clung to life-rafts and other floating objects in the choppy, oil-covered sea until rescue craft arrived, shortly after the collision due to the

accident's proximity to land. Of those aboard 836 survived, including the Captain: 79 bodies were recovered and 319 were listed as missing and presumed dead.

What was really surprising about this incident was the speed (within 48 hours after the sinking) with which the Soviet government released the details. Usually the Soviet government preferred to withhold information on major accidents in their waters, but this policy was changing under Mikhail Gorbachev.

Turkmenia
Far East Shipping Co, Vladivostock

Builders: V. E. B. Mathias-Thesen Werft, Wismar, East Germany, 1961.
Particulars: 4,720 gross tons, 401ft × 52ft.
Machinery: MAN diesels, twin screw, speed 18 knots.
Passengers: Approx 333 one-class passengers.

Date of disaster: 12 November 1986.

Fire at sea is amongst a shipowner's worst nightmares: loss of ship, and — more importantly — loss of life, is often quite likely. In a stretch of great misfortune, the Soviets had lost their *Mikhail Lermontov*, one of their biggest and finest liners, in February 1986; the aged *Admiral Nakhimov* quickly sank after a collision seven months later,

The ill-fated **Turkmenia** *anchored off Singapore during a cruise visit on 8 March 1983 (V. H. Young & L. A. Sawyer).*

in August; then, less than three months after that, their *Turkmenia* burned out in the western Pacific.

Running a 'youth cruise' with hundreds of students aboard at the time, the little *Turkmenia* was one of 18 sister and near-sister ships built by the Soviet Government in an East German shipyard. Headed by the *Mikhail Kalinin*, they ranked as the largest single class of deep-sea passenger ships anywhere, and also as the first brand new Soviet passenger ships in some 30 years.

Their operations were quite diverse: the Baltic and Black Sea routes, the Far East from Vladivostock down to Japan and Hong Kong, technical and military exchange voyages to the likes of Cuba, Indonesia and East Africa, and research and supply trips to the Arctic and Antarctic.

The *Turkmenia* spent almost all of her days in Far Eastern waters, being a rather familiar sight on the waterfronts of Yokohama, Kobe and Hong Kong. She carried regular passengers, including many on the Trans-Siberian Railway link from Moscow, as well as Government-sponsored travellers. She also made occasional cruises, visiting the South Pacific, Australia and New Zealand. While little actual detail is known

about this tragedy, it did spell the end of her sailing days. Towed back to Siberia, she was retired and reduced to a storage vessel.

Herald of Free Enterprise
P&O/Townsend Thoresen Ferry Co

Builders: Schichau, Unterweser AG, Bremerhaven, Germany, 1980.
Particulars: 7,951 gross tons, 131.91m x 23.19m, 433ft x 74.5ft
Machinery: 3 x 12 cylinder geared diesels by Sulzer Bros, speed 22 knots.
Passengers: 50 berthed, 1,300 unberthed.

Date of disaster: 6 March 1987.

Generally we have not included ferry disasters in this book. However, two made worldwide press and most likely will remain in the public's memory for some time to come. The first of these tragedies involved the illustrious P&O Group, which just three weeks before had taken over the Townsend Thoresen Ferry Company. Their *Herald of Free Enterprise* was being used on the Zeebrugge-Dover run at the time.

The ship had left for Dover at 19:00 local time when, some 45 minutes later, an at first

Tugs are moored alongside the ferry Herald of Free Enterprise, which capsized just after leaving the Belgian port of Zeebrugge (David Caulkin/Associated Press).

unexplained rush of water through the bow loading doors caused the ship to roll over on its port side in less than a minute. She had just cleared the then new outer breakwater at Zeebrugge, and in an extrordinarily fast rescue effort, coordinated between the local Belgian authorities (using helicopters as well as dozens of different craft), 408 passengers and crew were promptly rescued from the upturned hull of the vessel. In addition, 50 bodies were recovered almost immediately; another 120 victims were trapped on board, so salvage started almost immediately. Smit International, the well-known Dutch salvage firm, took on the project.

Weeks later, following extensive investigations and government inquiries, Townsend Thoresen was found to be fully responsible for this accident. The ship had gone to sea with her bow doors still open, and this had caused the immediate flooding of the entire car deck, and the ship's capsizing. By July the ship had been righted and moved to the naval base at Zeebrugge. In the final accounting, 197 had perished.

Once temporarily repaired, the ship was renamed *Flushing Range*, but rumours of her being rebuilt or even sold for further passenger service proved false. Under tow, she reached Kaohsiung in the winter of 1987 and was scrapped.

Logos
Educational Books Exhibit Ltd, British-based but Singapore flag
Previous name: *Umanak* (1949–70).

Builders: Elsinore Shipbuilding & Engineering Co, Elsinore, Denmark, 1949.
Particulars: 2,319 gross tons, 279ft x 44ft.
Machinery: B&W diesel, single screw, speed 10 knots.
Passengers: 62 one-class passengers (as built).

Date of disaster: 5 January 1988.

She was certainly amongst the world's most unusually specialised ships: a floating 'missionary book fair'. Owned by a West German evangelical group named Operation Mobilisation, but run by British Educational Books Ltd, based in Kent, she flew the Singapore flag and was rather appropriately named *Logos* — 'living word'. Historically, she had been the first post-Second World War passenger ship to be built for Denmark's State

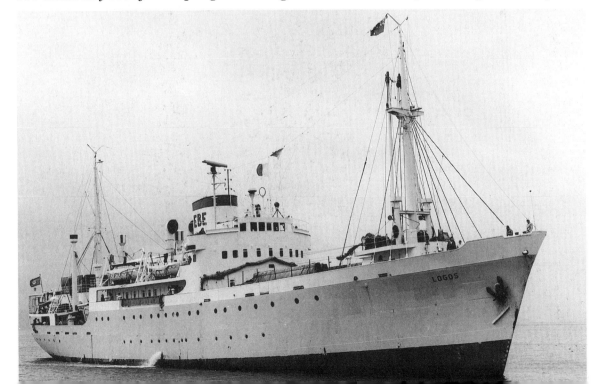

The 'missionary book fair' ship Logos at Wellington on 4 October 1979 (V. H. Young & L. A. Sawyer).

Smoke spews from the blazing **Priamurye** *after fire broke out while she was berthed at Osaka (Popperfoto/Reuter).*

Administration for the then colonial run between Copenhagen and ports in Greenland. With a special ice-strengthened hull, she had space for 62 passengers in a single class, as well as cargo. She was sold to Operation Mobilisation in 1970.

Logos met an untimely end when she was rounding the southern tip of South America, the Beagle Channel, which separates Chile and Argentina, en route from Ushuaia to Puerto Madryn, bound for a half-year tour of Argentine ports. Minus the customary Channel pilots (who had departed the ship early because of bad weather conditions), she struck a rock after midnight on 5 January 1988, ran aground and was soon declared a complete loss. The 135 passengers and crew were all rescued by the Chilean Navy, but her cherished cargo, some 200 tons of books, was lost.

Priamurye
Far East Shipping Co, Vladivostock

Builders: V. E. B. Mathias-Thesen Werft, Wismar, East Germany, 1961.
Particulars: 4,871 gross tons, 401ft x 52ft.
Machinery: MAN diesels, twin screw, speed 18 knots.
Passengers: Approx 333 one-class passengers.

Date of disaster: 18 May 1988.

Dockside fires can be as dangerous as those at sea. Flames can spread quickly, passengers and crew can be trapped aboard, and firefighters' water can often capsize and sometimes ruin a ship.

Soviet passenger ship misfortune continued when a fourth ship was lost within little more than two years. While on a special cruise from Vladivostock to Japanese ports sponsored by the Communist Youth League, the Priamurye caught fire at her Osaka berth. Her crew delayed calling Japanese fire units and

subsequently the blaze spread, finally taking 18 hours to bring under control; 11 of the 295 passengers perished. With the entire bridge and forward superstructure gutted, the ship — which had already been earmarked for early retirement — was towed away by a Soviet tug 11 days later. It is believed that she was broken up.

Jupiter
Epirotiki Lines, Piraeus
Previous name: *Moledet* (1961–71).

Builders: Chantiers de L'Atlantique, St Nazaire, France, 1961.
Particulars: 7,811 gross tons, 415ft x 65ft.
Machinery: S.E.M.T.-Pielstick diesel, single screw, speed 16 knots.

For a short time in the early 1970s the 7,811-ton **Jupiter** *was the largest passenger ship in the Epirotiki Lines fleet. She is seen while visiting Malta during a cruise* **(Michael Cassar).**

Passengers: 473 cruise passengers.

Date of disaster: 21 October 1988.

Collisions between ships can often have deadly results. The victim on this occasion, the *Jupiter,* had been built in 1961 at the big Chantiers de L'Atlantique shipyard at St Nazaire; in fact, just as the mighty *France* was being completed alongside. Then owned by Israel's state shipping company, the Zim Lines, she was named *Moledet;* designed to carry 596 passengers, all of them in Tourist Class, she was used on the Mediterranean migrant and tourist run between Marseille and Haifa.

With soaring Israeli operational costs against

a gradually declining trade, she was sold in 1971 to Epirotiki. Thoroughly refitted and refurbished as a cruise ship, she now carried 473 passengers, all in First Class quarters, on weekly Aegean Sea cruises from the Greek port of Piraeus in summer and on Caribbean voyages in winter. Unusually she sailed with two names — *Jupiter* was her known and cruising name, but *Zeus* was painted on the stern. (Another Epirotiki cruise ship, the little *Neptune*, has the name *Poseidon* on her stern).

Laid up in 1986 during the Mediterranean cruise slump following the terrorist hijacking of the *Achille Lauro*, the *Jupiter* later resumed cruising and charter sailings; her student sailings were in fact something of a successor to the educational cruises of the previously-mentioned *Uganda*. On 21 October 1988, just outside the port of Piraeus, the *Jupiter* was rammed by an Italian car-carrier, the 5,054-ton *Adige*, and sank within 40 minutes. It could have been a major tragedy since she was running an educational cruise charter and was carrying 500 British schoolchildren and their teachers, but only four lives were lost; the others were rescued quickly by harbour craft and other ships. With a large gash in her hull, the *Jupiter* remains in her watery grave outside the harbour.

Lavia
Virtue Shipping Co, Panama
Previous names: *Media* (1947–61), *Flavia* (1961–82), *Flavian* (1982–86).

Builders: John Brown & Company Ltd, Clydebank, Scotland, 1947.
Particulars: 15,465 gross tons, 556ft x 70ft.
Machinery: Steam turbines, twin screw, speed 18 knots.
Passengers: 1,120 maximum cruise passengers.

Date of disaster: 7 January 1989.

The reconditioning and repairing of ships, whether at a shipyard or a harbour anchorage, can be quite perilous. Delays complicated by deadlines can cause haste and sometimes carelessness, and fire is a frequent fate. So it was with the passenger ship *Lavia*, the former

Cunarder *Media* and later the Italian *Flavia*.

She was to be the Atlantic run's first brand new passenger ship since the Second World War. Built by the illustrious John Brown shipyard on the Clyde, she was actually planned as a freighter for a Cunard subsidiary, the Port Line, but the building contract was soon swung over to the parent firm, and she was redesigned as the 250-passenger, all-First Class *Media*. Along with lots of freight, she ran the Liverpool-New York service, beginning in August 1947; a twin sister, the *Parthia*, arrived in the following spring.

While she was the first Atlantic passenger ship as well as the first Cunarder to be fitted with fin stabilisers (in 1953), the first jets stole away her passengers, and bigger, faster freighters her cargo by the late '50s. Withdrawn by Cunard in 1961, she was sold to Italy's Cogedar Line for the still booming Australian migrant and around-the-world tourist trades. Gutted and completely rebuilt at Genoa, she was given new public rooms, lido decks, an extended bow and cabins for 1,320 passengers, all Tourist Class. As the renamed *Flavia*, she usually made 2½-month circumnavigations of the globe.

By 1968, as Cogedar was absorbed into the Costa Line fleet, the *Flavia* was reassigned to twice-weekly cruises between Miami, Nassau and Freeport. She was very popular, but in 1982, with her ageing turbines, she was sold to Hong Kong-Chinese owners, supposedly to become a 'casino cruise ship'. Renamed *Flavian*, she barely left her Hong Kong moorings.

Renamed again, as the *Lavia*, in 1986, she was finally being refitted when, in January 1989, a workers' fire erupted and quickly engulfed the old passenger quarters. Thirty-five workers and the ship's nine-man crew escaped, but the ship itself was damaged beyond repair. Four fireboats and 270 firemen using 22 water cannons battled the blaze. Overloaded with water, the *Lavia* capsized, ironically not far from where her former fleetmate, the *Queen Elizabeth* (then known as the *Seawise University*), had met her end 16 years earlier. The *Lavia* was later refloated and towed across to Kaohsiung, Taiwan, for scrapping.

A sad view of the fire-damaged Lavia, *with a fireboat alongside the still smouldering ship* (Bert Novelli Collection).

Half sunk in Hong Kong harbour, the Lavia *was later righted and sold to Taiwan scrappers* (Andrew Kilk Collection).

Chapter 10

The fateful nineties

In the passenger ship business, the 1990s is the age of cruise ships and ferries, bigger and better than ever. While 70,000-ton leisure liners now seem almost commonplace, the first 100,000-tonners are under way as we go to press. These are the first passenger ships to exceed the long-standing record of the original *Queen Elizabeth* at 83,673 gross tons. In the Baltic the largest ferry of all, the *Silja Europa*, is well over 10,000 tons larger than the immortal *Titanic* (46,000 tons). It is said that more people are travelling by ship than ever before. But while business booms and shipboard design and technology advances, there seems to have been no lessening of disasters.

Fire was the major cause of loss to passenger ships in the first half of the '90s. In fact, just as the decade began, two ferries — the *Sally Albatross*, then the *Scandinavian Star* — were swept by major blazes within two months of one another. Both ships were ruined. But it has also been an especially hideous fate for a good number of Greek and ex-Greek cruise ships — the *Melody, Pegasus, The Fiesta, Danae, Pallas Athena*, and even the hotel ship *Ramada* Al Salaam, which was attacked in home waters in Kuwait by Iraqi invaders.

Grounding nearly spelled the end of one popular cruise ship, the *Ocean Princess*, while another, the former *America* and later *Australis*, ended up on the rocks during her first voyage after a 15-year lay-up.

In vivid, sunlit colour, television brought into households around the world the spectacle of the *Oceanos* sinking off South Africa. She rose out of the sea, her bow pointing upwards, then took her final plunge. We continued to watch after she was gone, when just a few remains littered the otherwise choppy seas. Meanwhile, a year later, another Greek-owned cruise ship, the *Royal Pacific*, sank in South East Asian waters with only scant press attention. But coverage was expectedly extreme when the ferry *Estonia* sank on a blustery Baltic night and claimed well over 900 lives. It was the worst ferry tragedy yet, and overall one of the worst of any kind in recent years. While standards for all other bow-loading ferries were under review, new 1997 SOLAS (Safety of Life At Sea) standards will require many older cruise ships to be upgraded. Others, less fortunate and unable economically to conform, will be sent off to retirement. Greater safety at sea seems to be the priority as we near the millenium.

Sally Albatross
Rederi A/B Sally, Helsinki (P/R 'Sally Albatross')
Previous name: *Viking Saga* (1980–86).

Builders: Wartsila Shipyards, Turku, Finland, 1980.
Particulars: 14,330 gross tons, 475ft x 85ft.

Machinery: Pielstick-Wartsila diesels, twin screw, speed 21 knots.
Passengers: 1,104 in cabins; 896 deck.

Date of disaster: 9 January 1990.

When she was completed in the summer of 1980, the *Viking Saga* was one of the largest, most technologically advanced passenger ferries in the world. She sailed for Finland's Viking Line on the very busy overnight run between Stockholm and Helsinki, carrying 1,104 passengers in cabins as well as 896 'unberthed' passengers. Her large, drive-aboard garage could accommodate 540 private cars as well as 60 commercial vehicles. She and her twin sister, the *Viking Song*, were immensely successful.

However, large, deep-sea ferry construction, especially for that Baltic service, was advancing rapidly. By 1984 the *Viking Saga* was sold to Rederi A/B Sally, the Sally Line; and used for Baltic Sea cruises as the *Sally Albatross*. Successful in this role, she was more formally converted as a cruise ship during a refit in the winter of 1988 at Bremerhaven.

Two years later, during her annual mid-winter drydocking and overhaul at Stockholm's Finnboda Shipyard, she caught fire. Her upper-deck passenger quarters were destroyed beyond repair; blackened and scarred, she was later towed across to Finland and was scrapped almost completely. However, the lower section of her car deck, which included her machinery, was salvaged and used in the 1990–91 construction of her replacement, a larger *Sally Albatross*. But this ship was to meet with tragedy as well, as described on page 205.

Scandinavian Star
K/S Scandinavian Star, Nassau (operated by Da-No Line)

Previous names: *Massalia* (1971–84), *Stena Baltica* (1984), *Island Fiesta* (1984).

Builders: Dubigeon-Normandie SA, Nantes, France, 1971.
Particulars: 10,513 gross tons, 466ft x 71ft.
Machinery: Pielstick-Chantiers de L'Atlantique diesels, speed 20 knots.
Passengers: 810 maximum.

Date of disaster: 7 April 1990.

The *Scandinavian Star* was completed in the

A view showing clearly the extensive damage amidships suffered by the Sally Albatross *following her January 1990 fire* (Anders Ahlerup).

summer of 1971 as the *Massalia* for France's Nouvelle Cie de Paquebots for their Marseilles-Casablanca-Canary Islands passenger and ferry service. Then she carried 494 in First Class, 316 in Tourist Class and 260 private cars. In late 1983, she was sold to the Swedish-flag Stena Line, and went through three names within a year — *Stena Baltica, Island Fiesta* (for short cruises out of Florida), then *Scandinavian Star* (when she was operated as a 'day cruise ship' and floating casino for Florida's SeaEscape Cruises), carrying a maximum of 810 passengers.

On 16 March 1988 she suffered a serious engine room fire when 60 miles off the east coast of Mexico, and had to be towed back to Miami for major repairs. In March 1990 she was chartered to the Da-No Line for the ferry service between Frederikshavn and Oslo. She was on her fifth voyage when tragedy struck.

It was one of the worst disasters of its time,

and made worldwide headlines, prompting an international effort to improve both passenger ship safety standards and on board security. In a fire started by an arsonist aboard the ship, it was first reported that all the passengers and crew had been evacuated safely. In fact, at least 160 perished, including the ship's owner and his wife. It was also reported that language difficulties arose between the diverse nationalities amongst the passengers and crew, and soon led to chaos and an 'every man for himself' situation.

The ship burned for four days, and when she was finally towed into the port of Lysekil she was still smouldering. An exact death toll in the end could not be reached since the passenger lists were destroyed in the blaze, and furthermore even these did not give a full accounting of the many children aboard at the time.

Survivors later reported that there had been an earlier fire on board, which was extinguished before the arsonist struck a second time. In the tragic second blaze, surviving passengers reported that sprinkler systems aboard the vessel

The Scandinavian Star *ablaze, victim of an onboard arsonist* (**World Ship Society**).

did not work, that some lifeboats could not be lowered and that there were communication difficulties even amongst the crew-members. Four other ferries — the *Stena Saga, Dana Regina, Stena Nordica* and *Peter Wessel* — along with several cargo ships, answered the distress calls from the blazing ship.

Following the fire and an initial lay-up in Sweden, the *Scandinavian Star* was moved to a Copenhagen shipyard for a criminal investigation by Danish authorities. That August she was towed to Hull, appraised by ship repairers and provisionally renamed *Candi*. A month later she was moved to Southampton, awaiting possible buyers, and was finally sold in February 1994 for $2 million to International Shipping Partners. Renamed *Regal Voyager*, she was rebuilt as a cargo ferry at La Spezia, Italy.

Melody
Commercial Bank of Greece, Athens (the former owners being in receivership)
Previous names: *Djebel-Dira* (1948–70), *Phoenix* (1970).

Builders: Swan, Hunter & Wigham Richardson Ltd, Newcastle, England, 1948.
Particulars: 5,551 gross tons, 371ft x 51ft.
Machinery: Steam turbines, single screw, speed 16 knots.

Passengers: 283 cruise passengers.

Date of disaster: July 1990.

The waters in and around Piraeus, Greece are noted for their older, second-hand, often unrecognisable passenger ships. Frequently vintage vessels have undergone great structural alterations, and have then changed names, sometimes more than once, owners, colourings and funnel markings. Sighting such ships is a true test of even the most ardent passenger ship enthusiast and maritime historian. In the late 1980s, one such ship was the small *Melody*.

Launched in February 1948, the *Melody* initially sailed as the *Djebel-Dira* of Cie de Navigation Mixte. She was rather unusual at the time in being British-built for French owners. A combination passenger-cargo ship of comparatively little note, she ran on the Marseilles-Casablanca route with accommodations arranged for 56 First Class, 132 Third Class and 430 deck passengers. She had four cargo holds, two being insulated for chilled meat, fruits and vegetables, the others for wine and live sheep.

Along with many other French passenger ships of the time, in 1970 she was sold to Greek buyers, Sypros P. Bilinis, and renamed *Phoenix*. Stripped of her cargo holds and rebuilt for cruising, she was later renamed *Melody*, and ran cruises to the Greek islands, Turkey and Israel

Fire-damaged and half-sunk by the stern, the Melody has been abandoned off Atalanti Island near Piraeus, Greece (Jurgen Saupe).

Awaiting her next fate, either as a cruise ship or a floating hotel, the intended **Stella Polaris** *(formerly the* **Santa Paula***) is moored in Perama Bay, Greece, in 1973* **(Antonio Scrimali).**

until December 1980, when she was badly damaged in a severe storm en route to Haifa. Returned to Greece, she was laid up and left unrepaired for some time; meanwhile her owners, Athens Marine Cruises, went into bankruptcy. She was actually sold in 1988 to other Greek shipping interests, the IMS Shipping Co, and by 1990 was registered to Cougar Shipping Co, who used Honduran registry.

Having fallen into Greek Government receivership, she was virtually unmanned for a time and then, in July 1990, when some repairs were finally under way, she caught fire and later began to sink by the stern. Still half-sunk, she remains to this day abandoned off Atalanti Island. Nearby is another anchored, seemingly abandoned cruise ship, the *Bella Maria*, which had been the French *Azemmour* in earlier days.

Ramada al Salaam
National Hotel & Tourist Co, Kuwait
Previous name: *Santa Paula* (1958–72), *Stella Polaris* (1972-80), *Kuwait Mariott Hotel* (1980-88).
Builders: Newport News Shipbuilding &

Drydock Co, Newport News, Virginia, USA, 1958.
Particulars: 15,366 gross tons, 584ft x 84ft.
Machinery: Steam turbines, twin screw, speed 20 knots.
Passengers: Originally 300 all-First Class.

Date of disaster: February 1991.

Amidst the bombings, the fires and the general mass destruction of the Gulf War in 1990–91, details of individual events were often quite limited, even scarce. Certainly, the fate of a former American cruise ship moored in cement and used as a hotel was hardly a priority.

Built in 1958 at the Newport News Shipyard in Virginia and christened by Mrs Richard Nixon (her husband was then the Vice-President under Dwight D. Eisenhower), she was named *Santa Paula* for year-round 13-day cruises to the Caribbean from New York. Her twin sister was the *Santa Rosa* (rebuilt in 1990–91 after a long lay-up and currently sailing in the Alaskan and Caribbean cruise trades as the *Regent Rainbow*). Then owned by the Grace Line, the twin 15,000-ton, 300-passenger ships ran until 1971, when high US operational costs against sleek, new foreign-flag competitors spelled their end. The sisters were laid up and soon offered for sale.

The *Santa Paula* was sold in 1972 to the Mariott Hotel Group, then a large shareholder in Greece's Sun Line. Sent to Greece for rebuilding, she was to become Sun Line's largest cruise ship, the 900-passenger *Stella Polaris* (not to be confused with their current *Stella Solaris*, the former French *Cambodge*). However, as marine fuel oil prices suddenly and dramatically skyrocketed, the conversion was delayed, then cancelled altogether. She was handed back to Mariott, who, in turn, had her rebuilt at a Rijeka shipyard as a hotel ship. She arrived in Kuwait in the autumn of 1978, then, after further modifications, opened as the *Kuwait Mariott Hotel* in February 1980. She became the *Ramada al Salaam* hotel in 1988, and as such became caught up in the events of 1990-91.

During an Iraqi attack on Kuwait City in February 1991, the *Ramada al Salaam* was set on fire, burned out completely and remains, at the time of writing, an empty, blackened shell of its former self. Reports are that she will not be repaired and will most likely be demolished where she lies.

Pegasus
Epirotiki Lines, Piraeus
Previous names: *Svea Corona* (1975–84), *Sundancer* (1984).
Builders: Dubigeon-Normandie SA, Nantes, France, 1975.

Partially flooded and leaning over towards the pier, the fire-damaged Pegasus *is seen at Venice in July 1991* (Jurgen Saupe).

Particulars: 12,576 gross tons, 502ft x 72ft.
Machinery: Pielstick-Chantiers de L'Atlantique diesels, twin screw, speed 22 knots.
Passengers: 810 cruise passengers.

Date of disaster: 3 June 1991

Very occasionally, ships seem to 'return from the dead' — from fires, groundings, even sinkings. Somehow they are deemed worthy of expensive salvage, repairs and rebuilding. Certainly the Greek cruise ship *Pegasus* is a classic instance.

Having been a Baltic Sea ferry for nearly ten years, she became the Alaskan cruise ship *Sundancer* in 1984, but then, barely into service, she struck a rock off Vancouver Island. So seriously damaged was she that she was declared a complete loss and was about to be sold to scrappers when Epirotiki Lines bought the damaged ship instead. She was towed to Greece that December as the *Pegasus,* and was cruising again by 1987 — the Mediterranean and Black Seas in summer, the Caribbean and South America in winter.

However, more misfortune followed. While chartered to a German electrical firm as an exhibition ship and berthed in Venice, she was swept by fire and began to sink. Once again she was declared a complete loss and destined for the scrapyard; but once again, Epirotiki engineers thought differently. She was refloated and towed to Piraeus three months later, and was to have been refitted for further cruising. She was sold in the autumn of 1994 to another Greek shipowner, the Strintzis Line, and has undergone a $25 million refit to become the passenger-car ferry *Ionian Express.*

Oceanos
Epirotiki Lines, Piraeus
Previous names: *Jean Laborde* (1951–70), *Mykinai* (1970–71), *Ancona* (1971–74), *Brindisi Express* (1974), *Eastern Princess* (1974–76).

Builders: Forges et Chantiers de la Gironde, Bordeaux, France, 1951.
Particulars: 7,554 gross tons, 492ft x 64ft.
Machinery: Burmeister & Wain diesels, twin scew, speed 17 knots.
Passengers: 500 cruise passengers.

Date of disaster: 3-4 August 1991.

Another older ship, with a string of former names and several refits in her biography, the *Oceanos,* also belonged to Epirotiki Lines. She had a long and diverse history, starting life as one of four identical sister ships built as post-Second World War replacements for France's Messageries Maritimes. As the *Jean Laborde,* she carried three classes of passengers and cargo on the Marseilles-East Africa-Mauritius run until the late 1960s. In 1970 she was sold to the Greek-flag Efthymiadis Lines (a company later closed down because of negligence in operating its passenger ships) and was renamed *Mykinai,* then, a year later, *Ancona.* She was used in the Aegean as well as the Adriatic ferry service.

Renamed *Brindisi Express* in 1974, she was to have been rebuilt as an Adriatic ferry, but the project was later cancelled and the ship sold to the Helite Hellenic Italian Lines and renamed *Eastern Princess.* However, she was soon off to

Last moments of the Oceanos as she sinks off South Africa. Fortunately all 580 passengers and crew had been lifted to safety beforehand (Popperfoto/Reuter).

Eastern waters, running a short-lived cruise service between Singapore and Australia. She was back in the Mediterranean by the summer of 1976, when she was sold to Epirotiki; extensively rebuilt for First Class cruising with 500 berths. She became the *Oceanos* and ran mostly Greek islands cruises as well as some winter Caribbean sailings; she also ran some charter cruises in 1982 for Italy's Flotta Lauro.

The *Oceanos* was not quite 40 years old when, on 3 August 1991, she made headline news around the world. In high winds and rough seas she developed a leak in the engine room while on a charter cruise between East London and Durban. All power failed and soon the ship began to sink. Most embarrassingly for her owners, the Captain was among the first to leave the ship, supposedly to coordinate rescue efforts from the shore. In fact, the ship's entertainers were left to arrange rescue with the South African authorities and other ships. Colour video footage of this tragedy made by passengers soon found its way on to news broadcasts and into homes all over the world. Complicating the situation, it was Epirotiki's and therefore Greece's third cruise ship loss in two years.

On the following day, 4 August, no fewer than 14 helicopters from the South African Air Force began to evacuate the 580 passengers and crew still on board. The Dutch containership *Nedlloyd Mauritius* completed the rescue, and everyone was safe by the time the *Oceanos* lifted upwards and sank by the bow during the afternoon.

The Fiesta
Festival Shipping & Tourist Enterprises Ltd, Piraeus
Previous names: Theodor Herzl (1957–69), *Carnivale* (1969–75), *Freeport* (1975–76), *Vera Cruz I* (1976–90), *Sun Ambassador* (1990–91).
Builders: Deutsche Werft, Hamburg, West Germany, 1957.
Particulars: 10,595 gross tons, 487ft x 64ft.
Machinery: Steam turbines, twin screw, speed 18 knots.
Passengers: 960 maximum cruise passengers.

Date of disaster: 14 October 1991.

After extended service in North America as the cruise ship **Vera Cruz I***, she was being refitted as* **The Fiesta** *when she was destroyed by fire on 14 October 1991.* **(Luis Miguel Correia).**

Ship repairs and/or refit work is often done at small, overcrowded shipyards or at harbour anchorages with workboats and barges huddled alongside. The risk of an accident, particularly fire, is consequently high, and certainly Greek shipowners have been particularly vulnerable to these.

The Fiesta started her career as the 570-passenger *Theodor Herzl*, built as West German reparations to Israel. Along with some winter cruising she traded mostly on the Zim Lines' service between Marseilles, Italian ports and Haifa. In 1969 she was sold to American interests (the forerunners of Carnival Cruise Lines, which would not actually begin operations until 1972), and was assigned to a Liberian-flag subsidiary as the *Carnivale*. However, a planned conversion to a 750-passenger cruise ship never came to pass, and instead she spent some years at lonely anchorages, first at Toulon, then at La Spezia in Italy. She was finally refitted for cruising in 1975, sailing for Bahama Cruise Lines as the *Freeport* on overnight Florida-Bahamas sailings.

She was renamed *Vera Cruz I* a year later and subsequently sailed in Caribbean, Alaskan and Canadian waters. Her owners were later renamed as the Bermuda Star Line, and she spent a number of summers in New York-Bermuda service. Laid up again at the end of 1989, she was soon sold to Greek interests, who renamed her *Sun Ambassador*, then *The Fiesta* for a combination of Mediterranean and Caribbean cruising. In October 1991 she was being refitted at Drepatzona, Greece, for service under the Festival Cruises banner when a fast-spreading and very thorough fire finished her career. Sunk and declared a complete loss, the 487-foot-long hull was later raised and sold to local scrappers near Piraeus.

Danae
Independent Continental Lines (Costa Armatori Spa), Monrovia
Previous names: *Port Melbourne* (1955–72), *Therissos Express* (1972–74).

Builders: Harland & Wolff Ltd, Belfast, Northern Ireland, 1955.
Particulars: 16,310 gross tons, 533ft x 69ft.
Machinery: Doxford diesels, twin screw, speed 17 knots.
Passengers: 512 maximum cruise passengers.

Date of disaster: 10 December 1991.

On a visit to Perama Bay, that vast anchorage of ships near Piraeus in Greece, in the summer of 1993, we came across two, then recent, near-casualties of the cruising world. Moored side by side were the badly damaged *Ocean Princess* (see page 203), which had grounded in the Amazon River, and the *Danae*, formerly of Costa Cruises and damaged by fire while at a Genoa shipyard. Both ships were said to be beyond economic repair — revival rumours still surround the *Ocean Princess*, while the *Danae* has actually been repaired and resumed sailing.

After the fire, scrap merchants were said to be bidding for the *Danae*, but instead she was bought from insurance underwriters by Greek interests, who had her towed to Piraeus under the provisional name *Anar*. Now owned by the ever-expanding Lelakis Group, which owns Regency Cruises and most of their fleet of cruise liners, she was later renamed *Starlight Princess*. Rumours about her future were plentiful in that summer of '93. Variously it was reported that she would be repaired and sail for Regency, that she would cruise the Mediterranean for a newly formed company, and that she would be chartered to Seawind Cruise Lines to cruise the Caribbean. In fact she has since begun sailing on a German charter as the *Baltica*.

The *Danae* was built in 1955 as the British freighter *Port Melbourne*. Carrying only a dozen passengers but considerable freight (much of it refrigerated), she worked the Port Line's 'meat trade' between England, Australia and New Zealand until bought by the Greek-flag Carras Group in 1972. She was to have become the Adriatic Sea ferry *Therissos Express*, but there was evidently some rethinking as she laid at the Carras-owned shipyard at Chalkis in Greece for some time.

She finally emerged in 1974 as the luxury cruise ship *Danae* and sailed on worldwide itineraries for the short-lived Carras Cruises. She and her twin sister, the *Daphne*, the former *Port Sydney*, were said to have brought Greek cruising to new heights and standards. Both ships were chartered to Costa Cruises in 1979, then bought outright six years later. They now flew the Panamanian colours and were owned by a Panama-based

subsidiary of Costa. They went over to Liberian registry by 1990 and the *Danae* was run latterly by a Costa-Russian cooperative called Prestige Cruises. She was to have departed from Genoa on a long, luxurious cruise around continental South America, but following her fire, the *Daphne* was called upon to run the same itinerary.

Royal Pacific
Anchor of the Seas Ltd, Bahamas (Starlight Cruises Ltd)
Previous names: *Empress of Australia* (1965–85), *Empress* (1985–91).

Builders: Cockatoo Docks & Engineering Co Pty Ltd, Sydney, 1965.
Particulars: 13,176 gross tons, 468ft x 69ft.
Machinery: MAN diesels, twin screw, speed 21.5 knots.
Passengers: 623 maximum cruise passengers.

Date of disaster: 23 August 1992.

Cruising in Pacific waters, especially to South East Asian ports and particularly out of Singapore, had increased by the early 1990s, and a fleet of mostly second hand ships found new and further employment. One of these, the *Royal Pacific*, had an interesting career: Australian ferry, Greek ferry, American-based cruise ship and finally a Pacific cruise ship.

The largest passenger-carrying ship ever built in Australia, she was commissioned as the *Empress of Australia* in January 1965, and carried 250 berthed and 190 deck passengers on the

In her earlier days the cruise ship Royal Pacific *had been the* Empress of Australia, *the largest passenger ship ever built in Australia* (Luis Miguel Correia).

coastal trade between Sydney, Hobart, Bell Bay and Burnie. Twenty years later, in 1985, she made her longest voyage yet: to Greece and to new owners, Phineas Navigation Co Ltd of Limassol, Cyprus. Renamed *Empress,* she was quickly pressed into passenger and car ferry service between Cyprus and Lebanon.

In 1990–91 she was to have been chartered to the Swedish-flag Stena Line to become the *Stena Empress* for the Gothenburg-Copenhagen overnight service, but this plan never came to pass when her new Greek owners (now Falcon Maritime Co of Piraeus) decided to rebuild her as a cruise ship. By the summer of 1991 she was sailing for an affiliate, Starlight Cruises Ltd, for cruises on the Mexican Riviera between La Paz and Acapulco, and later from San Diego, California. She was moved to Pacific service in November 1991, reportedly for 'gambling cruises' out of Singapore, but it all ended on 23 August 1992, when, on a short 'cruise to nowhere', sailing 12 miles off Port Dickson, she collided with the 800-ton Taiwanese fish-factory-trawler *Terfu.* The Bahamas-registered cruise ship sank, and nine of the passengers and crew were lost.

Ocean Princess
Ocean Cruise Lines (Crosieres Paquet), Nassau
Previous name: *Italia* (1967–83).

Builders: Cantieri Navale Felszegi, Trieste, Italy, 1967.
Particulars: 12,218 gross tons, 490ft × 68ft.
Machinery: Sulzer diesels, twin screw, speed 20 knots.
Passengers: 476 cruise passengers.

Date of disaster: 1 March 1993.

Miscalculations by ships' captains and even local pilots can lead to tragedy; and the more remote the waterway, the greater the possibility of trouble. While the Amazon River has become increasingly popular as a cruise destination (with ships often going 1,000 miles up river to Manaus), these waters remain somewhat uncertain, and miscalculation was indeed a major part of the events that cut short the career of the gleaming white cruise ship *Ocean Princess.*

This nicely appointed vessel had always been a popular cruise ship. She was a product of the 1960s, the birth of the current cruise generation. Built by Italian bankers in 1967 and completed as the *Italia,* she was designed for the charter market. She was soon leased to the then new Princess Cruises, running American West Coast voyages to the Mexican Riviera and Alaska as the so-called *Princess Italia* (she was never formally renamed). Later she was chartered, then bought outright (1974), by the Costa Line. Keeping her popular name, she cruised almost everywhere: the Mediterranean, South America, even around-the-world trips.

In 1983 Greek-based, Panama-flag Ocean Cruise Lines bought her and renamed her *Ocean Princess.* In more recent years (her owners were sold to France's Paquet Cruises in 1990 and the ship changed to Bahamas registry), her cruising pattern became well established: Scandinavia in summer, the Caribbean, South America and even remote Antarctica in winter. It was during a late season Amazon cruise out of Buenos Aires and Rio de Janeiro in March 1993 that she grounded on the river bank about a mile downstream from Belem; it is believed that she hit an unmarked wreck. The collision was so severe that she ripped open part of her hull, flooded up to two passenger decks and throughout her engine room, and had to be evacuated. Declared a total

The sleek, engines-aft Ocean Princess *departing from Copenhagen on 9 June 1991* (Ove Neilsen).

loss, she was, however, pumped out, patched and towed to Greece. Under new owners, who bought her from the insurance underwriters, she became the *Sea Prince*, registered on the Caribbean island of St. Vincent.

We saw her in August 1993, laid up near Piraeus, stripped of her lifeboats, and scarred in mud and rust. Clearly she was a 'dead ship'. Small mountains of passenger furniture had been offloaded and were piled on the dockside, well exposed to the elements. A single ladder was fixed to the stern. Immediately alongside that same day was the fire-damaged but soon-to-be repaired former Costa cruise ship *Danae* (see page 201). Rumours as we went to press concerning a possible revival of the ex-*Ocean Princess* include her coming back to service as the *Regent Moon* for Regency Cruises, or as the *Seawind Spirit* for Seawind Cruise Lines.

American Star
Chaophraya Development & Transport Ltd, Panama

Previous names: *America* (1940–41), *West Point* (1941–46), *America* (1946–64), *Australis* (1964–78), *America* (1978), *Italis* (1978–80), *Noga* (1980–84), *Alferdoss* (1984–93).
Builders: Newport News Shipbuilding & Drydock Co, Newport News, Virginia, 1940.
Particulars: 26,353 gross tons, 723ft x 93ft.
Machinery: Steam turbines, twin screw, speed 23 knots.
Passengers: 2,258 maximum passengers, all one class.

Date of disaster: 18 January 1994.

The one-time flagship of the entire US merchant

marine and later flagship of the entire Greek passenger fleet, the renamed *American Star* had a long and diverse career spanning an amazing 54 years — as a Second World War troopship, transatlantic luxury liner, Australian migrant ship and finally as a cruise ship.

She is, however, perhaps best remembered as the *America*, built at the Newport News Shipyard in Virginia just as the Second World War started, in 1939–40. Diverted to the safety of trans-Panama Canal cruises for a time, she was soon handed over to the US Government and, painted in grey and with her capacity enlarged from 1,000 passengers to nearly 9,000 troops, she sailed for the next four years as the USS *West Point*. She travelled almost everywhere — Europe, the South Pacific, the Indian Ocean, South America. Often a target of enemy bombers and submarines, she was decommissioned intact in 1946, and was then rehabilitated for Atlantic service between New York, Southampton, Le Havre and Bremerhaven. Then a three-class ship, she was America's finest and largest liner until the arrival in June 1952, of the supership *United States*, the fastest passenger liner ever built. The 23-knot *America* became her consort.

In 1964 the Greek-flag Chandris Lines (owners of today's Celebrity and Fantasy Cruises) bought her for the Europe-Australia migrant trade. Rebuilt as the *Australis*, her capacity was more than doubled, jumping from 1,046 to 2,258, all Tourist Class. She sailed Australian and round-the-world services until 1977, then the following

The American Star *aground and broken in two on the west coast of Fuertaventura Island in the Canaries (Stamos C. Ioannou, courtesy William Rau).*

year she returned to New York, where, as the renamed *America*, she ran no more than two unsuccessful cruises. Her owners, the Venture Cruise Lines, were quickly forced into bankruptcy with claims of poor food, blocked toilets and even refuse in the swimming pool.

Chandris bought back their old flagship within months and, as the *Italis*, she was placed in Mediterranean cruising, losing her forward 'dummy' stack in a refit. However, by late 1979 she was too old and too expensive, so she went off to an anchorage in Perama Bay, that great basin of idle ships near Piraeus. She passed to other owners, becoming the *Noga*, the *Alferdoss* and finally the *American Star*.

For nearly 15 years she sat at her Greek moorings, lonely, largely forgotten and certainly falling into deepening decay. Over the years there were rumours that she would become a floating hotel in West Africa, a prison in Texas, a yacht club in Montreal, then in Hong Kong, a hotel at New York, a trade ship for the Chinese, a casino in Australia and, after considerable repairs, a reactivated cruise liner. Eventually in 1993 she did undergo some repairs in preparation for the long tow to Phuket in Thailand and her new career as a luxury hotel ship *American Star*. Her actual departure was long delayed, then, as the Suez Canal authorities refused permission for her passage, the 2,700-ton tug *Neftegaz* guided her out of the Mediterranean and through the Gibraltar Straits for the long tow around Africa and across the Indian Ocean. It was while under tow that the aged, creaking, almost empty former luxury ship met her end. In ferocious hurricane winds her towlines snapped and she drifted ashore on the west coast of Fuertaventura Island in the Canary Islands. Four crewmen, who were aboard the otherwise empty, darkened ship, were rescued by helicopter. Then, like some dead, beached whale, old age finally told — her 723-foot-long hull broke into three pieces. She was abandoned.

The three wrecked pieces of her hull will most likely be scrapped where they lie. It will be the end of the long life of a great lady of the sea.

Sally Albatross
Rederi A/B Sally, Helsinki (Oy Silja Line Ab)
Previous name: (parts used from the former *Viking Saga*.)

Builders: Rauma Yards O/Y, Rauma, Finland, 1992.
Particulars: 25,076 gross tons, 520ft x 85ft.
Machinery: Pielstick diesels, twin screw, speed 21 knots.
Passengers: 1,400 maximum.

Date of disaster: 4 March 1994.

A strikingly modern ship, the new *Sally Albatross* was constructed using the lower section of the car deck and the original machinery from the earlier ship of the same name that had been lost in a tragic fire at Stockholm in January 1990 (see page 194). This second *Sally Albatross* was a far more luxurious and better appointed ship, and unlike her predecessor she was intended for cruising from the start. In fact, during 1993 it was reported that she would to into charter service in North American waters, first as the *Crown Majesty* for the Boston-Bermuda services of Majesty Cruise Lines, then as the *Regent Moon* for the summer

The new ferry-cruise ship **Sally Albatross,** *incorporating parts of the earlier vessel of the same name, departing from Lisbon in 1993* **(Luis Miguel Correia).**

Alaskan service of Regency Cruises. However, remaining in Baltic waters instead, she met with tragedy during the following winter.

Returning to Tallinn during a 'day cruise' to Helsinki, she went aground in severe ice conditions and high winds, 2 hours south-west of Helsinki. At the time there were almost 1,101 mostly Finnish passengers and 158 crew on board. Since water had begun flooding the engine room, an evacuation was started and an SOS sent out. The Finnish icebreakers *Urko* and *Voima,* as well as the ferry *St Patrick II*, raced to the scene, and passengers left through the stern section of the flooding ship.

Later the *Sally Albatross* had a 13-degree and finally a 25-degree list at the stern. Further damage and more leaks were uncovered as she was carefully moved by the tug *Kraft* about 2 miles away, where she rested in up to 33 feet of sea-water. Now the engine room, passenger cabins and other spaces up to Deck 5 were flooded. Her owners, who called the accident a 'navigation error', were faced with a difficult decision: total loss, or salvage and repair.

After preliminary investigations by a Finnish company, the well-known Dutch salvage company, Smit International, was hired on 16 March to raise the half-sunken ship and move her to a drydock. Two months later, on 24 May, she was again floating on her own after being raised by the heavy-lift tug *Mobile Lifter*, and was taken

The Pallas Athena *as a burnt-out hulk lying outside Piraeus on 30 August 1994* (Jurgen Saupe).

to a drydock at Turku. However, her owners, convinced that she is an 'unlucky ship' (remembering the tragedy of the earlier *Sally Albatross* and the incorporation of parts of that ship in this second vessel), have decided that she will be sold once repaired. The repairs, which were to take over six months as we went to press, were reported to be costing over $36 million. Following these repairs and further improvements, she will start a four-year charter to Norwegian Cruise Lines of Miami. As the *Leeward,* she will make 3- and 4-day cruises to the Bahamas.

Pallas Athena
Epirotiki Lines, Piraeus
Previous names: *Flandre* (1952–68), *Carla C* (1968–86), *Carla Costa* (1986–92).

Builders: Ateliers et Chantiers de France, Dunkirk, France, 1952.
Particulars: 19,975 gross tons, 600ft x 80ft.
Machinery: Werkspoor diesels, twin screw, speed 19 knots.
Passengers: 754 all-First Class.

Date of disaster: 24 March 1994.

The French Line, the Compagnie Générale Transatlantique, had lost a good portion of their splendid fleet during the ruthless war years, including the ultra-luxurious *Normandie*. However, the celebrated *Ile De France* and the smaller *De Grasse* survived, then, through reparations, they inherited Germany's giant *Europa,* which was promptly rechristened *Liberté*. But for brand new tonnage, the Line's Parisian directors were more conservative, looking to medium-sized passenger ships, which included a pair of 800-passenger sister ships, the *Antilles* and the *Flandre*. The former, which sailed exclusively on the colonial West Indian run out of Le Havre, was destroyed by fire in January 1971 (see page 153).

The *Flandre* had troubles even at the start of her long and varied career. In the summer of 1952 she broke down on her intended gala transatlantic maiden voyage. She finally reached New York, but then broke down again. She couldn't even raise her own anchors or blast her whistle; instead, she had to be towed to her Manhattan pier.

After extensive and expensive repairs to the faulty engines, the *Flandre* sailed the North Atlantic between Le Havre, Southampton and New York. First partnered with the *Ile De France* and the *Liberté,* she later sailed with the stunning new *France* in 1962. She then joined her sister in Caribbean service before going to the Costa Line in 1968.

Rebuilt as a cruise ship and renamed *Carla C,* she went directly on charter to Princess Cruises and sailed from US West Coast ports as their *Princess Carla* (although never actually renamed). However, the Italians soon recalled their ship for their own Caribbean service. She underwent major surgery at Amsterdam in 1974, when her steam turbines were replaced by new Dutch diesels. Later renamed *Carla Costa,* Epirotiki bought her in 1992.

Running most seven-day cruises to the Aegean isles and Turkey as the *Pallas Athena,* she collided with Windstar's *Wind Spirit* in June 1993. When we saw her at Kusadasi two months later, she still had a nasty dent in her otherwise flared bow. But it was fire, historically always something of a problem to French-built passenger ships, that destroyed her. In March 1994, at Piraeus, a fire started in a passenger cabin and spread quickly. Her passengers had just disembarked and she was to sail again that same day, but she burned to a brown, twisted shell. Still smouldering, she was later towed out to open waters and declared a complete wreck.

The **Estonia** *berthed at Stockholm in August 1994, only a month or so before the tragedy that claimed over 900 lives* **(Mervyn Benford).**

Estonia
Estline (Estonian Steamship Lines)
Previous names: *Viking Sally* (1980–90), *Silja Star* (1990), *Wasa King* (1990–92).

Builders: Joseph L. Meyer GmbH & Co, Papenburg, Germany, 1980.
Particulars: 15,566 gross tons, 510ft x 79ft.
Machinery: MAN diesels, twin screw, speed 21 knots.
Passengers: 1,190 berthed in cabins, 810 unberthed.

Date of disaster: 28 September 1994.

She was built for the busy Baltic Sea trades as a rather ordinary vessel, but one that would make headline news around the world. When the *Estonia* sank on a blustery early autumn night while on a passage from Tallin to Stockholm, she claimed well over 900 lives. It was the worst tragedy yet involving a large, deep-sea ferry.

She started her sailing days in the summer of 1980 as the *Viking Sally* for the Sally Line's service between Stockholm, Mariehamm and Abo. A decade later she changed hands, going to O/Y Vassanlaivat of Mariehamm to become the *Silja Star,* then, in that same year, the *Wasa King.* In 1992 she was sold to the Estline, the Estonian Steamship Lines, a partnership between the

Estonian Government and a Swedish company, Nordstrum & Thulin AB.

The ship left Tallinn at 7 o'clock on the evening of 27 September. Earlier that same day inspectors had found problems with the seals lining her bow-loading door. Within an hour and a half, by 8.30pm, she ran into heavy weather. Many passengers retired to their cabins, and even the band stopped playing in the lounge. A rough few hours followed, then at about midnight an engineer detected that water was rushing through the front cargo-loading door. Crew members were alerted and pumps were turned on in the hold, but within about 15 minutes they were overwhelmed. An hour later, at 1.24 on the morning of the 28th, a distress call was sent out by the *Estonia*. The sea was very rough, winds were blowing at gale force and the ship had begun to list seriously. Then the engines lost power. At about 2 am the *Estonia* rolled over and sank quickly off the coast of Turku.

The first rescue vessel reached the scene about an hour later. 'One thing you really heard were the screams of women out in the sea,' recalled one of the survivors. Others told extraordinarily horrifying tales of stepping over wailing children and passing the elderly in their scramble to get off the ship. In the end most of the 140 survivors were men. The ship itself had plunged to a depth of 250 feet in the Baltic and her wreckage was videotaped three days later; the tapes confirmed suspicions that the huge front door had leaked, or perhaps even broken off.

While the *Estonia* now ranks as the worst ferry tragedy of recent times, there have been other disasters involving this type of passenger craft. On 26 September 1954 a Japanese ferry sank in Tsugaru Strait and claimed 1,172 lives. A ferry near Barisal, Bangladesh, sank on 20 April 1986, taking 262 to their deaths, and a Philippine ferry collided with a tanker on 20 December 1987 and 1,749 drowned as a result. Four hundred drowned when an Indian ferry sank in the Ganges River on 8 August 1988, and an Egyptian ferry claimed 460 lives when it collided with a coral reef near Safaga on 14 December 1991. On 16 February 1993 a heavily overcrowded Haitian ferry sank in local waters between Jeremie and Port-au-Prince, but without adequate passenger lists, an unknown number between 500 and 700 perished. And, of course, the previously mentioned *Herald of Free Enterprise* capsized off Belgium on 6 March 1987 and 189 were lost. In all, it is a very, very sad list.

Achille Lauro
StarLauro SpA, Naples
Previous name: Willem Ruys (1947–64)
Builders: De Schelde Shipyards, Flushing, Netherlands, 1938–47.
Particulars: 23,629 gross tns; 631ft x 82ft
Machinery: Sulzer diesels, twin screw
Passengers: 900 cruise passengers (maximum 1,652 berths)

Date of disaster: 30 November 1994.

The *Achille Lauro*'s history of misfortune ended in flames in the Indian Ocean. Nearly 1,000 passengers and crew fled to lifeboats as the listing, blistered cruiseship burned. Abandoned, she sank after an explosion on December 2.

Two deaths were reported. The ship blazed for nearly two days, tilting 40 degrees over to its port side before plunging to the bottom of the sea off the coast of Somalia. The ship reportedly sank during a salvage attempt by a Kenyan tug.

Laid down just before the start of World War II she was finally completed in 1947 as the *Willem Ruys* for the Royal Rotterdam Lloyd. She ran in the Rotterdam-East Indies service before, in 1959, being reassigned to around-the-world service. Her two Dutch running-mates, the *Johan Van Oldenbarnevelt* and the *Oranje,* also ended their days in flames. Both included in this book, the *Johan Van Oldenbarnevelt* became the Greek *Lakonia,* while the *Oranje* was rebuilt as Lauro's *Angelina Lauro.* Rebuilt by the Italians for the Europe-Australia migrant trade in 1964–65, the *Achille Lauro* was later converted for full-time cruising in 1973. She gained worldwide notoriety when Palestinian hijackers killed an American passenger in 1985. But the veteran liner's troubled past also included the death of an Italian fisherman whose boat was rammed in 1971, and two passengers who drowned trying to escape a 1981 fire.

Appendices

1 Summary of disasters

Country	Abandoned	Aground	Collision	Engine failure	Fire	Gun fire	Mine field	Missing	Storm	Terrorism	Torpedoed	Total
Argentina			1		2							3
Austria		1										1
Australia		1										1
Bahamas		1										1
Belgium					1							1
China (Taiwan)					1							1
Denmark		1	1		1							3
Egypt		1			1							2
England	1	39	13		9	1	1	1	2	1	2	70
Estonia									1			1
Finland		1			1							2
France		9	2	2	7			1	2			23
Germany		6			3							9
Greece		1	4	1	15				2	1		24
India					1				1			2
Indonesia					1							1
Italy	1	3	2	2	8	·					1	17
Japan		2										2
Kuwait					1							1
Liberia					1							1
Malaysia					3							3
Netherlands		2	1		2							5
New Zealand		2		1	1				1			5
Norway		1			3							4
Panama		1			1							2
Philippines		1										1
Portugal		4							1			5
Russia	1	1	1		2							5
Saudi Arabia					2							2
Singapore		1										1
Spain		4		1	3				1			9
Turkey					2							2
United States		4	3		4			1				12
Totals	**3**	**87**	**28**	**7**	**76**	**1**	**1**	**3**	**11**	**2**	**3**	**222**

2 Summary of casualties

	1900–09	1910–19	1920–29	1930–39	1940–49	1950–59	1960–69	1970–79	1980–89	1990–	Total
Abandoned									197		**197**
Aground	1,196	469	31	5		15			2		**1,718**
Collision	133	2,524	86	2		142	10		398	9	**3,304**
Engine failure		156	856								**1,012**
Fire	99	136		217			225	126	215		**1,018**
Minefield											
Missing	92+										**92+**
Storm	739	488	112				551	41		900	**2,831**
Terrorism							238				**238**
Torpedoed		1,392		112							**1,504**
Total	**2,259+**	**5,165**	**1,085**	**336**		**157**	**1,024**	**167**	**812**	**909**	**11,914+**

3 33 Largest ships in disasters

Ship	**Tonnage**	**Company**
Seawise University	83,673	C.Y. Tung
Titanic	46,328	White Star Line
L'Atlantique	42,512	Cie. Sudatlantique
Paris	34,569	French Line
Caribia	34,274	Universal Cruise Line
Leonardo Da Vinci	33,340	Italian Line
Lusitania	31,550	Cunard Line
Hanseatic	30,030	Hamburg Atlantic Line
Andrea Doria	29,083	Italian Line
American Star	26,353	Chaophraya Development & Transport Ltd
Lafayette	25,178	French Line
Sally Albatross	25,076	Rederi AB Sally
Caribia	24,496	Siosa Lines
Angelina	24,377	Costa Line
Achille Lauro	23,629	Star Lauro
President Hoover	21,936	Dollar Line
Columbus C	21,100	Costa Line
Celtic	20,904	White Star Line
Dakota	20,714	Great Northern SS Co
Empress of Canada	20,325	Canadian Pacific
Lakonia	20,314	Greek Line
Mikhail Lermontov	20,027	Baltic Shipping Co
Pallas Athena	19,975	Epirotiki Lines
Antilles	19,828	French Line
Reliance	19,618	Hamburg America Line
Bermuda	19,086	Furness Withy
Venezuela	18,769	Siosa Lines
Rasa Sayang	18,739	Michaelis Stroubakis
Homeric	18,563	Home Lines
Bianca C	18,427	Costa Line
Magdalena	17,547	Royal Mail Lines
Georges Philippar	17,539	Messageries Maritimes
Chidambaram	17,226	Shipping Corp of India
Admiral Nakhimov	17,053	Black Sea Shipping Co

4 Glossary

Amidship — midway point in a vessel between the bow and stern.

Bow — forward (front) part of a ship.

Bridge — area from which the Captain and his officers control the navigation of the ship.

Bulkhead — a vertical partition (or wall), in a port-starboard position or fore-and-aft direction which divides the ship into compartments.

First voyage — a ship's first trip on a new route.

Gross tons — amount of enclosed space in a ship, where the ton is 100 cubic feet volume.

Knot — unit of speed of a ship, equivalent to a distance of one nautical mile (6,080 ft) travelled per hour elapsed time.

Maiden voyage — first trip of a new ship.

Port — left-hand side of a ship looking forward.

Stabilizers — underwater fins on a ship designed to keep it as steady as possible in rough weather.

Positioning voyage — a journey made by a ship to a port from which a commercial journey is to be made.

Starboard — right-hand side of a ship looking forward.

Stern — aft (rear) part of a ship.

Watertight door — a heavy door which when closed prevents water from getting into or through to the next compartment.

Bibliography

'A Peril of the Sea.' *Evening Post,* Wellington, New Zealand, 15 September 1930.

Barnaby, K.C., *Some Ship Disasters and their Causes,* A.S. Barnes and Co, New York, 1973.

Bonsor, N.R.P., *North Atlantic Seaway,* Vol 1 Arco Publishing Company, New York, 1975.

Bonsor, N.R.P., *North Atlantic Seaway,* Vols 2–5. Brookside Publications, Jersey, 1978, 1979, 1980.

Bonsor, N.R.P., *South Atlantic Seaway,* Brookside Pubications, Jersey, 1983.

Braynard, Frank O., *Lives of the Liners,* Cornell Maritime Press, New York, 1947.

Cairis, Nicholas T., *North Atlantic Passenger Liners Since 1900,* Ian Allan, London, 1972.

Coleman, Terry, *The Liners,* G.P. Putman's Sons, New York, 1977.

Correia, Luis Miguel, 'O paquete 'LISBOA' de 1910'. *Revista de Marinha,* April 1984, pp 3–8.

Croall, James, *Disaster at Sea,* Stein and Day, New York, 1981.

Dunn Laurence, *Passenger Liners,* 2nd ed. Adlard Coles Ltd. London, 1965.

Haine, Edgar A., *Disaster at Sea,* Cornwall Books, East Brunswick, 1983.

Haws, Duncan, *Merchant Fleets in Profile,* Vols 1–5, Patrick Stephens Ltd, Cambridge, 1978–82.

Hocking Charles, *Dictionary of Disasters at Sea During the Age of Steam 1824–1962,* Vols I and II, Lloyd's Register of Shipping, London, 1969.

Hoehling, A.A., *They Sailed into Oblivion,* Thomas Yoseloff, New York, 1959.

Hoehling, A.A., *Great Ship Disasters,* Cowles Book Company Inc, New York, 1971.

Kludas, Arnold, *Great Passenger Ships of the World,* Vols 1–5, Patrick Stephens Ltd, Cambridge, 1975–1977.

Lord Walter, *A Night to Remember,* 3rd ed, Bantam Books, New York, 1978.

Maber, John M., *North Star to Southern Cross,* R. Stephenson & Sons Ltd, Prescot, 1967.

Maddocks, Melvin, *The Great Liners,* Time-Life Books, Alexandria, 1978.

Maxtone-Graham, John, *The Only Way to Cross,* The Macmillan Company, New York, 1972.

Mielke, Otto, *Disaster At Sea,* Fleet Publishing, New York, 1958.

Miller, William H., *The Great Luxury Liners 1927–1954,* Dover Publications Inc, New York, 1981.

Miller, William H., *Transatlantic Liners 1945–1980,* Arco Publishing Co, New York, 1981.

Mitchell, W.H. and Sawyer, L.A., *The Cape Run,* Terence Dalton Ltd, Lavenham, 1984.

Morris, Charles F., *Origins, Orient and Oriana,* Teredo Books Ltd, Brighton, 1983.

Moscow, Alvin, *Collision Course,* G.P. Putman's Sons, New York, 1959.

O'Starr Max, 'Yankee Pioneer'. *The Belgian Shiplover,* February 1975, pp 15–21.

Plowman, Peter, *Passenger Ships of Australia and New Zealand,* Vols 1–2, Conway Maritime Press, London, 1981.

Simpson, Colin, *The Lusitania,* Ballantine Books, New York, 1974.

Smith, Eugene W., *Passenger Ships of the World Past and Present,* George H. Dean Company, Boston, 1963.

Wall, Robert, *Ocean Liners,* E.P. Dutton, New York, 1977.

Witthoft, Hans Jurgen, *Hapag-Lloyd,* Koehlers Verlagsgesellschaft GmbH, Herford, 1979.

Documents

Federal Archives and Record Center, GSA. Bayonne, New Jersey for documents filed with the United States District Court for the Southern District of New York.

Great Britain, Shipping Casualties. *Report on the Loss of the* Titanic *(S.S.),* His Majesty's Stationery Office, London July 30 1912.

New Zealand Marine Department, Court of Inquiry. *Report, October 17, 1916* (M.13/298).

New Zealand Marine Department, Court of Inquiry. *Report, March 29, 1917* (M.13/322).

New Zealand Marine Department, Court of Inquiry. *Report, November 15, 1968* (H.51).

Periodicals

Dominion (Wellington newspaper).

Lloyd's Registry of Shipping.

Marine News (Journal of World Ship Society — England).

New York Times.

Sea Breezes.

Steamboat Bill (Journal of Steamship Historical Society of America).

The Illustrated London News.

The Times (London).

Index to vessels